SIDE by SIDE

Plus

Book & eText ①

Life Skills & Test Prep

Career & Academic Readiness

Expanded Reading & Writing

Digital FunZone & Audio

Steven J. Molinsky • Bill Bliss

Illustrated by Richard E. Hill

Side by Side Plus Book & eText 1

Pearson Education, 10 Bank Street, White Plains, NY 10606

Staff credits: The people who make up the *Side by Side Plus* team, representing content creation, design, manufacturing, marketing, multimedia, project management, publishing, rights management, and testing are Pietro Alongi, Allen Ascher, Rhea Banker, Elizabeth Barker, Lisa Bayrasli, Elizabeth Carlson, Jennifer Castro, Tracey Munz Cataldo, Diane Cipollone, Aerin Csigay, Victoria Denkus, Dave Dickey, Daniel Dwyer, Wanda España, Oliva Fernandez, Warren Fischbach, Pam Fishman, Nancy Flaggman, Patrice Fraccio, Irene Frankel, Aliza Greenblatt, Lester Holmes, Janet Johnston, Caroline Kasterine, Barry Katzen, Ray Keating, Renee Langan, Jaime Lieber, José Antonio Méndez, Julie Molnar, Alison Pei, Pamela Pia, Stuart Radcliffe, Jennifer Raspiller, Kriston Reinmuth, Mary Perrotta Rich, Tania Saiz-Sousa, Katherine Sullivan, Paula Van Ells, Kenneth Volcjak, and Wendy Wolf.

Contributing authors: Jennifer Bixby, Laura English, Megan Ernst, Elizabeth Handley, Meredith Westfall

Text composition: TSI Graphics, Inc.

Illustrations: Richard E. Hill

Photo credits: Original photography by Paul I. Tañedo and David Mager. Page v (computer) Oleksiy Mark/Fotolia, (tablet on left) Kuzmick/Fotolia, (tablet on right) Can Yesil/Fotolia; p. 6c (bottom right) Antonioguillem/Fotolia; p. 16b (7) WimL/Fotolia, (9) Mendolo/Fotolia; p. 16c (top left) Jack Z Young/ Shutterstock, (top right) RoMur/Fotolia, (bottom left) hurricanehank/Shutterstock, (bottom right) Monkey Business/Fotolia; p. 24a (top left) Blend Images/Alamy, (1) Marvin Dembinsky Photo Associates/Alamy, (2) Gina Sanders/Fotolia; p. 25 pablocalvog/Fotolia; p. 26 (top left) Juice Images/Alamy, (top right) Kim Steele/ Blend Images/Getty Images, (bottom left) Image Source/Getty Images, (bottom right) mimagephotography/ Shutterstock; p. 26b djma/Fotolia; p. 54 (top) Hill Street Studios/Blend Images/Getty Images, (bottom) Monkey Business/Fotolia; p. 54a (left) Dejan Ristovski/Shutterstock, (right) Monkey Business/Fotolia; p. 54b Rob Marmion/Shutterstock; p. 77 (left) Julie Campbell/Shutterstock, (middle) Ami Parikh/Shutterstock, (right) Greg Blomberg/Fotolia; p. 78 (top) John Warburton Lee/SuperStock, (middle top) jacky chapman/ Alamy, (middle bottom) Zoriah/The Image Works, (bottom) Zefa RF/Alamy; p. 78b (left) rabbit75_fot/Fotolia, (right) josefpittner/Fotolia; p. 98 (top) CandyBox Images/Fotolia, (middle top) Robert Churchill/iStockphoto/ Getty Images, (middle bottom) camihesse/Fotolia, (bottom) Image Source/Getty Images; p. 98b Jupiterimages/ Stockbyte/Getty Images; p. 106a (Ronald) Dmitry Kalinovsky/Shutterstock, (Kelly) WavebreakmediaMicro/ Fotolia; p. 114a aaron Belford/Shutterstock; p. 115 WoodyStock/Alamy; p. 116 (top left) Gary Conner/ Photodisc/Getty Images, (bottom left) Image Source/Getty Images, (middle) Pixel Embargo/Fotolia, (right) Steve Mason/Photodisc/Getty Images; p. 116b (left) Monkey Business/Fotolia, (right) Monkey Business/ Fotolia; p. 140 (top) A3528 Armin Weigel Deutsch Presse Agentur/Newscom, (middle) pressmaster/Fotolia, (bottom) IS2 from Image Source/Alamy; p. 140b (top left) DragonImages/Fotolia, (top right) Monkey Business/ Fotolia, (bottom left) Fuse/Getty Images, (bottom right) Sam D'Cruz/Fotolia; p. 165 (top) Philip Scalia/Alamy, (bottom left) Radharc Images/Alamy, (bottom right) Robert Landau/Alamy; P. 166 (top left) vannphoto/ Fotolia, (top middle) Chris Howes/Wild Places Photography/Alamy, (top right) ABW Photography/Purestock/ SuperStock, (bottom left) Caro/Alamy, (bottom middle) Ariel Skelley/Blend Images/Getty Images, (bottom right) Patti McConville/Alamy; p. 166a SelectStock/Vetta/Getty Images; p. 166b Blend Images/Shutterstock.

The authors gratefully acknowledge the contribution of Tina Carver in the development of the original *Side by Side* program.

Library of Congress Cataloging-in-Publication Data

Molinsky, Steven J.
   Side by side plus: book & etext / Steven J. Molinsky, Bill Bliss.
     volumes cm
   ISBN 978-0-13-382874-0 (bk. 1)
   1. English language—Conversation and phrase books. 2. English language—Textbooks for foreign speakers. I. Bliss, Bill. II. Title.
   PE1131.M584 2016
   428.3'4—dc23

                                          2015025452

ISBN-10: 0-13-382874-3
ISBN-13: 978-0-13382874-0

Printed in the United States of America
3   18

CONTENTS

Red type indicates standards-based lessons.

Red type indicates standards-based lessons.

Introducing the *Side by Side* Plus eText!

The **eText version** of the Student Book offers *instant-access point-of-use audio* and serves as the student's virtual speaking-practice companion. Teachers can "flip" the lesson plan by moving some of the core conversation practice to students' time outside of class, thereby gaining back valuable instruction time for the content and skills of the standards-based **Side by Side Plus** curriculum.

Welcome to the **FunZone**—a digital amusement park with attractions for each **Side by Side Plus** unit!

Stop by the *Picture Booth* for FlashCards practice and Picture/Word activities. *"Test Your Strength"* at our Vocabulary, Grammar, Reading, and Life Skills challenges. Step right up to the *Game Gallery* to play Concentration, Quiz Show, Crossword, and Lucky Letters games. Visit *ToonTown* for animation-based grammar activities. And don't miss the videos and music at the *ShowTime* stage.

The FunZone is optimized for computers and tablets. Students, BYOD—Bring Your Own Device.

Life Skills, Standards, Career Readiness, & Test Prep

Standards-based lessons in each unit's "yellow pages" apply students' language learning to their roles in the community, family, school, and at work—aligned with major adult education curriculum frameworks and assessment systems.

Real-life conversation practice stimulates interactive pair work. **Teamwork activities** promote cooperative learning as students share information and complete tasks.

Reading and writing activities include authentic realia and real-life writing tasks.

Check-up tests along with **vocabulary and skill checklists** enable students to assess their progress.

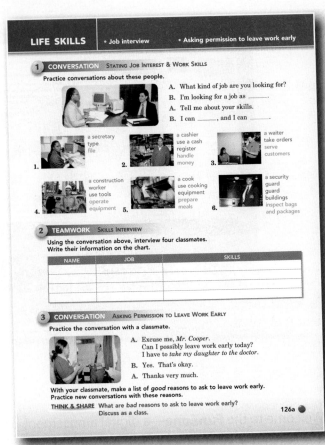

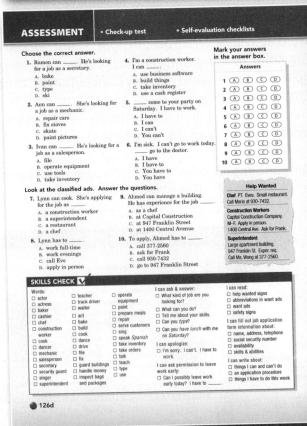

Reading & Writing Workshops

The new *Side by Side Plus* "blue pages" develop basic academic and career readiness skills.

Language Arts lessons offer guided discourse practice in academic communication about the English language. Students learn to "talk the talk" of the mainstream classroom.

Readings about school subjects, work, and life-skills topics build academic and career readiness while developing reading comprehension skills.

Writing activities offer systematic instruction in the Writing Process. Book 1 focuses on Pre-writing, Organizing Ideas, and Writing a First Draft. Upper levels of the program focus on Revising, Proofreading, and Publishing.

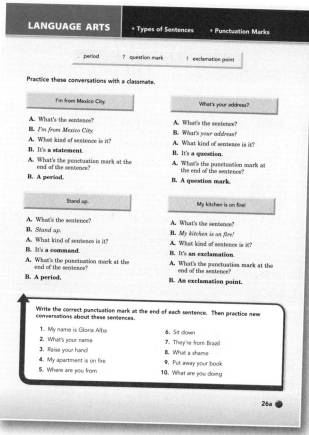

LANGUAGE ARTS • Types of Sentences • Punctuation Marks

. period ? question mark ! exclamation point

Practice these conversations with a classmate.

I'm from Mexico City.

A. What's the sentence?
B. *I'm from Mexico City.*
A. What kind of sentence is it?
B. It's **a statement**.
A. What's the punctuation mark at the end of the sentence?
B. **A period.**

What's your address?

A. What's the sentence?
B. *What's your address?*
A. What kind of sentence is it?
B. It's **a question**.
A. What's the punctuation mark at the end of the sentence?
B. **A question mark.**

Stand up.

A. What's the sentence?
B. *Stand up.*
A. What kind of sentence is it?
B. It's **a command**.
A. What's the punctuation mark at the end of the sentence?
B. **A period.**

My kitchen is on fire!

A. What's the sentence?
B. *My kitchen is on fire!*
A. What kind of sentence is it?
B. It's **an exclamation**.
A. What's the punctuation mark at the end of the sentence?
B. **An exclamation point.**

Write the correct punctuation mark at the end of each sentence. Then practice new conversations about these sentences.

1. My name is Gloria Alba
2. What's your name
3. Raise your hand
4. My apartment is on fire
5. Where are you from
6. Sit down
7. They're from Brazil
8. What a shame
9. Put away your book
10. What are you doing

26a

READING • Employment • Reading Comprehension

TELECOMMUTING

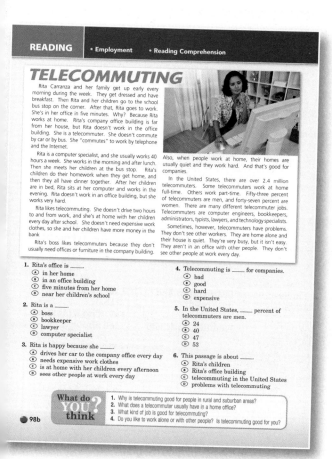

Rita Carranza and her family get up early every morning during the week. They get dressed and have breakfast. Then Rita and her children go to the school bus stop on the corner. After that, Rita goes to work. She's in her office in five minutes. Why? Because Rita works at home. Rita's company office building is far from her house, but Rita doesn't work in the office building. She is a telecommuter. She doesn't commute by car or by bus. She "commutes" to work by telephone and the Internet.

Rita is a computer specialist, and she usually works 40 hours a week. She works in the morning and after lunch. Then she meets her children at the bus stop. Rita's children do their homework when they get home, and then they all have dinner together. After her children are in bed, Rita sits at her computer and works in the evening. Rita doesn't work in an office building, but she works very hard.

Rita likes telecommuting. She doesn't drive two hours to and from work, and she's at home with her children every day after school. She doesn't need expensive work clothes, so she and her children have more money in the bank.

Rita's boss likes telecommuters because they don't usually need offices or furniture in the company building.

Also, when people work at home, their homes are usually quiet and they work hard. And that's good for companies.

In the United States, there are over 2.4 million telecommuters. Some telecommuters work at home full-time. Others work part-time. Fifty-three percent of telecommuters are men, and forty-seven percent are women. There are many different telecommuter jobs. Telecommuters are computer engineers, bookkeepers, administrators, typists, lawyers, and technology specialists.

Sometimes, however, telecommuters have problems. They don't see other workers. They are home alone and their house is quiet. They're very busy, but it isn't easy. They aren't in an office with other people. They don't see other people at work every day.

1. Rita's office is _____
   Ⓐ in her home
   Ⓑ in an office building
   Ⓒ five minutes from her home
   Ⓓ near her children's school

2. Rita is a _____
   Ⓐ boss
   Ⓑ bookkeeper
   Ⓒ lawyer
   Ⓓ computer specialist

3. Rita is happy because she _____
   Ⓐ drives her car to the company office every day
   Ⓑ needs expensive work clothes
   Ⓒ is at home with her children every afternoon
   Ⓓ sees other people at work every day

4. Telecommuting is _____ for companies.
   Ⓐ bad
   Ⓑ good
   Ⓒ hard
   Ⓓ expensive

5. In the United States, _____ percent of telecommuters are men.
   Ⓐ 24
   Ⓑ 40
   Ⓒ 47
   Ⓓ 53

6. This passage is about _____
   Ⓐ Rita's children
   Ⓑ Rita's office building
   Ⓒ telecommuting in the United States
   Ⓓ problems with telecommuting

What do YOU think?
1. Why is telecommuting good for people in rural and suburban areas?
2. What does a telecommuter usually have in a home office?
3. What kind of job is good for telecommuting?
4. Do you like to work alone or with other people? Is telecommuting good for you?

98b

THE WRITING PROCESS • Pre-writing • Organizing Ideas • Writing a First Draft

Marisol is writing a paragraph about life in her home. She's using the writing process. She's pre-writing, organizing ideas, and writing a first draft.

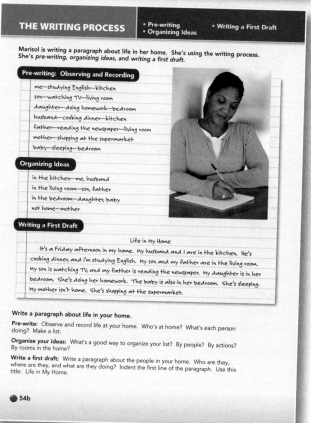

Pre-writing: Observing and Recording

me—studying English—kitchen
son—watching TV—living room
daughter—doing homework—bedroom
husband—cooking dinner—kitchen
father—reading the newspaper—living room
mother—shopping at the supermarket
baby—sleeping—bedroom

Organizing Ideas

in the kitchen—me, husband
in the living room—son, father
in the bedroom—daughter, baby
not home—mother

Writing a First Draft

Life in My Home

It's a Friday afternoon in my home. My husband and I are in the kitchen. He's cooking dinner, and I'm studying English. My son and my father are in the living room. My son is watching TV, and my father is reading the newspaper. My daughter is in her bedroom. She's doing her homework. The baby is also in her bedroom. She's sleeping. My mother isn't home. She's shopping at the supermarket.

Write a paragraph about life in your home.

Pre-write: Observe and record life at your home. Who's at home? What's each person doing? Make a list.

Organize your ideas: What's a good way to organize your list? By people? By actions? By rooms in the home?

Write a first draft: Write a paragraph about the people in your home. Who are they, where are they, and what are they doing? Indent the first line of the paragraph. Use this title: Life in My Home.

54b

Scope and Sequence

Unit	Topics, Vocabulary, & Math	Grammar	Functional Communication	Listening & Pronunciation	Writing
1	• Personal information • Meeting people • Alphabet • Spelling names aloud • Cardinal numbers in addresses & telephone numbers	• To be: Introduction	• Meeting people	• Listening for personal information • Pronouncing linked sounds	• Writing about yourself: Name, address, phone number, country of origin • Filling out a form • Addressing an envelope
2	• Classroom objects • Rooms in the home • Cities, countries, & nationalities • Places around town • Classroom actions • Giving & following instructions	• To be + location • Subject pronouns	• Greeting people	• Listening for information about people's locations • Pronouncing reduced *and*	• Making a list of classroom objects • Writing information in a chart
3	• Everyday activities • Calling directory assistance • Calling 911 • Using a telephone directory	• Present continuous tense	• Checking understanding	• Listening and responding correctly to questions about people's actions • Pronouncing reduced *What are* & *Where are*	• Writing about your current activities and the activities of friends • Writing emergency telephone numbers
Gazette Reading & Writing Workshop	• Titles & nicknames • Common leisure activities: playing instruments, sports, & games • Culture concept: Greetings around the world • Telephone numbers • Civics: A Nation of Immigrants	• To be • Present continuous tense	• Describing people's activities	• Listening to messages on a telephone answering machine	• Writing an e-mail or instant message to tell about yourself • Types of sentences • Punctuation marks
4	• Everyday activities • Places around town • Civics: Community service	• To be: Short answers • Possessive adjectives	• Attracting someone's attention	• Listening & responding correctly to questions about activities • Pronouncing deleted *h*	• Writing about a place in your community • Writing names & addresses of places in a chart
5	• Describing people & things • Weather • Reading a weather map • Fahrenheit & Celsius temperatures	• To be: Yes/No questions, Short Answers • Adjectives • Possessive nouns	• Calling someone you know on the telephone	• Listening & responding correctly to requests for information • Pronouncing yes/no questions with *or*	• Filling out a form • Writing a friendly letter describing the weather and current activities • Writing information in a chart
6	• Describing activities & events • Family members • Reading a family tree diagram	• To be: Review • Present continuous tense: Review • Prepositions of location	• Introducing people	• Listening & making deductions • Pronouncing stressed and unstressed words	• Writing a story about a scene • Writing about a favorite photograph
Gazette Reading & Writing Workshop	• Family relations • Classroom activities • Culture concept: Extended & nuclear families • Social Studies: The family	• To be • Possessive adjectives	• Describing family members and family relationships	• Listening to and interpreting correctly radio weather forecasts	• Writing about your family • Writing a message to tell about weather and current activities • The Writing Process

CORRELATION and PLACEMENT KEY

Side by Side Plus 1 correlates with these standards-based curriculum levels and assessment system score ranges.

For correlation keys to other major state and local curriculum frameworks, please visit:
http://pearsoneltusa.com/molinskyandbliss

NRS (National Reporting System) Educational Functioning Level	Low Beginning
BEST Plus 2.0 (Basic English Skills Test)	362–427 (SPL 2)
BEST Literacy	21–52 (SPL 2)
CASAS Reading	181–190
CASAS Listening	181–189
CASAS Writing	136–145
TABE CLAS-E Reading & Writing	395–441
TABE CLAS-E Listening & Speaking	408–449

Life Skills, Civics, & Test Preparation	EFF	SCANS	CCRS	CASAS	LAUSD	Florida*
• Personal information & forms • Information on an envelope • Common abbreviations in addresses • Forms of identification	• Gather information • Cooperate with others	• Sociability • Acquire & evaluate information	RI/RL.1.1, RI.1.4, SL.K.2, SL.K.3, SL.K.6, SL.1.1(a-c), SL.1.4, SL.1.6, L.1.1(a, b, g, k), L.1.2.b, L.1.6	0.1.2, 0.1.4, 0.1.6, 0.2.1, 0.2.2, 2.4.1, 5.1.4, 7.4.7	1, 2, 3, 4, 5, 7, 8, 11b, 41, 58, 59, 60	2.01.04, 2.01.05, 2.05.01, 2.05.02, 2.08.01, 2.15.05, 2.16.02, 2.16.05
• Classroom items • Simple classroom commands • School personnel • School locations • Locating classroom items • Taking inventory	• Manage resources • Work together • Give direction	• Identify resources • Participate as a team member • See things in the mind's eye	RI/RL.1.1, RI.1.4, SL.K.2, SL.K.3, SL.K.6, SL.1.1(a-c), SL.1.4, SL.1.6, L.1.1(a, b, c, d, g, j, k), L.1.6	0.1.2, 0.1.4, 0.1.5, 6.0.2, 7.3.1, 7.3.2, 7.4.7	5, 9a, 15, 16, 17, 18, 59	2.05.01, 2.05.02, 2.08.01, 2.16.01, 2.16.02, 2.16.05, 2.16.08, 2.16.09, 2.16.12
• Common classroom & home activities • Asking about home activities • Calling directory assistance • Calling 911 • Using a telephone directory	• Seek input from others • Identify a strong sense of family	• Identify goal-relevant activities	RI/RL.1.1, RI.1.4, RI.1.7, W.1.3, SL.K.2, SL.K.3, SL.K.6, SL.1.1(a-c), SL.1.4, SL.1.6, L.1.1(a, b, c, d, e, g, k), L.1.2.a, L.1.6	0.1.4, 0.1.5, 0.1.6, 0.2.4, 2.1.1, 2.1.2, 2.5.1, 7.4.7	9c, 11a, 12, 13, 19, 59	2.05.02, 2.06.01, 2.06.03, 2.06.05, 2.06.06, 2.10.02, 2.14.07, 2.16.01, 2.16.02, 2.16.05, 2.16.08, 2.16.12
• Identifying people by appropriate titles • Interpreting telephone messages on an answering machine	• Respect others & value diversity • Use technology	• Acquire & evaluate information • Work with cultural diversity • Work with technology	RI/RL.1.1, RI.1.2, RI.1.4, RI.1.7, W.1.2, SL.K.2, (a-c), SL.K.3, SL.1.4, SL.K.6, SL.1.1(a-c), SL.1.6, L.1.1 (k, l), L.1.2.c, L.1.2.d, L.1.6	0.1.4, 0.2.3, 0.2.4, 2.1.7, 2.7.2, 4.5.4	1, 4, 9c, 12	2.05.02, 2.06.02, 2.08.01, 2.14.07, 2.16.01, 2.16.02
• Common classroom & home activities • Asking about home activities • Learning skill: Alphabetizing • Civics: Community service	• Meet family responsibilities • Work within the big picture • Observe critically	• Identify goal-relevant activities • Responsibility • Understand a social system	RI/RL.1.1, RI.1.2, RI.1.4, W.1.2, W.1.3, SL.K.2, SL.K.3, SL.K.6, SL.1.1(a-c), SL.1.4, SL.1.6, L.1.1(a, b, d, g, k), L.1.6	0.1.4, 0.2.4, 5.6.1, 7.2.3, 7.4.5, 7.4.7	9d, 12, 13, 22, 58, 59	2.07.08, 2.16.05, 2.16.10, 2.16.12
• Describing people, things, & weather • Using the telephone • Interpreting a thermometer • Weather reports • Reading a weather map	• Seek input from others	• Sociability	RI/RL.1.1, RI.1.3, RI.1.4, RL.1.7, W.1.3, SL.K.2, SL.K.3, SL.K.6, SL.1.1(a-c), SL.1.4, SL.1.6, L.1.1(a, b, d, f, g, h, k), L.1.6	0.1.2, 0.2.2, 1.1.5, 2.1.8, 2.3.3, 7.4.7	6, 7, 28, 29, 59	2.05.01, 2.05.02, 2.06.01, 2.06.02, 2.13.01, 2.13.03, 2.16.01, 2.16.07, 2.16.11
• Family relations • Common activities • Greeting & introducing • Learning skill: Categorizing • Eye contact & gestures	• Identify family relationships • Express sense of self • Cooperate with others	• Sociability • Self-esteem • Participate as a team member	RI/RL.1.1, RI.1.4, RI.1.7, W.1.2, W.1.3, SL.K.2, SL.K.3, SL.K.6, SL.1.1(a-c), SL.1.4, SL.1.6, L.1.1(b, d, e, g, h, j, k), L.1.6	0.1.1, 0.1.2, 0.1.4, 0.2.1, 0.2.4, 7.2.3, 7.4.7	6, 9b, 59	2.05.01, 2.05.02, 2.14.01, 2.16.02, 2.16.08, 2.16.11, 2.16.12
• Family relations • Common classroom activities • Weather forecasts	• Identify family relationships • Respect others & value diversity • Use technology	• See things in the mind's eye • Identify goal-relevant activities • Work with cultural diversity	RI/RL.1.1, RI.1.2, RI.1.4, RI.1.7, W.1.2 (a-c), W.1.3, SL.K.2, SL.1.1(a-c), L.1.6	0.1.5, 0.2.3, 2.3.3, 2.7.2	6, 12, 28	2.14.01, 2.16.02

EFF: Equipped for the Future (Content standards, Common activities, & Role maps)
SCANS: Secretary's Commission on Achieving Necessary Skills (U.S. Department of Labor)
CCRS: College and Career Readiness Standards for Adult Education (U.S. Department of Education)
CASAS: Comprehensive Adult Student Assessment System
LAUSD: Los Angeles Unified School District (ESL Beginning High content standards)
Florida: Adult ESOL Low Beginning Standardized Syllabi

(*Florida benchmarks 2.15.06, 2.15.07, 2.15.08, 2.16.01, 2.16.02, 2.16.05, 2.16.12, 2.17.01, 2.17.02, and 2.17.03 are covered in every unit and therefore are not included in the listings above.)

Scope and Sequence

Unit	Topics, Vocabulary, & Math	Grammar	Functional Communication	Listening & Pronunciation	Writing
7	• Places around town • Locating places • Describing neighborhoods • Describing apartments • Reading a simple map • Apartment ads • Cardinal numbers indicating quantity	• Prepositions • There is /There are • Singular/Plural introduction	• Expressing gratitude	• Listening for information about neighborhoods & apartments • Using rising intonation to check understanding	• Writing a description of a neighborhood • Writing about your apartment building or home
8	• Clothing • Colors • Shopping for clothing • Money • Price tags • Cardinal numbers indicating money denominations, prices, & clothing sizes • Store receipts	• Singular/Plural • Adjectives • This/That/These/Those	• Complimenting	• Listening for information about clothing items • Pronouncing emphasized words	• Writing a description of clothing and colors
Gazette Reading & Writing Workshop	• Clothing, colors, and cultures • Culture concept: People's homes around the world • Civics concept: Urban, suburban, and rural communities • Interpreting percents in a pie chart	• Singular/Plural • Adjectives • Statements and questions with Verb To Be	• Describing clothing • Complimenting • Describing homes	• Listening for information in public address announcements in stores	• Writing an e-mail or instant message to describe your neighborhood
9	• Language & nationalities • Everyday activities • Civics: Staying informed	• Simple present tense	• Hesitating	• Listening for –s vs. non –s endings in verbs contained in sentences • Blending with does	• Writing about your city, language, and daily activities • Writing information in a chart
10	• Days of the week • Habitual actions • People's interests & activities • Work schedules • Bus destination signs	• Simple present tense: Yes/No questions, Negatives, Short answers	• Starting a conversation	• Listening for information about people's habitual actions • Pronouncing reduced of	• Writing about usual activities during the week and on the weekend • Writing about a work schedule
Gazette Reading & Writing Workshop	• Languages around the world • Interpreting tables with number facts in millions • Culture concept: Exercising around the world • Employment: Telecommuting	• Simple present tense • Subject and verb agreement	• Describing everyday activities and interests	• Listening for information in a recorded telephone announcement	• Writing an e-mail or instant message to tell about activities & interests
11	• Calendar • Describing frequency of actions • Describing people • Time expressions • Interpreting percentages related to adverbs of frequency	• Object pronouns • Simple present tense: –s vs. non –s endings • Have/Has • Adverbs of frequency	• Reacting to information	• Pronouncing past tense endings • Pronouncing deleted h • Listening and making deductions	• Writing about close friends • Writing about daily activities
12	• Feelings & emotions • Describing usual & unusual activities • The education system • School personnel & locations	• Contrast: Simple present & present continuous tenses	• Reacting to bad news	• Listening to distinguish questions about current vs. habitual actions • Pronouncing reduced to	• Writing about a typical day in a city or town
Gazette Reading & Writing Workshop	• Traffic: A global problem • Culture concept: Modes of transportation around the world • Interpreting tables with number facts in millions • The education system: Public schools	• Simple present tense • Statements and questions with the simple present tense	• Describing a problem • Describing customary activities	• Listening for information in radio news reports	• Writing an e-mail or instant message to tell about yourself, family, & personal appearance

Life Skills, Civics, & Test Preparation	EFF	SCANS	CCRS	CASAS	LAUSD	Florida
• Identifying & locating places in the community • Identifying rooms, furniture, & fixtures in a residence • Inquiring about residences, rentals, & neighborhoods • Interpreting a map • Apartment ads	• Seek input from others • Provide for family's safety & needs • Cooperate with others	• Identify resources • Acquire & evaluate information • See things in the mind's eye (map) • Participate as a team member	RI/RL.1.1, RI.1.4, RI.1.7, W.1.2, SL.K.2, SL.K.3, SL.K.6, SL.1.1(a-c), SL.1.4, SL.1.6, L.1.1(a, b, c, g, j, k), L.1.2.a, L.1.6	0.1.2, 0.1.4, 1.1.3, 1.4.1, 1.4.2, 2.2.1, 2.5.1, 2.5.3, 6.0.2, 7.4.7	9d, 22, 23, 38, 39, 59	2.05.01, 2.08.01, 2.09.04, 2.11.06, 2.11.08, 2.12.01, 2.12.02, 2.16.06, 2.16.08, 2.16.09
• Clothing • Asking for help • Identifying clothing needs • Money: Coins, Currency • Clothing labels: Sizes, Prices, Colors • Price tags • Store receipts	• Manage resources • Seek & receive assistance • Resolve conflict & negotiate • Be friendly & courteous • Meet family responsibilities	• Identify resources • Serve clients/ customers • Negotiate • Problem solving • Sociability	RI/RL.1.1, RI.1.4, RI.1.7, SL.K.3, SL.K.6, SL.1.1(a-c), SL.1.4, SL.1.6, L.1.1(b, c, d, f, k), L.1.5.a, L.1.6	0.1.4, 1.1.6, 1.1.9, 1.2.1, 1.6.4, 1.3.9, 6.1.1, 7.4.7	9d, 30, 31, 33, 34, 59	2.08.01, 2.08.04, 2.11.01, 2.11.03, 2.11.04, 2.15.01, 2.16.04, 2.16.06, 2.16.07, 2.16.09
• Clothing • Store announcements • Describing housing and neighborhoods	• Respect others & value diversity • Analyze & use information • Work with symbolic information • Use technology	• Work with cultural diversity • See things in the mind's eye (pie chart) • Sociability	RI/RL.1.1, RI.1.2, RI.1.4, RI.1.7, W.1.2, (a-c), SL.K.2, SL.K.3, SL.1.4, SL.K.6, SL.1.6, SL.1.1(a-c), L.1.1.l, L.1.2(c, d), L.1.6	0.1.4, 0.2.3, 1.1.3, 1.3.7, 1.3.9, 1.4.1, 2.7.2, 6.4.2, 6.7.4, 6.8.1	33, 34	2.08.01, 2.11.06, 2.15.01
• Asking for and giving personal information: Name, city, language, daily activities • Common activities • Social interactions • Civics: Staying informed	• Express sense of self • Promote values, ethics, & cultural heritage • Cooperate	• Sociability • Self-esteem • Participate as a team member	RI/RL.1.1, RI.1.4, W.1.3, SL.K.2, SL.K.3, SL.K.6, SL.1.1(a-c), SL.1.4, SL.1.6, L.1.1(b, c, d, e, g, k), L.1.4.c, L.1.6	0.1.4, 0.2.1, 0.2.4, 7.3.1, 7.3.2, 7.4.7	13, 59	2.05.02, 2.16.01, 2.16.02, 2.16.05
• Common activities • Ordering in a fast food restaurant • Days of the week • Work schedules • Bus routes & signs	• Allocate time • Offer input on interests • Identify strong sense of family	• Allocate time • Self-management • Sociability	RI/RL.1.1, RI.1.4, RI.1.7, W.1.3, SL.K.2, SL.K.3, SL.K.6, SL.1.4, SL.1.1(a-c), SL.1.6, L.1.1(a, b, d, e, k), L.1.6	0.1.2, 0.1.3, 0.1.4, 0.2.4, 2.2.1, 2.2.2, 2.2.3, 2.6.4, 4.1.6, 4.2.1, 6.7.3, 7.4.7	12, 13, 14a, 24, 37, 55, 59	2.02.04, 2.03.03, 2.05.02, 2.05.03, 2.08.03, 2.09.01, 2.14.07, 2.16.01, 2.16.02, 2.16.05
• Describe common activities • Interpreting recorded telephone announcements	• Analyze & use information • Work with numbers • Respect others & value diversity • Use technology	• See things in the mind's eye (map) • Acquire & evaluate information • Work with cultural diversity • Work with technology	RI/RL.1.1, RI.1.2, RI.1.4, RI.1.7, W.1.2, SL.K.2, SL.K.6, SL.1.1(a-c), SL.1.4, SL.1.6, L.1.1(c, e), L.1.6	0.2.3, 1.1.3, 2.1.7, 2.6.1, 2.7.2, 6.8.1	12, 23	2.05.02, 2.08.01
• Family relations • Family responsibilities • Describing oneself • Describing people at work • Asking for tableware (Workbook)	• Allocate time • Express sense of self • Identify strong sense of family • Be friendly	• Allocate time • Self-esteem • Sociability	RI/RL.1.1, RI.1.4, W.1.2, SL.K.3, SL.K.6, SL.1.1(a-c), SL.1.4, SL.1.6, L.1.1(a, b, c, d, e, f, g, k), L.1.2.i, L.1.6	0.1.2, 0.1.4, 0.2.4, 7.4.7, 7.5.5	6, 12, 13, 59	2.02.02, 2.02.04, 2.05.02, 2.05.03, 2.08.03, 2.16.01, 2.16.03, 2.16.05, 2.16.07
• Describing states of being • Asking about home activities • School personnel & locations	• Identify problems • Work within the big picture • Identify community resources	• Self-management • Creative thinking • Understand a workplace system	RI/RL.1.1, RI.1.2, RI.1.4, SL.K.3, SL.K.6, SL.1.1(a-c), SL.1.4, SL.1.6, L.1.1(b, e, f, k), L.1.4.c, L.1.6	0.1.4, 0.2.4, 2.2.2, 2.2.3, 7.4.7	16, 17, 24, 59, 60	2.01.01, 2.05.01, 2.05.02, 2.14.02, 2.16.02, 2.16.07
• Describing modes of travel to work and school • Interpreting traffic information & other information in radio newscasts	• Identify problems & solutions • Respect others & value diversity • Work with numbers • Use technology	• Acquire & evaluate information • Work with cultural diversity	RI/RL.1.1, RI.1.2, RI.1.4, RI.1.7, W.1.2, SL.K.2, SL.K.6, SL.1.1(a-c), SL.1.4, SL.1.6, L.1.1.l, L.1.2(a, c, d), L.1.6	0.2.3, 2.2.3, 2.7.2, 6.8.1	13, 24	2.08.01, 2.16.02

Scope and Sequence

Unit	Topics, Vocabulary, & Math	Grammar	Functional Communication	Listening & Pronunciation	Writing
13	• Occupations • Expressing ability • Looking for a job • Help Wanted signs • Want ads • Responding to questions in a simple job interview • Applying for a driver's license	• Can • Have to	• Apologizing • Expressing obligation • Invitations	• Listening for information about occupational skills • Pronouncing *can* & *can't*	• Filling out a job application form • Writing about how to apply for a passport, marriage license, or loan • Writing about what you have to do this week • Making lists of skills
14	• Describing future plans & intentions • Weather forecasts • Telling time • Months of the year • Seasons • Dates • Job application forms • Ordinal numbers	• Future: Going to • Time expressions • Want to	• Asking the time • Congratulating • Expressing wants • Making predictions	• Listening for time expressions • Pronouncing *going to* & *want to*	• Writing about plans for tomorrow • Writing months of the year • Writing dates • Filling out a form
Gazette **Reading & Writing Workshop**	• Time zones • Culture concept: Notions of time and punctuality in different cultures • Employment: Part-time workers	• Verb: To be • Simple present tense • Future: Going to • Statements and questions with *Can*	• Describing occupation	• Listening for movie listing information in a recorded telephone announcement	• Writing an e-mail or instant message to tell about plans for the weekend • Capitalization
15	• Past actions & activities • Ailments • Making a doctor's appointment • A medical exam • Medical appointment cards • Medicine labels • Numbers: Interpreting a thermometer, medicine labels, & a dosage cup • Staying healthy	• Past tense: Regular verbs, Introduction to irregular verbs	• Saying how you feel • Describing an event	• Listening to distinguish statements in the present tense vs. the past tense • Pronouncing past tense endings	• Writing about a party • Writing about your meals yesterday
16	• Reporting past actions & activities • Giving reasons • Giving excuses • Job applications • Using clock times in a narrative	• Past tense: Yes/No questions, Short answers, WH- questions, More irregular verbs • Time expressions	• Giving an excuse	• Listening for specific information to complete a checklist • Pronouncing *Did you*	• Writing about your activities yesterday • Filling out a job application form
17	• Television commercials • Biographies & autobiographies • Basic foods & food groups • Ordering a meal • Reading a simple menu • Supermarket ads • Food labels	• To be: Past tense	• Recommending products • Describing physical states & emotions • Telling about the past	• Listening to distinguish present vs. past facts • Using correct intonation with yes/no questions and WH- questions	• Writing a brief autobiography about major life events (born, grew up, went to school, studied, moved) • Writing about your childhood • Making a shopping list
Gazette **Reading & Writing Workshop**	• Advertisements • Opposites • Culture concept: Shopping around the world • Consumer Economics: Shopping with coupons	• Tense review • Adjectives	• Describing products • Telling about activities in the past	• Listening for information in radio advertisements	• Writing an e-mail or instant message to tell about what you did today • The Writing Process

Life Skills, Civics, & Test Preparation	EFF	SCANS	CCRS	CASAS	LAUSD	Florida
• Occupations, abilities, & skills • Asking permission at work • Calling to explain absence • Help wanted signs • Want ads • Police/safety commands & signs	• Express sense of self • Plan: Set a goal • Define what one is trying to achieve • Be tactful • Reflect & evaluate • Work within the big picture	• Identify human resources (work skills) • Self-management: Assess self accurately • Self-esteem • Understand an organizational system • Participate as a team member	RI/RL.1.1, RI.1.4, RI.1.7, W.1.2, SL.K.2, SL.K.3, SL.K.6, SL.1.1(a-c), SL.1.4, SL.1.6, L.1.1(a, b, d, k), L.1.6	0.1.2, 0.1.3, 0.2.4, 1.9.1, 2.2.2, 2.5.4, 2.5.7, 3.1.1, 3.3.3, 3.4.1, 4.1.2, 4.1.3, 4.1.5, 4.1.6, 4.1.8, 4.3.1, 4.4.1, 7.4.7	10, 14b, 42, 48, 49, 50, 51, 52, 53, 54, 57, 59, 60	2.01.01, 2.01.02, 2.01.03, 2.01.04, 2.01.07, 2.02.01, 2.02.03, 2.03.03, 2.05.01, 2.10.01, 2.10.03, 2.14.07, 2.15.05
• Asking & telling time • The calendar • Ordinal numbers • Months of the year • Filling out a form • National holidays in the United States & Canada (Workbook)	• Create & pursue vision & goals • Make a prediction • Identify opportunities for family members to succeed	• Identify goal-relevant activities • Self-management: Set personal goals	RI/RL.1.1, RI.1.4, RI.1.7, SL.K.2, SL.K.3, SL.K.6, SL.1.1(a-c), SL.1.4, SL.1.6, L.1.1(a, b, d, e, k), L.1.2(b, i), L.1.6	0.1.1, 0.1.2, 0.2.2, 0.2.4, 2.3.1, 2.3.2, 2.3.3, 2.5.4, 2.7.1, 4.1.6, 4.2.1, 7.4.7	3, 7, 13, 25, 26, 40, 55, 59, 60	2.01.03, 2.02.04, 2.05.02, 2.08.01, 2.08.03, 2.09.02, 2.14.07, 2.15.05, 2.16.02, 2.16.03
• Identifying time zones • Identifying occupations • Interpreting movie listings in telephone recorded announcements	• Analyze & use information • Work with symbolic information • Respect others & value diversity • Use technology	• Acquire & evaluate information • Identify human resources (occupations) • Work with cultural diversity • Responsibility	RI/RL.1.1, RI.1.2, RI.1.4, RI.1.7, W.1.2, SL.K.2, SL.K.6, SL.1.1(a-c), SL.1.4, SL.1.6, L.1.1(e, l), L.1.2(a, b, c, d), L.1.6	0.2.3, 2.1.3, 2.1.7, 2.6.2, 2.7.2, 4.1.8	13, 23, 50	2.01.01, 2.06.02, 2.08.02, 2.13.03
• Medical care: Parts of the body • Ailments • Calling for medical appointments • Calling for emergency assistance • Over-the-counter medications • Drug labels & dosages • Filling/Refilling prescriptions • Interpreting a Fahrenheit thermometer • Interpreting a dosage cup	• Provide for family's safety & physical needs • Seek & receive assistance	• Self-management • Responsibility	RI/RL.1.1, RI.1.2, RI.1.4, RI.1.7, W.1.2, SL.K.2, SL.K.3, SL.K.6, SL.1.1(a-c), SL.1.4, SL.1.6, L.1.1(a, b, d, e, k), L.1.2(e, i), L.1.4.c, L.1.6	1.3.7, 2.1.2, 2.1.8, 2.3.2, 2.5.1, 3.1.1, 3.1.2, 3.1.3, 3.3.1, 3.3.2, 3.4.1, 3.5.9, 7.3.1, 7.4.7	19, 20, 21, 27, 32, 43, 44, 45, 46, 59, 60	2.06.05, 2.07.01, 2.07.02, 2.07.03, 2.07.04, 2.07.05, 2.07.06, 2.07.10, 2.08.01, 2.08.03, 2.16.02
• Apologizing for lateness at work • Providing information about education & employment record • Safety procedures: Earthquake, Clothing on fire (Workbook) • Eye contact & gestures (Workbook)	• Allocate time • Balance individual roles & needs with those of the organization • Develop & express sense of self	• Responsibility • Integrity • Allocate time	RI/RL.1.1, RI.1.4, RI.1.7, SL.K.2, SL.K.3, SL.K.6, SL.1.1(a-c), SL.1.4, SL.1.6, L.1.1(a, b, e, k), L.1.6	0.1.1, 0.1.6, 1.3.7, 3.4.2, 4.1.2, 4.1.5, 4.3.1, 7.4.7	11c, 32, 47, 54, 59, 60	2.01.02, 2.01.03, 2.02.01, 2.03.03, 2.05.01, 2.05.02, 2.15.05, 2.16.02
• Basic foods & food groups • Food ads & labels • Learning skill: Categorizing • Common containers (Workbook) • System of weights using ounces & pounds (Workbook)	• Promote family members' growth & development • Express sense of self • Use math to solve problems	• Self-management • Serve clients/customers • Responsibility • Self-esteem	RI/RL.1.1, RI.1.4, RI.1.7, W.1.3, SL.K.2, SL.K.3, SL.K.6, SL.1.1(a-c), SL.1.4, SL.1.6, L.1.1(a, b, c, d, e, f, k), L.1.5.a, L.1.6	0.1.2, 0.1.3, 0.2.1, 0.2.4, 1.3.8, 1.6.1, 2.6.4, 6.1.1, 7.4.7	35, 36, 37, 59, 60	2.05.02, 2.07.09, 2.07.11, 2.11.01, 2.16.02, 2.16.05, 2.16.07, 2.16.10
• Interpreting advertisements	• Respect others & value diversity • Use technology	• Acquire & evaluate information • Work with cultural diversity	RI/RL.1.1, RI.1.2, RI.1.4, RI.1.7, W.1.2, SL.K.2, SL.1.1(a-c), L.1.1, L.1.2, L.1.6	0.2.3, 1.1.7, 1.2.1, 1.2.5, 1.3.1, 2.7.2, 7.2.3	22, 34	2.11.01, 2.16.07, 2.16.10

1

To Be: Introduction

- **Personal Information**
- **Cardinal Numbers**
- **Meeting People**
- **Filling Out a Form**

- **Forms of Identification**
- **Addressing an Envelope**
- **Abbreviations in Addresses**

VOCABULARY PREVIEW

(1)
Aa	Bb	Cc	Dd	Ee	Ff	Gg
Hh	Ii	Jj	Kk	Ll	Mm	Nn
Oo	Pp	Qq	Rr	Ss	Tt	Uu
Vv	Ww	Xx	Yy	Zz		

(2) 0   1   2   3   4   5   6   7   8   9   10

1. alphabet

2. numbers

3. name

235 Main Street

4. address

741-8906

5. telephone number
phone number

What's Your Name?

* What's = What is
  235 = two thirty-five
  741-8906 = seven four one – eight nine "oh" six

Answer these questions.

1. What's your name?

   _____.

2. What's your address?

   _____.

3. What's your phone number?

   _____.

4. Where are you from?

   _____.

Now practice with other students in your class.

ROLE PLAY *A Famous Person*

Interview a famous person. Make up addresses, phone numbers, and cities. Use your imagination! Practice with another student. Then present your role play to the class.

A. What's your name?

B. My name is _____.

A. _____ address?

B. _____.

A. _____ phone number?

B. _____.

A. Where are you from?

B. _____.

a famous actor

a famous actress

a famous athlete

the president*
of your country

How to Say It!

Meeting People

A. Hello. My name is *Peter Lewis.*

B. Hi. I'm *Nancy Lee.* Nice to meet you.

A. Nice to meet you, too.

Practice conversations with other students.

* president / prime minister / leader

3

WHAT'S YOUR NAME?

My name is David Carter. I'm American. I'm from San Francisco.

My name is Mrs. Grant. My phone number is 549-2376.

My name is Ms. Martinez. My telephone number is (213) 694-5555. My fax number is (213) 694-5557.

My name is Peter Black. My address is 378 Main Street, Waterville, Florida. My license number is 921DCG.

My name is Susan Miller. My apartment number is 4-B.

My name is Mr. Santini. My e-mail address is TeacherJoe@worldnet.com.*

My name is William Chen. My address is 294 River Street, Brooklyn, New York. My telephone number is 469-7750. My social security number is 044-35-9862.

* "TeacherJoe at worldnet-dot-com"

✔ READING CHECK-UP

MATCH

____ 1. name
____ 2. address
____ 3. phone number
____ 4. apartment number
____ 5. social security number
____ 6. e-mail address

a. 549-2376
b. 4-B
c. TeacherJoe@worldnet.com
d. William Chen
e. 378 Main Street
f. 044-35-9862

LISTENING

Listen and choose the correct answer.

1. a. Mary Black
   b. Mrs. Grant
2. a. 265 River Street
   b. 265 Main Street
3. a. 5-C
   b. 9-D

4. a. 295-4870
   b. 259-4087
5. a. 032-98-6175
   b. 032-89-6179
6. a. maryb@worldnet.com
   b. garyd@worldnet.com

INTERVIEW *Spelling Names*

Practice the conversation.

A. What's your last name?
B. *Kelly.*
A. How do you spell that?
B. *K-E-L-L-Y.*
A. What's your first name?
B. *Sarah.*
A. How do you spell that?
B. *S-A-R-A-H.*

Now interview students in your class.

	LAST NAME	FIRST NAME
1.		
2.		
3.		
4.		
5.		
6.		
7.		
8.		

PRONUNCIATION Linked Sounds

Listen. Then say it.

My name is Maria.

My address is 10 Main Street.

My apartment number is 3B.

Say it. Then listen.

My name is David.

My address is 9 River Street.

My phone number is 941-2238.

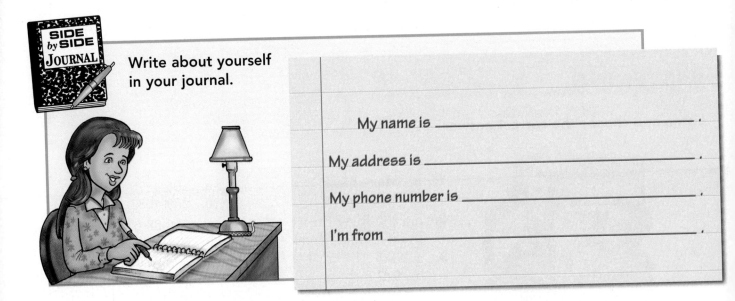

SIDE by SIDE JOURNAL

Write about yourself in your journal.

My name is _____ .

My address is _____ .

My phone number is _____ .

I'm from _____ .

GRAMMAR FOCUS

TO BE: AM/IS/ARE

am	I'm from Mexico City. (I am)
is	What's your name? (What is) My name is Maria.
are	Where are you from?

Choose the correct word.

1. My name (are   is) Carlos.
2. Where (are   is) you from?
3. I (are   am) from Los Angeles.
4. My phone number (are   is) 954-3376.
5. (I   I'm) from Miami.

I'M/MY/YOU/YOUR

I'm My	I'm from San Francisco. My name is Maria.
you your	Where are you from? What's your name?

Choose the correct word.

6. (I'm   My) address is 25 Center Street.
7. (I'm   My) from Chicago.
8. What's (you   your) social security number?
9. Where are (you   your) from?
10. Hello. (I'm   My) David Wong.

1 CONVERSATION   GIVING PERSONAL INFORMATION

Look at the form. Practice the conversation with a classmate.

A. What's your first name?

B. _____.

A. What's your last name?

B. _____.

A. How do you spell that?

B. _____.

A. What's your address?

B. _____.

A. What's your apartment number?

B. _____.

A. What's your city?

B. _____.

A. What's your state?

B. _____.

A. What's your zip code?

B. _____.

Registration Form

NAME	Edward	H.	Ramirez
	First	Middle Initial	Last

ADDRESS	94 River Street		7D
	Number Street		Apartment Number
	Los Angeles	CA	90036
	City	State	Zip Code

2 WRITING   FILLING OUT A FORM

Fill out the form with your personal information.

Registration Form

NAME			
	First	Middle Initial	Last

ADDRESS			
	Number Street		Apartment Number
	City	State	Zip Code

3 **TEAMWORK** ASKING FOR AND GIVING PERSONAL INFORMATION

Work with a classmate. Interview each other. Ask these questions.
Write the information on the form.

What's your first name? How do you spell it?
What's your last name? How do you spell it?
What's your address?
What's your apartment number?
What's your city?
What's your state?
What's your zip code?

First   Middle Initial   Last

Number   Street   Apartment Number

City   State   Zip Code

4 **WRITING** ADDRESSING AN ENVELOPE

Address this envelope to your classmate.

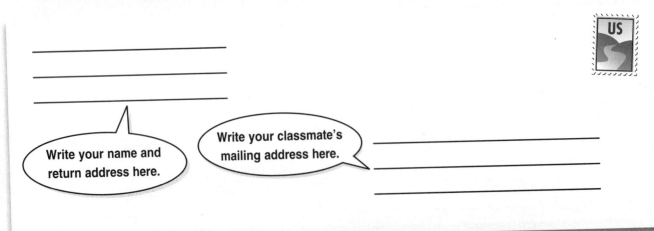

Write your name and return address here.

Write your classmate's mailing address here.

Look at these forms of identification (I.D.) and answer the questions.

a driver's license

a social security card

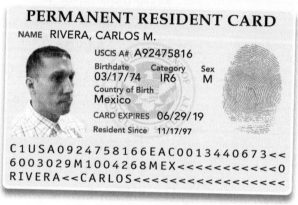

a permanent resident card

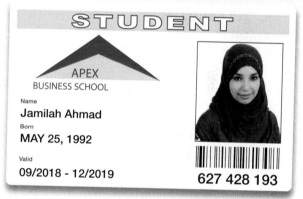

a student I.D. card

1. What is Susan Johnson's address? _____

2. What is Mr. Rivera's first name? _____

3. What is Peter Chen's social security number? _____

4. What is the name of Jamilah Ahmad's school? _____

THINK & SHARE What are *your* forms of identification? Why are they important?

ABBREVIATIONS IN ADDRESSES

Study these abbreviations.

St.	Street	N.	North
Ave.	Avenue	S.	South
Blvd.	Boulevard	E.	East
Apt.	Apartment	W.	West

Read these addresses.

63 E. Main St.
81 S. Central Ave.
417 N. Washington Ave., Apt. 42
246 W. Hollywood Blvd., Apt. 17D
937 S. River St., Apt. 8F

COMMUNITY CONNECTIONS What are other abbreviations in addresses in your community?

Look at the envelope. Choose the correct answer.

1. first name
   A. Dallas
   B. Diaz
   C. Blanca
   D. Texas

2. last name
   A. Texas
   B. M.
   C. Center
   D. Diaz

3. address
   A. 275 Center Street
   B. Texas
   C. Blanca M. Diaz
   D. 75211

4. city
   A. Texas
   B. Dallas
   C. Center
   D. Diaz

5. state
   A. Blanca
   B. 2B
   C. Texas
   D. Center

6. apartment number
   A. 75211
   B. 275
   C. 2
   D. 2B

Blanca M. Diaz
275 Center Street, Apt. 2B
Dallas, Texas 75211

Mark your answers in the answer box.

Choose the correct answer.

7. e-mail address
   A. 25 Park Street
   B. David Chen
   C. Chen@worldnet.com
   D. 3-A

8. social security number
   A. 549-3428
   B. 034-98-3547
   C. 6-G
   D. 275

9. fax number
   A. (555) 248-3974
   B. 5-C
   C. 03765
   D. fox25@worldnet.com

10. zip code
    A. 028-76-3962
    B. 2B
    C. (414) 555-4978
    D. 02847

	Answers			
1	A	B	C	D
2	A	B	C	D
3	A	B	C	D
4	A	B	C	D
5	A	B	C	D
6	A	B	C	D
7	A	B	C	D
8	A	B	C	D
9	A	B	C	D
10	A	B	C	D

SKILLS CHECK

Words:
- [ ] name
- [ ] first name
- [ ] last name
- [ ] address
- [ ] e-mail address
- [ ] telephone number
- [ ] phone number
- [ ] apartment number
- [ ] fax number
- [ ] driver's license
- [ ] permanent resident card
- [ ] social security card
- [ ] student I.D. card

Questions:
- [ ] What's your name?
- [ ] What's your last name?
- [ ] What's your first name?
- [ ] How do you spell that?
- [ ] What's your address?
- [ ] What's your phone number?
- [ ] Where are you from?

I can say:
- [ ] Hello.
- [ ] Hi.
- [ ] My name is _____.
- [ ] I'm _____.
- [ ] My address is _____.
- [ ] My phone number is _____.
- [ ] I'm from _____.
- [ ] Nice to meet you.

I can write:
- [ ] the letters of the alphabet
- [ ] numbers 0–10
- [ ] personal information
- [ ] addresses
- [ ] telephone numbers
- [ ] people's first and last names

2

To Be + Location
Subject Pronouns

- **Classroom Objects**
- **Classroom Actions**
- **Rooms in the Home**
- **Cities, Countries, Nationalities**
- **Places Around Town**
- **Giving and Following Instructions**

VOCABULARY PREVIEW

1. pen
2. pencil
3. book
4. desk
5. computer
6. bank
7. supermarket
8. post office
9. restaurant
10. library
11. living room
12. dining room
13. kitchen
14. bedroom
15. bathroom

In the Classroom

1. pen
2. book
3. pencil
4. notebook
5. bookshelf

6. globe
7. map
8. board
9. wall

10. clock
11. bulletin board
12. computer
13. table

14. chair
15. ruler
16. desk
17. dictionary

Where Is It?

(Where is) Where's the book?	(It is) It's on the desk.

1. Where's the pen?

2. Where's the board?

3. Where's the globe?

4. Where's the ruler?

5. Where's the pencil?

6. Where's the clock?

7. Where's the notebook?

8. Where's the dictionary?

9. Where's the bulletin board?

Make a List!

Work with another student. Make a list of all the objects in your classroom. Present your list to the class. Who has the best list?

1. living room
2. dining room
3. kitchen

4. bedroom
5. bathroom
6. attic

7. yard
8. garage
9. basement

Where Are You?

Where	am	I			?
	is	he she it			
	are	we you they			

(I am)	I'm
(He is)	He's
(She is)	She's
(It is)	It's
(We are)	We're
(You are)	You're
(They are)	They're

in the kitchen.

Where are you?

I'm in the kitchen.

Where are you?

We're in the living room.

Where are Mr. and Mrs. Jones?

They're in the yard.

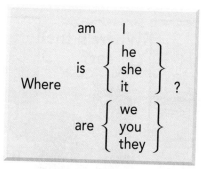

1. Where are you?

2. Where are you?

3. Where are Jim and Pam?

4. Where are you?

5. Where are Mr. and Mrs. Park?

6. Where are you?

7. Where are you?

8. Where are you and Ben?

9. Where are Mr. and Mrs. Hernandez?

11

Where's Bob?

* Where's = Where is

1. Where's Tim?

2. Where's Rosa?

3. Where's the newspaper?

4. Where's Peggy?

5. Where's the telephone book?

6. Where's Harry?

7. Where's Ellen?

8. Where's Kevin?

9. Where's the cell phone?

READING

THE STUDENTS IN MY ENGLISH CLASS

The students in my English class are very interesting. Henry is Chinese. He's from Shanghai. Linda is Puerto Rican. She's from San Juan. Mr. and Mrs. Kim are Korean. They're from Seoul.

George is Greek. He's from Athens. Carla is Italian. She's from Rome. Mr. and Mrs. Sato are Japanese. They're from Tokyo. My friend Maria and I are Mexican. We're from Mexico City.

Yes, the students in my English class are very interesting. We're from many different countries . . . and we're friends.

✓ READING CHECK-UP

TRUE OR FALSE?

_____ 1. Linda is Korean.

_____ 2. George is Greek.

_____ 3. Henry is from Mexico City.

_____ 4. Mr. Kim is from Seoul.

_____ 5. Carla is Chinese.

_____ 6. The students in the class are from many countries.

How About You?

Tell about the students in YOUR English class. Where are they from?

How to Say It!

Greeting People

A. Hi. How are you?
B. Fine. And you?
A. Fine, thanks.

Practice conversations with other students.

Where Are They?

Ask and answer questions based on these pictures.

1. _____ Albert?

_____ .

2. _____ Carmen?

_____ .

3. _____ Walter and Mary?

_____ .

4. _____ you?

_____ .

5. _____ you?

_____ .

6. _____ Kate?

_____ .

7. _____ Mr. and Mrs. Lee?

_____ .

8. _____ monkey?

_____ .

9. _____ I?

_____ .

Now add people and places of your own.

10. _____ ?

_____ .

11. _____ ?

_____ .

12. _____ ?

_____ .

READING

George

Maria

SOCIAL SECURITY

Mr. and Mrs. Sato

our English teacher

ALL THE STUDENTS IN MY ENGLISH CLASS ARE ABSENT TODAY

All the students in my English class are absent today. George is absent. He's in the hospital. Maria is absent. She's at the dentist. Mr. and Mrs. Sato are absent. They're at the social security office. Even our English teacher is absent. He's home in bed!

What a shame! Everybody in my English class is absent today. Everybody except me.

 READING *CHECK-UP*

WHAT'S THE ANSWER?

1. Where's George?
2. Where's Maria?
3. Where are Mr. and Mrs. Sato?
4. Where's the English teacher?

How About You?

Tell about YOUR English class:
Which students are in class today?
Which students are absent today?
Where are they?

LISTENING

WHAT'S THE WORD?

Listen and choose the correct answer.

1. a. bank   b. park
2. a. hospital   b. library
3. a. He's   b. She's
4. a. He's   b. She's
5. a. We're   b. They're
6. a. We're   b. They're

WHERE ARE THEY?

Listen and choose the correct place.

1. a. living room   b. dining room
2. a. bathroom   b. bedroom
3. a. garage   b. yard
4. a. bathroom   b. bedroom
5. a. kitchen   b. living room
6. a. bedroom   b. basement

PRONUNCIATION Reduced *and*

Mr. and Mrs.

Listen. Then say it.

Mr. and Mrs. Jones

Mr. and Mrs. Park

Jim and Pam

You and Ben

Say it. Then listen.

Mr. and Mrs. Lee

Mr. and Mrs. Miller

Walter and Mary

Jim and I

 **SIDE by SIDE JOURNAL**

Draw a picture of your apartment or house. Label the rooms.

 Project

Work with another student. Draw a picture of your classroom. Label all the objects.

GRAMMAR FOCUS

SUBJECT PRONOUNS
TO BE + LOCATION

	am	I?
Where	is	he? she? it?
	are	we? you? they?

(I am)	I'm	
(He is) (She is) (It is)	He's She's It's	in the kitchen.
(We are) (You are) (They are)	We're You're They're	

Choose the correct words.

1. A. Where (is are) Mrs. Chen?
   B. (He's She's) in the library.

2. A. Where (am are) you?
   B. (I'm It's) in the kitchen.

3. A. Where (am is) Mr. Grant?
   B. (She's He's) in the classroom.

4. A. Where (is are) the pen?
   B. (It's They're) on the desk.

5. A. Where (are am) Mr. and Mrs. Kim?
   B. (He's They're) in the restaurant.

6. A. Where (is are) you and John?
   B. (We're They're) in the park.

1 SPEAKING CLASSROOM INSTRUCTIONS

Practice these classroom instructions

Stand up.

Go to the board.

Write your name and address.

Erase the board.

Sit down.

Take out your book.

Open your book.

Raise your hand.

Close your book.

Put away your book.

2 SPEAKING REQUESTING OBJECTS & GIVING INSTRUCTIONS

Practice sentences with these classroom objects.

Please give me your _____.

1.   2.   3.   4.   5.

Practice more sentences with these classroom objects.

Point to the _____.

6.   7.   8.   9.   10.

3 TEAMWORK GIVING & FOLLOWING INSTRUCTIONS

Work with a classmate. Practice giving and following the instructions on pages 16a and 16b.

4 NUMBERS COUNTING OBJECTS

Take inventory! How many are there in your classroom?
Count the objects, and write the number.

NUMBER	ITEM	NUMBER	ITEM	NUMBER	ITEM	NUMBER	ITEM
	boards		chairs		computers		globes
	bulletin boards		clocks		desks		maps

SHARE & SOLVE   What objects are NOT in your classroom? Is this a problem?
Discuss in class. Then talk with someone in your school office.

Read about these people and answer the questions.

Lan is Chinese.
She's from Beijing.
Beijing is a city in China.

Muhammad is Somalian.
He's from Mogadishu.
Mogadishu is in Somalia.

Helen is Greek.
She's from Athens, Greece.

Alex is Russian.
He's from Moscow.
Moscow is a city in Russia.

Karina is Bolivian.
She's from La Paz.
La Paz is in Bolivia.

Marcelo is Brazilian.
He's from São Paulo, Brazil.

1. Who is from Bolivia? _____

2. Where is Mogadishu? _____

3. What city is Marcelo from? _____

4. What country is Lan from? _____

5. Who is Russian? _____

6. What is Helen's nationality? _____

Fill in the chart with information about these people.

NAME	NATIONALITY	CITY	COUNTRY	C ONTINENT

ACADEMIC SKILLS

Look at a world map. Find the countries in this lesson. What continent is each country part of? Write this information in the chart.

Continents	
Africa	Europe
Antarctica	North America
Asia	South America
Australia	

CHART IT!

Make a new chart like the one above. Interview other students and write their information on the chart.

What's your nationality?
What city are you from?
What country are you from?
What continent is your country part of?

Choose the correct answer.

Mark your answers in the answer box.

1. Go to the _____.
   A. pen
   B. board
   C. clock
   D. ruler

2. Open your _____.
   A. pencil
   B. ruler
   C. book
   D. table

3. The computer is on the _____.
   A. table
   B. clock
   C. board
   D. wall

4. The map is on the _____.
   A. pencil
   B. wall
   C. clock
   D. ruler

5. The car is in the _____.
   A. bedroom
   B. living room
   C. attic
   D. garage

6. Mrs. Park is from _____.
   A. Mexican
   B. Korean
   C. Korea
   D. Greek

7. I'm _____.
   A. Puerto Rico
   B. Puerto Rican
   C. San Juan
   D. Mexico City

8. São Paulo is a _____ in Brazil.
   A. city
   B. country
   C. continent
   D. nationality

Answers

1	A	B	C	D
2	A	B	C	D
3	A	B	C	D
4	A	B	C	D
5	A	B	C	D
6	A	B	C	D
7	A	B	C	D
8	A	B	C	D
9	A	B	C	D
10	A	B	C	D

Look at the I.D. card. Choose the correct answer.

9. What kind of I.D. card is this?
   A. a driver's license
   B. a student I.D. card
   C. a permanent resident card
   D. a social security card

10. What information is on Carlos Rivera's I.D. card?
   A. address
   B. social security number
   C. zip code
   D. nationality

PERMANENT RESIDENT CARD
NAME RIVERA, CARLOS M.
USCIS A# A92475816
Birthdate 03/17/74   Category IR6   Sex M
Country of Birth Mexico
CARD EXPIRES 06/29/19
Resident Since 11/17/97
C1USA0924758166EAC0013440673<<
6003029M1004268MEX<<<<<<<<<<0
RIVERA<<CARLOS<<<<<<<<<<<<<<<

SKILLS CHECK ✔

Words:

☐ board	☐ pen	☐ living room
☐ book	☐ pencil	☐ yard
☐ bookshelf	☐ ruler	
☐ bulletin board	☐ table	☐ bank
☐ chair	☐ wall	☐ hospital
☐ clock		☐ library
☐ computer	☐ attic	☐ movie theater
☐ desk	☐ basement	☐ park
☐ dictionary	☐ bathroom	☐ post office
☐ globe	☐ bedroom	☐ restaurant
☐ map	☐ dining room	☐ supermarket
☐ notebook	☐ garage	☐ zoo
	☐ kitchen	

I can ask & answer:
- ☐ Where are *you*?
- ☐ Where's *Bob*?

- ☐ What's your nationality?
- ☐ What city are you from?
- ☐ What country are you from?

- ☐ Hi. How are you?
  Fine. And you?
  Fine, thanks.

I can:
- ☐ give & follow classroom instructions
- ☐ make a list of classroom objects
- ☐ draw and label a picture
- ☐ find countries on a world map
- ☐ make a chart

Present Continuous Tense

- **Everyday Activities**
- **Calling Directory Assistance**
- **Calling 911**
- **Using a Telephone Directory**

VOCABULARY PREVIEW

1. eating
2. drinking
3. cooking
4. reading
5. studying
6. teaching
7. singing
8. sleeping
9. swimming
10. planting
11. watching TV
12. listening to music
13. playing cards
14. playing baseball
15. playing the piano

What Are You Doing?

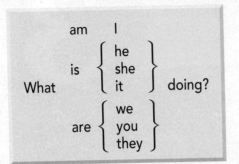

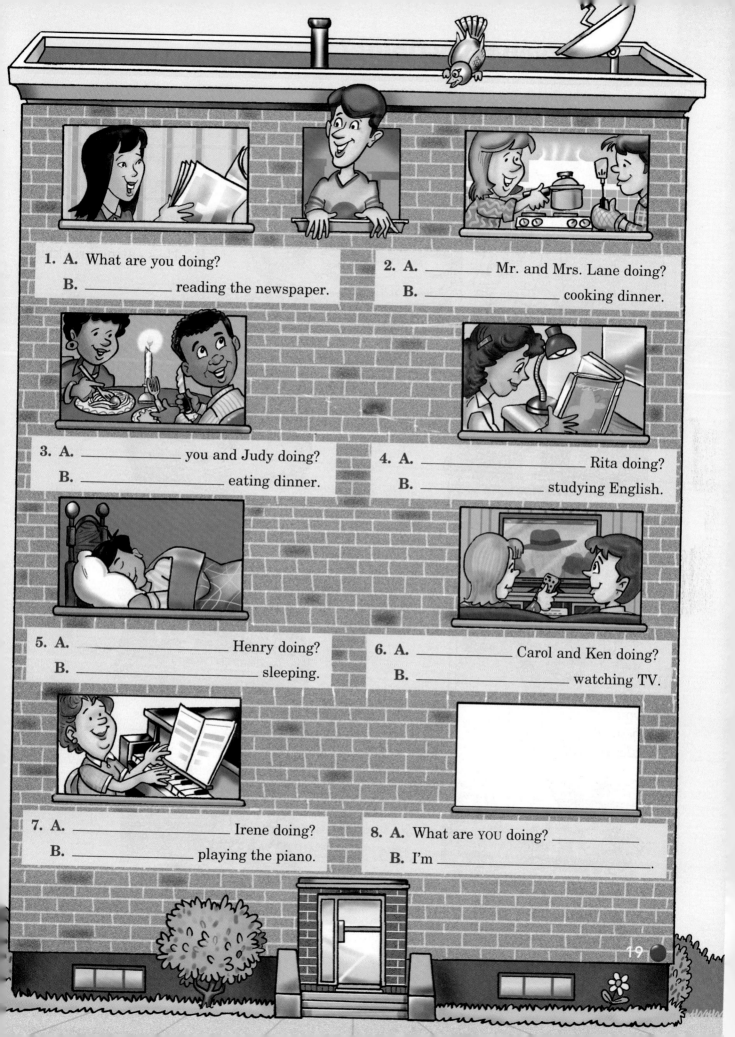

1. **A.** What are you doing?
   B. _____ reading the newspaper.

2. **A.** _____ Mr. and Mrs. Lane doing?
   B. _____ cooking dinner.

3. **A.** _____ you and Judy doing?
   B. _____ eating dinner.

4. **A.** _____ Rita doing?
   B. _____ studying English.

5. **A.** _____ Henry doing?
   B. _____ sleeping.

6. **A.** _____ Carol and Ken doing?
   B. _____ watching TV.

7. **A.** _____ Irene doing?
   B. _____ playing the piano.

8. **A.** What are YOU doing? _____
   B. I'm _____.

What's Everybody Doing?

A. Where's Walter?

B. He's in the kitchen.

A. What's he doing?

B. He's eating breakfast.

1. *Karen*
park
eating lunch

2. *Mr. and Mrs. Clark*
dining room
eating dinner

3. *you*
bedroom
playing the guitar

4. *you*
living room
playing cards

5. *Gary and Jane*
yard
playing baseball

6. *Miss Baker*
cafeteria
drinking milk

7. *you*
   library
   studying English

8. *Ms. Johnson*
   classroom
   teaching mathematics

9. *Marvin*
   bathroom
   singing

10. *Martha*
    hospital
    watching TV

11. *your friend*
    park
    listening to music

12.

How to Say It!

Checking Understanding

A. Where's *Walter*?
B. He's in the *kitchen*.
A. In the *kitchen*?
B. Yes.

Practice conversations with other students.

Action Game!

What am I doing?

You're playing the guitar.

Pantomime an everyday activity for the class. Ask students, "What am I doing?"

IN THE PARK

The Jones family is in the park today. The sun is shining, and the birds are singing. It's a beautiful day!

Mr. Jones is reading the newspaper. Mrs. Jones is listening to the radio. Sally and Patty Jones are studying. And Tommy Jones is playing the guitar.

The Jones family is very happy today. It's a beautiful day, and they're in the park.

AT HOME IN THE YARD

The Chen family is at home in the yard today. The sun is shining, and the birds are singing. It's a beautiful day!

Mr. Chen is planting flowers. Mrs. Chen is drinking lemonade and reading a book. Emily and Jason Chen are playing with the dog. And Jennifer Chen is sleeping.

The Chen family is very happy today. It's a beautiful day, and they're at home in the yard.

✔ READING CHECK-UP

TRUE OR FALSE?

_____ 1. The Jones family is at home in the yard today.

_____ 2. Mrs. Chen is planting flowers.

_____ 3. Patty Jones is studying.

_____ 4. Jason Chen is reading a book.

_____ 5. The Chen family is singing.

_____ 6. The Jones family and the Chen family are very happy today.

Q & A

Using this model, make questions and answers based on the stories on page 22.

A. *What's Mr. Jones doing?*
B. *He's reading the newspaper.*

LISTENING

Listen and choose the correct answer.

1. a. She's studying.
   b. I'm studying.
2. a. He's eating.
   b. She's eating.
3. a. He's watching TV.
   b. She's watching TV.

4. a. We're cooking dinner.
   b. They're cooking dinner.
5. a. We're planting flowers.
   b. They're planting flowers.
6. a. You're playing baseball.
   b. We're playing baseball.

IN YOUR OWN WORDS

FOR WRITING AND DISCUSSION

AT THE BEACH

The Martinez family is at the beach today. Using this picture, tell a story about the Martinez family.

Listen. Then say it.

What are you doing?

What are Jim and Jane doing?

Where are Mary and Fred?

Where are you and Judy?

Say it. Then listen.

What are they doing?

What are Carol and Ken doing?

Where are Mr. and Mrs. Lane?

Where are you and Henry?

SIDE by SIDE JOURNAL

What are you doing now?
What are your friends doing?
Write about it in your journal.

GRAMMAR FOCUS

PRESENT CONTINUOUS TENSE

	am	I	
What	is	he she it	doing?
	are	we you they	

(I am)	I'm	
(He is) (She is) (It is)	He's She's It's	eating.
(We are) (You are) (They are)	We're You're They're	

Match the questions and answers.

____ **1.** What's Mr. Baker doing?

____ **2.** What are Susan and Jane doing?

____ **3.** What are you and Sam doing?

____ **4.** What's Ms. Garcia doing?

____ **5.** What are you doing?

____ **6.** What am I doing?

a. She's reading a book.

b. We're eating lunch.

c. He's cooking dinner.

d. You're playing the piano.

e. They're studying.

f. I'm watching TV.

Complete the sentences.

7. A. What _____ Mr. Yamamoto doing?

   B. _____ sleeping.

8. A. What _____ Mr. and Mrs. Wu doing?

   B. _____ eating breakfast.

9. A. What _____ I doing?

   B. _____ swimming.

10. A. _____ are you and Carol doing?

   B. _____ playing cards.

11. A. _____ _____ you doing?

   B. _____ reading a book.

12. A. _____ _____ Ms. Lopez doing?

   B. _____ listening to music.

1   CONVERSATION   CALLING DIRECTORY ASSISTANCE

Practice the conversation with a classmate. Use your information.

A. Nationwide 4-1-1 Directory Assistance. City and state, please.
B. _____, _____.
A. Say the name of the business you want, or say, "Residence."
B. Residence.
A. Okay. For a residence, say just the person's first and last name.
B. _____ _____.
A. The number is area code (_ _ _) _ _ _ – _ _ _ _.

2   CONVERSATION   CALLING 911

Practice conversations with a classmate. Use your information.

A. 9-1-1 Emergency Operator.
B. _____
A. What's the address?
B. _____.
A. What's your name?
B. _____.
A. Telephone number?
B. _____.
A. Okay. We'll be there right away.

1. My apartment is on fire!

2. My father is having a heart attack!

3   COMMUNITY CONNECTIONS   EMERGENCY NUMBERS

Write these emergency telephone numbers.

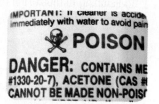

IMPORTANT: If cleaner is accide... immediately with water to avoid pain

☠ **POISON**

DANGER: CONTAINS ME... #1330-20-7), ACETONE (CAS #... CANNOT BE MADE NON-POIS...

Police: _____   Fire: _____   Ambulance: _____   Poison Control Center: _____

Choose the correct answer.

1. I'm reading the ___.
A. piano
B. dinner
C. TV
D. newspaper

2. We're studying ___.
A. cards
B. TV
C. English
D. lunch

3. He's ___ breakfast.
A. reading
B. eating
C. studying
D. playing

4. She's ___ the piano.
A. drinking
B. sleeping
C. playing
D. cooking

5. They're drinking ___.
A. milk
B. cards
C. mathematics
D. the guitar

6. The number for ___ is 4-1-1.
A. an ambulance
B. the police
C. the emergency operator
D. directory assistance

Mark your answers in the answer box.

Answers

1 (A) (B) (C) (D)
2 (A) (B) (C) (D)
3 (A) (B) (C) (D)
4 (A) (B) (C) (D)
5 (A) (B) (C) (D)
6 (A) (B) (C) (D)
7 (A) (B) (C) (D)
8 (A) (B) (C) (D)
9 (A) (B) (C) (D)
10 (A) (B) (C) (D)

Look at this page from a telephone directory. Choose the correct answer.

```
Milford Ann  87 Central Ave............ 449–6283
Miller Alan  25 Pond Ave ................. 782–4529
    Ann  15 Main St.............................. 782–3398
    Brian  177 Center St....................... 449–3207
    Carl  33 Pine Rd ............................ 449–3962
    Diane  778 Central Ave.................. 782–8933
    Edward  96 Grove St...................... 784–8920
    Grace  353 Washington ................. 782–4427
    Hugo  29 First St............................ 784–3309
    Ivan  15 River Rd............................ 449–8299
    Julia G  333 8th Ave....................... 784–1157
    Michael  99 Highland St ................ 449–0909
Millet Joseph  2485 Lee Blvd. ......... 447–2831
```

7. Alan Miller's address is ___.
A. 15 Main Street
B. 33 Pine Road
C. 96 Grove Street
D. 25 Pond Avenue

8. Grace Miller's phone number is ___.
A. 449-3962
B. 782-4427
C. 784-1157
D. 782-3398

9. 784-3309 is the phone number of ___.
A. Hugo Miller
B. Carl Miller
C. Michael Miller
D. Brian Miller

10. 15 Main Street is the address of ___.
A. Ann Milford
B. Ivan Miller
C. Ann Miller
D. Brian Miller

SKILLS CHECK ✓

Words:
☐ cooking dinner
☐ drinking milk/lemonade
☐ eating breakfast/lunch/dinner
☐ listening to music/the radio
☐ planting flowers
☐ playing baseball
☐ playing cards
☐ playing the guitar/the piano
☐ reading a book/the newspaper
☐ singing
☐ sleeping

☐ studying English
☐ swimming
☐ teaching
☐ watching TV

I can ask & answer:
☐ What are you doing?
☐ What's he/she doing?
☐ What are they doing?
☐ Where are you?
☐ Where's *Walter*?
☐ Where are *Mr. and Mrs. Clark*?

I can check my understanding:
☐ *In the kitchen?*

I can use the telephone to:
☐ call directory assistance
☐ call 911

I can write:
☐ emergency telephone numbers

I can write about:
☐ daily activities

FACT FILE

Titles

Mr. is a title for a man.
Ms., Mrs., and **Miss** are titles for a woman.

Nicknames

My name is David.
My nickname is Dave.

COMMON NICKNAMES

Name	Nickname	Name	Nickname
James	Jim	Elizabeth	Liz, Betty
Peter	Pete	Jennifer	Jenny
Robert	Bob	Judith	Judy
Timothy	Tim	Katherine	Kathy, Kate
Thomas	Tom	Patricia	Patty
William	Bill	Susan	Sue

Global Exchange

SungHee: Hello. My name is Sung Hee. I'm Korean. I'm from Seoul. I'm a student. Right now I'm in my English class. I'm looking for a keypal in a different country.

DanielR: Hi, Sung Hee! My name is Daniel. My nickname is Danny. My last name is Rivera. I'm Mexican. I'm from Mexico City. I'm a student. Right now I'm at home. I'm at my computer, and I'm listening to music. I'm also looking for a keypal. Tell me about your school and your English class.

Send a message over the Internet. Tell about yourself. Look for a keypal.

I'm playing _____ .

Instruments

 the violin

 the clarinet

 the trumpet

Sports

 soccer

 tennis

 basketball

Games

 chess

 checkers

 tic tac toe

Greetings

Right now, all around the world, people are greeting each other in different ways.

They're shaking hands.

They're kissing.

They're bowing.

They're hugging.

How are people in your country greeting each other today?

LISTENING

You have seven messages!

You Have Seven Messages!

Messages

_c_ **①**	**a.**	Mrs. Lane 731–0248
___ **②**	**b.**	Linda Lee 969–0159
___ **③**	**c.**	Henry Drake 427–9168
___ **④**	**d.**	Dad
___ **⑤**	**e.**	Patty
___ **⑥**	**f.**	Jim 682–4630
___ **⑦**	**g.**	Kevin Carter 298–4577

What Are They Saying?

WELCOME

HILL

. period   ? question mark   ! exclamation point

Practice these conversations with a classmate.

I'm from Mexico City.

A. What's the sentence?

B. *I'm from Mexico City.*

A. What kind of sentence is it?

B. It's **a statement**.

A. What's the punctuation mark at the end of the sentence?

B. **A period.**

What's your address?

A. What's the sentence?

B. *What's your address?*

A. What kind of sentence is it?

B. It's **a question**.

A. What's the punctuation mark at the end of the sentence?

B. **A question mark.**

Stand up.

A. What's the sentence?

B. *Stand up.*

A. What kind of sentence is it?

B. It's **a command**.

A. What's the punctuation mark at the end of the sentence?

B. **A period.**

My kitchen is on fire!

A. What's the sentence?

B. *My kitchen is on fire!*

A. What kind of sentence is it?

B. It's **an exclamation**.

A. What's the punctuation mark at the end of the sentence?

B. **An exclamation point.**

Write the correct punctuation mark at the end of each sentence. Then practice new conversations about these sentences.

1. My name is Gloria Alba
2. What's your name
3. Raise your hand
4. My apartment is on fire
5. Where are you from
6. Sit down
7. They're from Brazil
8. What a shame
9. Put away your book
10. What are you doing

A Nation of Immigrants

The United States is a nation of immigrants. Immigrants in the United States are from many different countries around the world. They are from Asia, Central America, South America, the Middle East, Africa, and Europe.

Immigrants are "foreign-born." About forty million foreign-born people are in the United States. Foreign-born people are about thirteen percent of the population.

Where are immigrants from? Twenty-nine percent of U.S. immigrants are from Mexico. Twenty-five percent are from Southeast Asia.

Nine percent are from the Caribbean. Eight percent are from South America. Four percent are from the Middle East. And nineteen percent are from other areas.

The states with a large number of foreign-born people are California, New York, Texas, Florida, and New Jersey. Over ten million immigrants are in California. The immigrant population is growing in the United States. Many immigrants are now living in Tennessee, South Carolina, Kentucky, Alabama, Mississippi, and other states.

60 Percent of All Immigrants Are in Five States

California 10.2 million 25%

New York 4.3 million 11%

New Jersey 1.9 million 5%

Florida 3.7 million 9%

Texas 4.2 million 10%

1. Immigrants are from _____.
- A. the United States
- B. California and Texas
- C. six different countries
- D. many different countries

2. Immigrants are _____.
- A. children
- B. foreign-born
- C. not from Mexico
- D. 40 percent of the population

3. _____ percent of immigrants are from South America.
- A. Eight
- B. Thirteen
- C. Nineteen
- D. Twenty-nine

4. Twenty-five percent of immigrants are from _____.
- A. Mexico
- B. the Caribbean
- C. Southeast Asia
- D. the Middle East

5. According to the map, 3.7 million immigrants are in _____.
- A. Texas
- B. Florida
- C. California
- D. New Jersey

6. This passage is about _____.
- A. immigrants in the United States
- B. immigrants from South America
- C. foreign-born people around the world
- D. foreign-born people in California and New York

APPLY YOUR KNOWLEDGE

1. In your city or town, where are immigrants from?

2. Is the immigration population in your city or town very large?

4

To Be: Short Answers
Possessive Adjectives

- **Everyday Activities**
- **Places Around Town**

- **Civics: Community Service**

VOCABULARY PREVIEW

1. brushing
2. cleaning
3. feeding

4. fixing
5. painting

6. reading
7. washing

I'm Fixing My Sink

I	my
he	his
she	her
it	its
we	our
you	your
they	their

Hi! What are you doing?

I'm fixing **my** sink.

What's Bob doing?

He's fixing **his** car.

What's Mary doing?

She's cleaning **her** room.

What are you doing?

We're cleaning **our** apartment.

What are **your** children doing?

They're doing **their** homework.

Are You Busy?

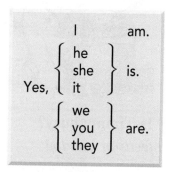

Yes,	I am.
	he / she / it is.
	we / you / they are.

Are you busy?

Yes, I am. I'm washing my hair.

1. Is Frank busy?
cleaning his apartment

2. Is Helen busy?
feeding her cat

3. Are you busy?
fixing our TV

4. Are Jim and Lisa busy?
painting their bedroom

5. Are you busy?
doing my homework

6. Is Richard busy?
washing his clothes

7. Are Ed and Ruth busy?
painting their garage

8. Is Timmy busy?
feeding his dog

9. Are you busy?
doing our exercises

10. Are you busy?
fixing my bicycle

11. Is Karen busy?
washing her car

12. Is Anwar busy?
cleaning his yard

13. Are your children busy?
brushing their teeth

14. Are you busy?
washing our windows

15. Is Wendy busy?
reading her e-mail

How to Say It!

Attracting Someone's Attention

A. Jane?
B. Yes?
A. What are you doing?
B. I'm doing my exercises.

Practice conversations with other students.

TALK ABOUT IT! *Where Are They, and What Are They Doing?*

Use these models to talk about the picture with other students in your class.

A. Where's *Mr. Molina*?

B. *He's* in the *park*.

A. What's *he* doing?

B. *He's listening to the radio.*

A. Where are *Mr. and Mrs. Sharp*?

B. They're in the *laundromat*.

A. What are they doing?

B. They're *washing their clothes.*

A BUSY DAY

Everybody at 159 River Street is very busy today. Mr. Price is cleaning his bedroom. Ms. Hunter is painting her bathroom. Ricky Gomez is feeding his cat. Mr. and Mrs. Wong are washing their clothes. Mrs. Martin is doing her exercises. And Judy and Larry Clark are fixing their car.

I'm busy, too. I'm washing my windows . . . and of course, I'm watching all my neighbors. It's a very busy day at 159 River Street.

✔ READING *CHECK-UP*

TRUE OR FALSE?

___ 1. Mr. Price is in his bedroom.

___ 2. Ricky is eating.

___ 3. Mr. and Mrs. Clark are in their apartment.

___ 4. Mrs. Martin is doing her exercises.

___ 5. Their address is 195 River Street.

Q & A

Using this model, make questions and answers based on the story.

A. *What's Mr. Price doing?*
B. *He's cleaning his bedroom.*

LISTENING

Listen and choose the correct answer.

1. a. The newspaper.
    b. Breakfast.

2. a. Her e-mail.
    b. Dinner.

3. a. The dining room.
    b. Soccer.

4. a. Their kitchen.
    b. Basketball.

5. a. TV.
    b. My clothes.

6. a. His neighbors.
    b. His windows.

IN YOUR OWN WORDS

FOR WRITING AND DISCUSSION

A BUSY DAY

Everybody at 320 Main Street is very busy today. Tell a story about them, using this picture and the story on page 32 as a guide.

PRONUNCIATION Deleted *h*

Listen. Then say it.

She's fixing her car.

She's cleaning her room.

He's feeding his dog.

He's washing his windows.

Say it. Then listen.

He's painting his apartment.

She's doing her homework.

He's brushing his teeth.

She's reading her e-mail.

Go to a place in your community—a park, a library, a supermarket, or someplace else. Look at the people. What are they doing? Write about it in your journal.

GRAMMAR FOCUS

To Be: Short Answers

	I	am.
Yes,	he she it	is.
	we you they	are.

Possessive Adjectives

I'm		my	
He's		his	
She's		her	
It's	cleaning	its	room.
We're		our	
You're		your	
They're		their	

Match the questions and answers.

____ **1.** Is Mr. Montero busy?

____ **2.** Are Bob and Ellen busy?

____ **3.** Is Mrs. Green busy?

____ **4.** Are you and Rita busy?

____ **5.** Are you busy?

a. Yes, they are.

b. Yes, I am.

c. Yes, we are.

d. Yes, he is.

e. Yes, she is.

Complete the sentences.

6. I'm cleaning _____ apartment.

7. Mr. Sato is painting _____ garage.

8. Mrs. Miller is feeding _____ cat.

9. David and I are washing _____ windows.

10. My children are doing _____ homework.

11. Are you brushing _____ teeth?

Read the news article and answer the questions.

Community Service Day

Today is Community Service Day in Madison. Many people all over the city are doing something to help the community. Students at Madison High School are cleaning around their school.

People in West Town are painting walls in their neighborhood. People at the library are washing all the windows. Children are planting flowers in Wilson Park, and students from the Clark Building Trades School are fixing an old home. It's a very busy day in the community!

1. What are students at the high school doing?
  A. They're fixing an old home.
  B. They're washing windows.
  C. They're painting.
  D. They're cleaning around their school.

2. Where are children planting flowers?
  A. at the Building Trades School
  B. at the high school
  C. in a park
  D. at the library

3. What are people doing in West Town?
  A. They're painting walls.
  B. They're planting flowers.
  C. They're cleaning their neighborhood.
  D. They're washing windows.

4. What are people washing at the library?
  A. books
  B. windows
  C. people
  D. an old home

COMMUNITY CONNECTIONS Write the names and addresses of these places in *your* community.

PLACE	NAME	ADDRESS
library		
high school		
park		
hospital		

THINK & WRITE Today is Community Service Day in *your* community. Write about it, using the news article above as a guide.

Choose the correct answer.

1. I'm washing my ____.
   - A. homework
   - B. TV
   - C. yard
   - D. windows

2. She's feeding her ____.
   - A. car
   - B. kitchen
   - C. cat
   - D. teeth

3. We're doing our ____.
   - A. radio
   - B. homework
   - C. laundromat
   - D. park

4. He's painting the ____.
   - A. breakfast
   - B. TV
   - C. wall
   - D. dog

5. They're cleaning the ____.
   - A. park
   - B. homework
   - C. TV
   - D. exercises

6. She's fixing her ____.
   - A. car
   - B. newspaper
   - C. exercises
   - D. neighbors

7. We're ____ our apartment.
   - A. feeding
   - B. doing
   - C. cleaning
   - D. brushing

8. They're ____ their kitchen.
   - A. feeding
   - B. painting
   - C. brushing
   - D. reading

9. We're ____ our exercises.
   - A. cleaning
   - B. painting
   - C. washing
   - D. doing

10. I'm ____ my e-mail.
   - A. painting
   - B. reading
   - C. watching
   - D. washing

Mark your answers in the answer box.

	Answers			
1	A	B	C	D
2	A	B	C	D
3	A	B	C	D
4	A	B	C	D
5	A	B	C	D
6	A	B	C	D
7	A	B	C	D
8	A	B	C	D
9	A	B	C	D
10	A	B	C	D

SKILLS CHECK ✓

Words:
- ☐ brushing *my* teeth
- ☐ cleaning *his* apartment/garage/ living room/room/yard
- ☐ doing *her* exercises/homework
- ☐ feeding *our* cat/dog
- ☐ fixing *your* bicycle/car/sink/TV
- ☐ painting *their* bathroom/ bedroom/kitchen/living room
- ☐ washing *my* car/clothes/ hair/windows

- ☐ building trades school
- ☐ health club
- ☐ high school
- ☐ laundromat
- ☐ library
- ☐ park

- ☐ community
- ☐ community service day
- ☐ neighbor
- ☐ neighborhood

I can ask & answer:
- ☐ What are you doing?
- ☐ What's he/she doing?
- ☐ What are they doing?

- ☐ Are you busy?
- ☐ Is he/she busy?
- ☐ Are they busy?

I can greet someone:
- ☐ Hi!

I can attract someone's attention:
- ☐ *Jane?*

I can write:
- ☐ names & addresses of places in the community

I can write about:
- ☐ daily activities
- ☐ activities in the community

5

To Be: Yes/No Questions
Short Answers

Adjectives
Possessive Nouns

- **Describing People and Things**
- **Weather**

- **Reading a Weather Map**
- **Fahrenheit and Celsius Temperatures**

VOCABULARY PREVIEW

 ①    ②    ③    ④

 ⑤    ⑥    ⑦    ⑧

 ⑨    ⑩    ⑪    ⑫

1. tall – short
2. young – old
3. heavy/fat – thin
4. new – old

5. married – single
6. handsome – ugly
7. beautiful/pretty – ugly
8. large/big – small/little

9. noisy/loud – quiet
10. expensive – cheap
11. easy – difficult
12. rich – poor

35

Tall or Short?

(I am)	I'm
(He is)	He's
(She is)	She's
(It is)	It's
(We are)	We're
(You are)	You're
(They are)	They're

} tall.

Bob   Bill

A. Is Bob tall or short?

B. He's tall.

A. Is Bill tall or short?

B. He's short.

Ask and answer these questions.

Kate   Peggy

1. Is Kate young or old?
2. Is Peggy young or old?

Howard   Mike

3. Is Howard heavy or thin?
4. Is Mike fat or thin?

Howard's car   Mike's car

5. Is Howard's car new or old?
6. Is Mike's car new or old?

Gloria   Jennifer

7. Is Gloria married or single?
8. Is Jennifer married or single?

Robert   Captain Crook

9. Is Robert handsome or ugly?

10. Is Captain Crook handsome or ugly?

Robert's house   George's apartment

13. Is Robert's house large or small?

14. Is George's apartment big or little?

the food at the   the food at
Plaza Restaurant   Burger Town

17. Is the food at the Plaza Restaurant expensive or cheap?

18. Is the food at Burger Town expensive or cheap?

Marvin   Larry

21. Is Marvin rich or poor?

22. Is Larry rich or poor?

Vanessa   Hilda

11. Is Vanessa beautiful or ugly?

12. Is Hilda pretty or ugly?

Kate's neighbors   Peggy's neighbors

15. Are Kate's neighbors noisy or quiet?

16. Are Peggy's neighbors loud or quiet?

the questions in   the questions in
Chapter 5   Chapter 17

19. Are the questions in Chapter 5 easy or difficult?

20. Are the questions in Chapter 17 easy or difficult?

Now ask and answer your own questions.

Tell Me About . . .

Am	I			
Is	he she it			tall?
Are	we you they			

Yes,	I		am.
	he she it		is.
	we you they		are.

No,	I'm		not.
	he she it		isn't.
	we you they		aren't.

Are you married?

No, I'm not. I'm single.

Tell me about your new car. Is it large?

No, it isn't. It's small.

Tell me about your new neighbors. Are they quiet?

No, they aren't. They're noisy.

1. **A.** Tell me about your computer.
   _____ new?

   B. No, _____. _____.

2. **A.** Tell me about your new boss.
   _____ young?

   B. No, _____. _____.

3. **A.** Tell me about your neighbors.
   _____ noisy?
   B. No, _____. _____.

4. **A.** Tell me about the Plaza Restaurant.
   _____ cheap?
   B. No, _____. _____.

5. **A.** Tell me about your brother.
   _____ tall?
   B. No, _____. _____.

6. **A.** Tell me about your sister.
   _____ single?
   B. No, _____. _____.

7. **A.** Tell me about Nancy's cat.
   _____ pretty?
   B. No, _____. _____.

8. **A.** Tell me about Ron and Betty's dog.
   _____ little?
   B. No, _____. _____.

9. **A.** Tell me about the questions in your English book.
   _____ difficult?
   B. No, _____. _____.

10. **A.** Tell me about Santa Claus.
    _____ thin?
    B. No, _____. _____.

How's the Weather Today?

How's the weather today in YOUR city?

How to Say It!

Calling Someone You Know on the Telephone

A. Hello.
B. Hello. Is this *Julie*?
A. Yes, it is.
B. Hi, *Julie*. This is *Anna*.
A. Hi, *Anna*. . . .

Practice conversations with other students.

The Weather Is Terrible Here!

A. Hi, Jack. This is Jim. I'm calling from Miami.

B. From Miami? What are you doing in Miami?

A. I'm on vacation.

B. How's the weather in Miami? Is it sunny?

A. No, it isn't. It's raining.

B. Is it hot?

A. No, it isn't. It's cold.

B. Are you having a good time?

A. No, I'm not. I'm having a TERRIBLE time. The weather is TERRIBLE here!

B. I'm sorry to hear that.

A. Hi, _____. This is _____. I'm calling from _____.

B. From _____? What are you doing in _____?

A. I'm on vacation.

B. How's the weather in _____? Is it _____?

A. No, it isn't. It's _____.

B. Is it _____?

A. No, it isn't. It's _____.

B. Are you having a good time?

A. No, I'm not. I'm having a TERRIBLE time. The weather is TERRIBLE here!

B. I'm sorry to hear that.

1. *British Columbia*
   cool?
   snowing?

2. *Tahiti*
   hot?
   sunny?

You're on vacation, and the weather is terrible! Call a student in your class. Use the conversation above as a guide.

DEAR MOTHER

Royal Sludge Hotel

Dear Mother,

I'm writing from our hotel at Sludge Beach. Ralph and I are on vacation with the children for a few days. We're happy to be here, but to tell the truth, we're having a few problems.

The weather isn't very good. In fact, it's cold and cloudy. Right now I'm looking out the window, and it's raining cats and dogs.

The children aren't very happy. In fact, they're bored and they're having a terrible time. Right now they're sitting on the bed, playing tic tac toe and watching TV.

The restaurants here are expensive, and the food isn't very good. In fact, Ralph is at a clinic right now. He's having problems with his stomach.

All the other hotels here are beautiful and new. Our hotel is ugly, and it's very, very old. In fact, right now a repairperson is fixing the bathroom sink.

So, Mother, we're having a few problems here at Sludge Beach, but we're happy. We're happy to be on vacation, and we're happy to be together.

See you soon.

Love,

Ethel

✔ READING CHECK-UP

TRUE OR FALSE?

___ 1. The weather is beautiful.

___ 2. The children are happy.

___ 3. The children are watching TV.

___ 4. The restaurants are cheap.

___ 5. Ralph is at the hotel right now.

___ 6. Their hotel is old.

___ 7. A repairperson is fixing the window.

___ 8. Ethel is watching the cats and dogs.

LISTENING

WHAT'S THE ANSWER?

Listen and choose the correct answer.

1. a. It's large.   b. It's heavy.
2. a. It's married.   b. It's beautiful.
3. a. They're quiet.   b. They're sunny.
4. a. It's young.   b. It's warm.
5. a. It's small.   b. It's easy.
6. a. It's good.   b. It's raining.

TRUE OR FALSE?

Listen to the conversation. Then answer *True* or *False*.

1. Louise is calling Betty.
2. The weather is hot and sunny.
3. The hotel is old.
4. The food is very good.
5. Louise is watching TV.

PRONUNCIATION Yes/No Questions with *or*

Listen. Then say it.

Is Bob tall or short?

Is Kate young or old?

Are they noisy or quiet?

Is it hot or cold?

Say it. Then listen.

Is the car new or old?

Are you married or single?

Is it sunny or cloudy?

Are they large or small?

How's the weather today? What are you doing now? Write a letter to a friend and tell about it.

GRAMMAR FOCUS

To Be: Yes/No Questions

Am	I	
Is	he she it	tall?
Are	we you they	

To Be: Short Answers

	I	am.
Yes,	he she it	is.
	we you they	are.

	I'm	not.
No,	he she it	isn't.
	we you they	aren't.

Complete the sentences.

1. A. _____ he tall?
   B. Yes, _____ _____.

2. A. _____ they new?
   B. Yes, _____ _____.

3. A. _____ she short?
   B. No, _____ _____.

4. A. _____ you and Roberto busy?
   B. Yes, _____ _____.

5. A. _____ your homework difficult?
   B. No, _____ _____.

6. A. _____ your neighbors quiet?
   B. No, _____ _____.

7. A. _____ you single?
   B. Yes, _____ _____.

8. A. _____ it raining?
   B. Yes, _____ _____.

9. A. _____ you heavy?
   B. No, _____ _____.

10. A. _____ you and Alicia busy?
    B. No, _____ _____.

11. A. _____ your sister married?
    B. Yes, _____ _____.

12. A. _____ Mr. Lee in Miami?
    B. No, _____ _____.

Look at the weather map. Practice conversations with a classmate.

Seattle
50°F/10°C

Minneapolis
30°F/-1°C

Detroit
49°F/9°C

Boston
32°F/0°C

Salt Lake City
45°F/7°C

Chicago
50°F/10°C

Philadelphia
48°F /9°C

New York
45°F/7°C

San Francisco
62°F/17°C

Denver
34°F/1°C

St. Louis
51°F/11°C

Washington, DC
56°F/12°C

Los Angeles
69°F/21°C

San Diego
72°F/22°C

Phoenix
68°F/20°C

Dallas
72°F/22°C

Atlanta
74°F/23°C

Houston
80°F/27°C

New Orleans
83°F/28°C

Miami
85°F/27°C

Sunny	Partly Cloudy	Cloudy	Raining	Foggy	Snowing

A. What's the weather today in _____?
   (city)

B. It's _____.
   (weather)

A. What's the temperature today in _____?
   (city)

B. It's _____ degrees Fahrenheit, _____ degrees Celsius.
   (temperature)   (temperature)

F = Fahrenheit
C = Celsius

COMMUNITY CONNECTIONS Look in a newspaper. What's the weather today in different cities? Fill in the chart.

CITY	WEATHER	TEMP.*	CITY	WEATHER	TEMP.

* Temperature

Choose the correct answer.

1. Our car is ____.
   A. married
   B. thin
   C. old
   D. single

2. The homework is ____.
   A. handsome
   B. difficult
   C. cheap
   D. rich

3. Our neighbors are ____.
   A. expensive
   B. easy
   C. cloudy
   D. noisy

4. Our new apartment is ____.
   A. beautiful
   B. poor
   C. married
   D. heavy

Mark your answers in the answer box.

Answers
1 Ⓐ Ⓑ Ⓒ Ⓓ
2 Ⓐ Ⓑ Ⓒ Ⓓ
3 Ⓐ Ⓑ Ⓒ Ⓓ
4 Ⓐ Ⓑ Ⓒ Ⓓ
5 Ⓐ Ⓑ Ⓒ Ⓓ
6 Ⓐ Ⓑ Ⓒ Ⓓ
7 Ⓐ Ⓑ Ⓒ Ⓓ
8 Ⓐ Ⓑ Ⓒ Ⓓ
9 Ⓐ Ⓑ Ⓒ Ⓓ
10 Ⓐ Ⓑ Ⓒ Ⓓ

Seattle 50°F/10°C
Boston 32°F/0°C
New York 30°F/-1°C
Los Angeles 85°F/27°C
Dallas 70°F/20°C
Atlanta 48°F/9°C
Miami 90°F/32°C

Look at the weather map. Choose the correct answer.

5. In Los Angeles, it's ____.
   A. cloudy
   B. sunny
   C. snowing
   D. raining

6. It's snowing in ____.
   A. Atlanta
   B. New York
   C. Boston
   D. Dallas

7. In Seattle, it's ____.
   A. raining
   B. partly cloudy
   C. cold
   D. hot

8. It's cold in ____.
   A. Seattle
   B. Dallas
   C. Miami and Boston
   D. New York and Boston

9. It's cloudy in ____.
   A. Miami
   B. Atlanta and Los Angeles
   C. Atlanta and Dallas
   D. Dallas and Boston

10. It's sunny and hot in ____.
   A. Atlanta and Boston
   B. Los Angeles and Boston
   C. Miami and Los Angeles
   D. Atlanta and Dallas

SKILLS CHECK ✓

Words:
- ☐ beautiful
- ☐ big
- ☐ cheap
- ☐ difficult
- ☐ easy
- ☐ expensive
- ☐ fat
- ☐ handsome
- ☐ heavy

- ☐ large
- ☐ little
- ☐ loud
- ☐ married
- ☐ new
- ☐ noisy
- ☐ old
- ☐ poor
- ☐ pretty

- ☐ quiet
- ☐ rich
- ☐ short
- ☐ single
- ☐ small
- ☐ tall
- ☐ thin
- ☐ ugly
- ☐ young

- ☐ cloudy
- ☐ cold
- ☐ cool
- ☐ hot
- ☐ raining
- ☐ snowing
- ☐ sunny
- ☐ warm

- ☐ Celsius
- ☐ Fahrenheit

I can ask & answer:
- ☐ Is *he tall* or *short*?
- ☐ Are *they noisy* or *quiet*?
- ☐ Is *he/she/it old*?
- ☐ Are *we/you/they quiet*?
- ☐ How's the weather in ____?
- ☐ What's the weather today in ____?
- ☐ What's the temperature today in ____?

I can:
- ☐ call someone I know on the telephone
- ☐ read a weather map
- ☐ use Fahrenheit & Celsius temperatures

I can write about:
- ☐ the weather
- ☐ what people are doing

6

To Be: Review
Present Continuous Tense: Review
Prepositions of Location

- **Family Members**
- **Reading a Family Tree Diagram**

- **Describing Activities and Events**
- **Introducing People**

VOCABULARY PREVIEW

1. wife
2. husband

parents
3. mother
4. father

children
5. daughter
6. son
7. sister
8. brother

grandparents
9. grandmother
10. grandfather

grandchildren
11. granddaughter
12. grandson

13. aunt
14. uncle
15. niece
16. nephew
17. cousin

My Favorite Photographs

A. Who is he?

B. He's my father.

A. What's his name?

B. His name is Paul.

A. Where is he?

B. He's in Paris.

A. What's he doing?

B. He's standing in front of the Eiffel Tower.

Using these questions, talk about the following photographs.

Who is he? What's his name? Where is he? What's he doing?	Who is she? What's her name? Where is she? What's she doing?	Who are they? What are their names? Where are they? What are they doing?

1. *my mother*
   in the park
   riding her bicycle

2. *my parents*
   in the dining room
   having dinner

3. *my son*
at the beach
swimming

4. *my daughter*
in front of our house
washing her car

5. *my wife*
in the yard
planting flowers

6. *my husband*
in our living room
sleeping on the sofa

7. *my sister and brother*
in the kitchen
baking a cake

8. *my grandmother and grandfather*
at my wedding
crying

9. *my aunt and uncle*
in Washington, D.C.
standing in front of the White House

10. *my cousin*
in front of his apartment building
skateboarding

11. *my niece*
    at school
    acting in a play

12. *my nephew*
    in his bedroom
    sitting on his bed and playing the guitar

13. *my friend*
    in his apartment
    playing a game on his computer

14. *my friends*
    at my birthday party
    singing and dancing

ON YOUR OWN *Your Favorite Photographs*

This is a photograph of my sister and me. My sister's name is Amanda. We're in the park. Amanda is feeding the birds, and I'm sitting on a bench and listening to music.

Bring in your favorite photographs to class. Talk about them with other students. Ask the other students about *their* favorite photographs.

ARTHUR IS VERY ANGRY

It's late at night. Arthur is sitting on his bed, and he's looking at his clock. His neighbors are making a lot of noise, and Arthur is VERY angry.

The people in Apartment 2 are dancing. The man in Apartment 3 is vacuuming his rug. The woman in Apartment 4 is playing the drums. The teenagers in Apartment 5 are listening to loud music. The dog in Apartment 6 is barking. And the people in Apartment 7 are having a big argument.

It's very late, and Arthur is tired and angry. What a terrible night!

✔ READING CHECK-UP

Q & A

Using this model, make questions and answers based on the story.

A. *What's the man in Apartment 3 doing?*
B. *He's vacuuming his rugs.*

CHOOSE

1. Arthur's neighbors are ____.
   a. noisy
   b. angry

2. The man in Apartment 3 is ____.
   a. painting
   b. cleaning

3. The people in Apartment 5 are ____.
   a. young
   b. old

4. The dog in Apartment 6 isn't ____.
   a. sleeping
   b. making noise

5. The woman in Apartment 4 is ____.
   a. playing cards
   b. playing music

6. Arthur isn't very ____.
   a. happy
   b. tired

TOM'S WEDDING DAY

Today is a very special day. It's my wedding day, and all my family and friends are here. Everybody is having a wonderful time.

My wife, Jane, is standing in front of the fireplace. She's wearing a beautiful white wedding gown. Uncle Harry is taking her photograph, and Aunt Emma is crying. (She's very sentimental.)

The band is playing my favorite popular music. My mother is dancing with Jane's father, and Jane's mother is dancing with my father.

My sister and Jane's brother are standing in the yard and eating wedding cake. Our grandparents are sitting in the corner and talking about "the good old days."

Everybody is having a good time. People are singing, dancing, and laughing, and our families are getting to know each other. It's a very special day.

✔ **READING** *CHECK-UP*

WHAT'S THE ANSWER?

1. Where is Jane standing?
2. What's she wearing?
3. What's Uncle Harry doing?

4. What's Aunt Emma doing?
5. What's Tom's mother doing?
6. What are their grandparents doing?

LISTENING

QUIET OR NOISY?

Listen to the sentence. Are the people quiet or noisy?

1. a. quiet   b. noisy
2. a. quiet   b. noisy
3. a. quiet   b. noisy
4. a. quiet   b. noisy
5. a. quiet   b. noisy
6. a. quiet   b. noisy

WHAT DO YOU HEAR?

Listen to the sound. What do you hear? Choose the correct answer.

1. a. They're studying.   b. They're singing.
2. a. He's crying.   b. He's doing his exercises.
3. a. She's vacuuming.   b. She's washing her clothes.
4. a. They're barking.   b. They're laughing.
5. a. She's playing the piano.   b. She's playing the drums.

IN YOUR OWN WORDS

FOR WRITING AND DISCUSSION

JESSICA'S BIRTHDAY PARTY

Today is a very special day. It's Jessica's birthday party, and all her family and friends are there. Using this picture, tell a story about her party.

How to Say It!

Introducing People

A. I'd like to introduce *my brother*.
B. Nice to meet you.
C. Nice to meet you, too.

Practice conversations with other students.

PRONUNCIATION Stressed and Unstressed Words

Listen. Then say it.

He's pláying the guitár.

She's ácting in a pláy.

She's ríding her bícycle.

He's sleéping on the sófa.

Say it. Then listen.

We're báking a cáke.

They're sítting in the yárd.

He's wáshing his cár.

She's sítting on her béd.

SIDE by SIDE JOURNAL

Write in your journal about your favorite photograph.

This is a photograph of _____ .

In this photograph, _____ .

It's my favorite photograph because _____ .

GRAMMAR FOCUS

TO BE

Who is	he? she?
Who are	they?

He's my father. She's my wife.
They're my parents.

PRESENT CONTINUOUS TENSE

What's	he she	doing?
What are	they	doing?

He's She's	sleeping.
They're	swimming.

PREPOSITIONS OF LOCATION

She's in the park.	He's sitting on his bed.
He's at the beach.	We're in front of our house.

Complete the sentences.

1. A. Who _____ he?
   B. _____ my brother.
2. A. Who _____ they?
   B. _____ my grandparents.
3. A. Who is _____?
   B. _____ my daughter.
4. A. Who _____ _____?
   B. He's my son.

5. A. What's she _____?
   B. _____ baking.
6. A. What _____ they doing?
   B. _____ dancing.
7. A. _____ he doing?
   B. _____ vacuuming.
8. A. What's _____ _____?
   B. She's having dinner.

9. We're reading _____ the living room.
10. He's sleeping _____ the sofa.
11. I'm standing _____ _____ _____ my car
12. My friends are crying _____ my wedding

1 READING A DIAGRAM A FAMILY TREE

**Look at the family tree.
Complete the story.**

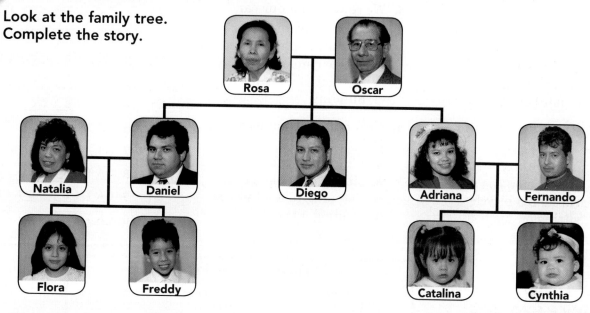

The Serrano family is a large family. Oscar is Rosa's _____ ¹. Rosa is the _____² of Daniel, Diego, and Adriana. Oscar is their _____³. Daniel is married. His _____⁴ is Natalia. They have two children. The name of their _____⁵ is Flora, and the name of their _____⁶ is Freddy. Adriana is Flora and Freddy's _____⁷. Adriana and Fernando have two _____⁸, Catalina and Cynthia. Flora, Freddy, Catalina, and Cynthia are _____⁹. They are Rosa and Oscar's _____¹⁰. Rosa is their _____¹¹, and Oscar is their _____¹². Diego is not married. He's single. Diego is the _____¹³ of Flora, Freddy, Catalina, and Cynthia.

2 TEAMWORK FAMILY RELATIONSHIPS

**Work with a classmate.
Ask and answer questions
about the family tree.**

A. Who is *Daniel?*

B. *Daniel is Rosa and Oscar's son, Natalia's husband, Flora and Freddy's father, Diego and Adriana's brother, and Catalina and Cynthia's uncle.*

3 CONVERSATION INTRODUCING PEOPLE

**Practice conversations in groups of three.
Introduce family members and friends.**

A. This is my *husband, Alex.*

B. Nice to meet you.

C. Nice to meet you, too.

Choose the correct answer.

1. Our daughter is swimming ____.
A. in the kitchen
B. at the beach
C. in our living room
D. in her bedroom

2. My son is ____ in the park.
A. baking
B. sleeping on the sofa
C. riding his bicycle
D. sitting on his bed

3. We're washing our car ____.
A. in our kitchen
B. at our daughter's wedding
C. in Apartment 4
D. in front of our apartment building

4. He's making a lot of noise. He's ____.
A. planting flowers
B. sitting on a bench
C. listening to loud music
D. reading a book

Answers

1 (A) (B) (C) (D)
2 (A) (B) (C) (D)
3 (A) (B) (C) (D)
4 (A) (B) (C) (D)
5 (A) (B) (C) (D)
6 (A) (B) (C) (D)
7 (A) (B) (C) (D)
8 (A) (B) (C) (D)
9 (A) (B) (C) (D)
10 (A) (B) (C) (D)

Look at the family tree. Choose the correct answer.

Richard ——— Irene
Jane —— David   Tom —— Carol
Timmy —— Patty   Sarah —— Kevin

5. Jane is Timmy and Patty's ____.
A. mother
B. sister
C. grandmother
D. father

6. David is Richard and Irene's ____.
A. daughter
B. son
C. grandson
D. uncle

7. Timmy and Patty are David's ____.
A. parents
B. uncle and aunt
C. grandchildren
D. children

8. Tom is Timmy and Patty's ____.
A. aunt
B. cousin
C. uncle
D. grandfather

9. Sarah is Patty and Timmy's ____.
A. cousin
B. aunt
C. grandmother
D. sister

10. Sarah and Kevin are Irene's ____.
A. children
B. grandchildren
C. parents
D. grandparents

SKILLS CHECK ✓

Words:
☐ mother
☐ father
☐ parents
☐ son
☐ daughter
☐ children
☐ brother
☐ sister
☐ grandmother
☐ grandfather
☐ grandparents
☐ grandson
☐ granddaughter
☐ grandchildren
☐ wife
☐ husband
☐ aunt
☐ uncle
☐ niece
☐ nephew
☐ cousin

I can ask & answer:
☐ Who is he/she?
☐ What's his/her name?
☐ Where is he/she?
☐ What's he/she doing?

☐ Who are they?
☐ What are their names?
☐ Where are they?
☐ What are they doing?

I can introduce people:
☐ I'd like to introduce ____.
  Nice to meet you.
  Nice to meet you, too.

☐ This is my *husband, Alex.*

I can:
☐ read a family tree diagram

I can write about:
☐ a party
☐ a favorite photograph

A Family Tree

Betty and Henry Wilson's family tree is very large

A family tree is a diagram of the people in a family. This is the Wilson family tree. All the members of the Wilson family are on this family tree—parents, children, grandparents, grandchildren, aunts, uncles, cousins, nieces, and nephews.

Betty and Henry are the parents of Sally, Linda, and Tom. Linda is single. Sally is married. Her husband's name is Jack. Sally and Jack are the parents of Jimmy and Sarah. Jimmy is their son, and Sarah is their daughter.

Tom is also married. His wife's name is Patty. Patty and Tom are the parents of Julie and Kevin. Julie is their daughter, and Kevin is their son.

Jimmy, Sarah, Julie, and Kevin are cousins. They are also the grandchildren of Betty and Henry. (Betty and Henry are their grandparents.)

Jack is Julie and Kevin's uncle. Sally is their aunt. Tom is Jimmy and Sarah's uncle. Patty is their aunt. Linda is also the aunt of Jimmy, Sarah, Julie, and Kevin.

Jimmy is the nephew of Linda, Patty, and Tom. Sarah is their niece. Julie is the niece of Sally, Jack, and Linda. Kevin is their nephew.

Draw your family tree. Then write about it.

I'm _____ .

■ reading

■ writing

■ raising my hand

■ opening my book

■ closing my book

■ erasing the board

■ using a calculator

Today's Weather

_d_ **1** hot
____ **2** snowing
____ **3** warm and sunny
____ **4** cool and sunny
____ **5** cold and cloudy

a. Atlanta
b. Chicago
c. Toronto
d. Honolulu
e. Los Angeles

AROUND THE WORLD

Extended and Nuclear Families

This is an **extended family.** The grandparents, parents, and children are all together in one apartment. An uncle, an aunt, and two cousins are in another apartment in the same building. Extended families are very common around the world.

This is a **nuclear family.** Only the mother, father, and children are in this home. The grandparents, aunts, uncles, and cousins are in different homes. Nuclear families are very common in many countries.

Is your family a nuclear family or an extended family? Which type of family is common in your country? In your opinion, what are some good things and bad things about these different types of families?

Global Exchange

Ken425: It's a beautiful day in our city today. It's warm and sunny. The people in my family are very busy. My brother and sister are cleaning our apartment. My mother is washing the windows, and my father is fixing the bathroom sink. I'm cooking dinner for my family. How about you? What's the weather today? What are you doing? What are other people in your family doing?

Send a message to a keypal. Tell about the weather, and tell about what you and others are doing today.

FACT FILE

Family Relationships

wife's mother husband's mother }	=	mother-in-law
wife's father husband's father }	=	father-in-law
son's wife	=	daughter-in-law
daughter's husband	=	son-in-law
wife's sister husband's sister }	=	sister-in-law
wife's brother husband's brother }	=	brother-in-law

What Are They Saying?

The Family

Social groups are important in a community. A school is a social group. A church is a social group. A family is also a social group.

In the United States, families are often different. Some families are large, and other families are small. Many families are two-parent families. In some two-parent families, a mother and a father are married to each other. In other two-parent families, the mother and the father aren't married but they are living together. Some families are same-sex families. Both parents are men, or both parents are women.

Some families are single-parent families with just one parent—a mother or a father. In these families, sometimes the parents are divorced. They aren't married anymore. The children are at home with one parent.

In some families, both parents are working. In other families, one family member is at home with the children and the other is working.

In a strong family, healthy food, good clothing, and a clean home are important. In a strong family, parents are always teaching and children are always learning. Parents are teaching their children important lessons about life, and children are learning what is right and what is wrong. A strong family is important for children. It is also important for a community.

	1970	2012
Average number of children per family	2.3	1.9
Percentage of homes with married parents and children	40%	20%
Percentage of homes with a single parent and children	11%	18%
Percentage of married parents with both parents working	56%	75%

1. An example of a two-parent family is a family with _____.
   A. a mother and a grandmother
   B. a mother and a father
   C. a divorced father
   D. a single mother

2. In some families, the mother and father are not married, but they are _____.
   A. living together
   B. divorced
   C. working
   D. single parents

3. Divorced parents are _____.
   A. married
   B. not married
   C. a husband and a wife
   D. a two-parent family

4. In a strong family, parents are always _____ their children.
   A. calling
   B. writing to
   C. having problems with
   D. teaching

5. In 2012, _____ percent of homes are married parents with children.
   A. 18
   B. 20
   C. 40
   D. 75

6. This passage is about _____.
   A. large families
   B. divorced couples
   C. different kinds of families
   D. social groups in a community

APPLY YOUR KNOWLEDGE
1. What type of family are you in?
2. What social groups are you in?

Marisol is writing a paragraph about life in her home. She's using the writing process. She's *pre-writing*, *organizing ideas*, and *writing a first draft*.

Pre-writing: Observing and Recording

me—studying English—kitchen

son—watching TV—living room

daughter—doing homework—bedroom

husband—cooking dinner—kitchen

father—reading the newspaper—living room

mother—shopping at the supermarket

baby—sleeping—bedroom

Organizing Ideas

in the kitchen—me, husband

in the living room—son, father

in the bedroom—daughter, baby

not home—mother

Writing a First Draft

Life in My Home

It's a Friday afternoon in my home. My husband and I are in the kitchen. He's cooking dinner, and I'm studying English. My son and my father are in the living room. My son is watching TV, and my father is reading the newspaper. My daughter is in her bedroom. She's doing her homework. The baby is also in her bedroom. She's sleeping. My mother isn't home. She's shopping at the supermarket.

Write a paragraph about life in your home.

Pre-write: Observe and record life at your home. Who's at home? What's each person doing? Make a list.

Organize your ideas: What's a good way to organize your list? By people? By actions? By rooms in the home?

Write a first draft: Write a paragraph about the people in your home. Who are they, where are they, and what are they doing? Indent the first line of the paragraph. Use this title: Life in My Home.

7

Prepositions
There Is/There Are
Singular/Plural: Introduction

- Places Around Town
- Locating Places in the Community
- Describing Neighborhoods
- Reading a Simple Map
- Describing Apartments
- Apartment Ads

VOCABULARY PREVIEW

1. bakery
2. barber shop
3. book store
4. bus station
5. cafeteria
6. clinic
7. department store
8. drug store
9. hair salon
10. health club
11. hotel
12. laundromat
13. school
14. train station
15. video store

Where's the Restaurant?

A. Where's the restaurant?
B. It's **next to** the bank.

A. Where's the school?
B. It's **between** the library and the park.

A. Where's the supermarket?
B. It's **across from** the movie theater.

A. Where's the post office?
B. It's **around the corner from** the hospital.

1. Where's the bank?

3. Where's the restaurant?

5. Where's the hotel?

7. Where's the clinic?

2. Where's the post office?

4. Where's the hospital?

6. Where's the gas station?

8. Where's the bakery?

Is There a Laundromat in This Neighborhood?

There's (There is) a bank on Main Street.
Is there a bank on Main Street?

A. Excuse me. Is there a laundromat in this neighborhood?

B. Yes. There's a laundromat on Main Street, next to the supermarket.

1. drug store?

2. clinic?

3. department store?

4. hair salon?

5. book store?

6. post office?

How to Say It!

Expressing Gratitude

A. Thank you. / Thanks.
B. You're welcome.

Practice some conversations on this page again.
Express gratitude at the end of each conversation.

Is there . . . ?	Yes, there is. No, there isn't.

Is there a restaurant in your neighborhood?

No, there isn't.

Is there a cafeteria in your neighborhood?

Yes, there is.

Where is it?

It's on Central Avenue, across from the bank.

Draw a simple map of your neighborhood. With another student, ask and answer questions about your neighborhoods.

Some places you can talk about:

bakery	clinic	hospital	post office
bank	department store	hotel	restaurant
barber shop	drug store	laundromat	school
book store	fire station	library	supermarket
bus station	gas station	movie theater	train station
cafeteria	hair salon	park	video store
church	health club	police station	

Is There a Stove in the Kitchen?

A. Is there a stove in the kitchen?

B. Yes, there is. There's a very nice stove in the kitchen.

A. Oh, good.

A. Is there a refrigerator in the kitchen?

B. No, there isn't.

A. Oh, I see.

1. *a window in the kitchen?*
Yes, . . .

2. *a fire escape?*
No, . . .

3. *a closet in the bedroom?*
Yes, . . .

4. *an elevator* in the building?*
No, . . .

5. *an air conditioner* in the bedroom?*
Yes, . . .

6. *a superintendent in the building?*
No, . . .

7. *a bus stop near the building?*
No, . . .

8. *a jacuzzi in the bathroom?*
Yes, . . .

* **a** stove   **an** elevator
  a closet   **an** air conditioner

How Many Bedrooms Are There in the Apartment?

| How many windows are there in the bedroom? | There's one window in the bedroom. There are two windows in the bedroom. |

A. Tell me, how many bedrooms are there in the apartment?

B. There are two bedrooms in the apartment.

A. Two bedrooms?

B. Yes. That's right.

1. *floors*
   building

2. *windows*
   living room

3. *closets*
   apartment

4. *apartments*
   building

5. *washing machines*
   basement

6. *bathrooms*
   apartment

   * two and a half

SUPERINTENDENT

BUS STOP

Is there a window? Yes, there is. / No, there isn't.	Are there any windows? Yes, there are. / No, there aren't.

You're looking for a new apartment. Practice with another student. Ask questions about the apartment on page 61.

Ask the landlord:

1. a stove in the kitchen?
2. a refrigerator in the kitchen?
3. a superintendent in the building?
4. an elevator in the building?
5. a fire escape?
6. a satellite dish on the roof?
7. a mailbox near the building?
8. a bus stop near the building?

Ask a tenant in the building:

9. children in the building?
10. cats in the building?
11. mice in the basement?
12. cockroaches in the building?
13. broken windows in the building?
14. holes in the walls?
15. washing machines in the basement?

Ask the landlord:

16. rooms—in the apartment?
17. floors—in the building?
18. closets—in the bedroom?
19. windows—in the living room?

READING

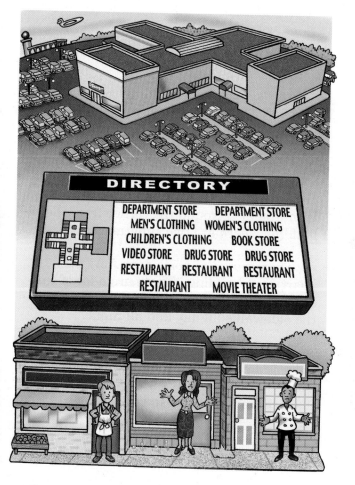

THE NEW SHOPPING MALL

Everybody in Brewster is talking about the city's new shopping mall. The mall is outside the city, next to the Brewster airport. There are more than one hundred stores in the mall.

There are two big department stores. There are many clothing stores for men, women, and children. There's a book store, and there's a video store. There are two drug stores, and there are four restaurants. There's even a large movie theater.

Almost all the people in Brewster are happy that their city's new shopping mall is now open. But some people aren't happy. The owners of the small stores in the old center of town are very upset. They're upset because many people aren't shopping in the stores in the center of town. They're shopping at the new mall.

✔ READING CHECK-UP

CHOOSE

1. Everybody in Brewster is _____.
   a. at the airport
   b. outside the city
   c. talking about the mall

2. In the mall, there are _____.
   a. two video stores
   b. two drug stores
   c. two restaurants

3. In the mall, there are _____.
   a. book stores and cafeterias
   b. restaurants and drug stores
   c. clothing stores and video stores

4. The store owners in the center of town are upset because _____.
   a. people aren't shopping in their stores
   b. people aren't shopping at the mall
   c. they're very old

How About You?

Is there a shopping mall in your city or town?
Are there small stores in your city or town?
Tell about stores where you live.

AMY'S APARTMENT BUILDING

Amy's apartment building is in the center of town. Amy is very happy there because the building is in a very convenient place.

Across from the building, there's a bank, a post office, and a restaurant. Next to the building, there's a drug store and a laundromat. Around the corner from the building, there are two supermarkets.

There's a lot of noise near Amy's apartment building. There are a lot of cars on the street, and there are a lot of people on the sidewalks all day and all night.

However, Amy isn't very upset about the noise in her neighborhood. Her building is in the center of town. It's a very busy place, but it's a convenient place to live.

 READING *CHECK-UP*

WHAT'S THE ANSWER?

1. Where is Amy's apartment building?
2. What's across from her building?
3. Is there a laundromat near her building?
4. Why is there a lot of noise near Amy's building?
5. Why is Amy happy there?

TRUE OR FALSE?

1. Amy's apartment is in a convenient place.
2. There's a drug store around the corner from her building.
3. There are two supermarkets in her neighborhood.
4. There are a lot of cars on the sidewalk.
5. The center of town is very noisy.

How About You?

Tell about YOUR neighborhood.
Is it convenient? Is it very busy?
Is it noisy or quiet?

IN YOUR OWN WORDS

FOR WRITING AND DISCUSSION

EDWARD'S APARTMENT BUILDING

Edward's apartment building is in the center of town. Edward is very happy there because the building is in a very convenient place. Using this picture, tell about Edward's neighborhood.

LISTENING

WHAT PLACES DO YOU HEAR?

Listen and choose the correct places.

Example: (a.) supermarket   b. school   (c.) video store

1. a. park   b. bank   c. laundromat
2. a. fire station   b. police station   c. gas station
3. a. school   b. department store   c. clothing store
4. a. bank   b. drug store   c. book store
5. a. hotel   b. hair salon   c. hospital

TRUE OR FALSE?

Listen to the conversation. Then answer *True* or *False*.

1. There are four rooms in the apartment.
2. There are two closets in the bedroom.
3. There are four windows in the kitchen.
4. There's a superintendent in the building.
5. There are three washing machines.
6. There's an elevator in the building.

Listen. Then say it.

Two bedrooms?

Five closets?

Next to the bank?

On Main Street?

Say it. Then listen.

Three windows?

Twenty floors?

Across from the clinic?

On Central Avenue?

In your journal, write about your apartment building or home. Tell about the building and the neighborhood.

GRAMMAR FOCUS

THERE IS/THERE ARE

There's one window in the bedroom.

Is there a laundromat in this neighborhood?
   Yes, there is.
   No, there isn't.

There are two windows in the bedroom.

Are there any children in the building?
   Yes, there are.
   No, there aren't.

SINGULAR/PLURAL: INTRODUCTION

There's one bedroom in the apartment.
There are two bedrooms in the apartment.

PREPOSITIONS

It's next to the bank.
It's across from the movie theater.
It's between the library and the park.
It's around the corner from the hospital.

Complete the sentences.

1. A. _____ there a clinic in this neighborhood?
   B. Yes, _____ _____.

2. A. _____ there cats in the building?
   B. Yes, _____ _____.

3. A. Is _____ a stove in the kitchen?
   B. No, _____ _____.

4. A. Are _____ mice in the basement?
   B. No, _____ _____.

5. A. How many rooms _____ there in the apartment?
   B. _____ _____ four rooms.

6. A. How many closets are _____ in the bedroom?
   B. _____ one closet in the bedroom.

7. The hospital is _____ the corner from the park.
8. The restaurant is _____ to the post office.
9. The hotel is _____ the bakery and the bank.
10. The gas station is across _____ the library.
11. The drug store is next _____ the laundromat.

LIFE SKILLS
• Locating places in the community
• Reading a simple map

1 CONVERSATION ASKING FOR & GIVING LOCATION

Look at the map. Practice the conversations with a classmate.

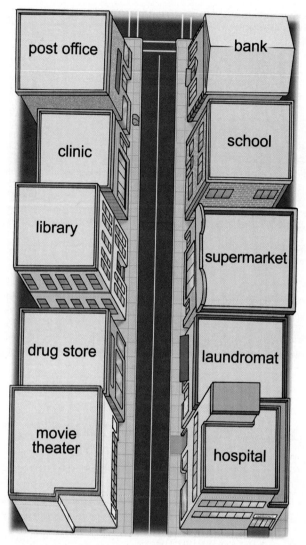

A. Excuse me. I'm looking for a post office.

B. Go that way. There's a post office on the left, next to the clinic.

A. On the left, next to the clinic?

B. Yes.

A. Thank you.

A. Excuse me. I'm looking for a laundromat.

B. Go that way. There's a laundromat on the right, across from the drug store.

A. On the right, across from the drug store?

B. Yes.

A. Thank you.

2 TEAMWORK ASKING FOR & GIVING LOCATION

Work with other classmates. Practice new conversations about the places on the map. Use these expressions.

> on the left
> on the right
>
> next to the ____
> across from the ____
> between the ____ and the ____

A. Excuse me. I'm looking for a _____.

B. Go that way. There's a _____

_____, _____.

A. _____, _____?

B. Yes.

A. Thank you.

66a

3 CONVERSATION GIVING & FOLLOWING DIRECTIONS

Practice the conversations with a classmate. Follow the directions on the map.

A. Excuse me. Is there a library near here?

B. Yes. Go that way one block on Wilson Avenue and turn left on Oak Street. The library is on the left.

A. Thanks very much.

B. You're welcome.

A. Excuse me. Is there a bus station near here?

B. Yes. Go that way two blocks on Wilson Avenue and turn right on Maple Street. The bus station is on the right.

A. Thanks very much.

B. You're welcome.

4 TEAMWORK GIVING & FOLLOWING DIRECTIONS

Work with other classmates. Practice new conversations about the places on the map.
Use these expressions.

go that way _____ block(s) on _____
         (number)   (street)

turn right/left on _____
               (street)

on the right

on the left

A. Excuse me. Is there a _____ near here?

B. Yes. _____.

A. Thanks very much.

B. You're welcome.

LIFE SKILLS READING

• Reading a map   • Reading apartment ads

READING A MAP

Look at the map on page 66b and answer the questions.

1. Where is the police station?
A. on Maple Street
B. on Lake Avenue
C. on Pine Street
D. on Elm Street

2. Where is the supermarket?
A. next to the laundromat
B. across from the hospital
C. next to the train station
D. across from the movie theater

3. What ISN'T on Grand Avenue?
A. the movie theater
B. the post office
C. the train station
D. the hospital

4. Is there a supermarket near this laundromat?
A. Yes. Go that way one block.
B. Yes. Go that way two blocks.
C. Yes. Go that way three blocks.
D. No, there isn't.

ABBREVIATIONS IN HOUSING ADS

Match the words and abbreviations.

_____ **1.** apt.   **a.** garage

_____ **2.** BA   **b.** apartment

_____ **3.** BR   **c.** bathroom

_____ **4.** gar.   **d.** large

_____ **5.** lge.   **e.** bedroom

_____ **6.** kit.   **f.** air conditioning

_____ **7.** elev.   **g.** living room

_____ **8.** AC   **h.** kitchen

_____ **9.** nr.   **i.** elevator

_____ **10.** liv. rm.   **j.** near

READING A CLASSIFIED AD

Look at the ad and answer the questions.

$500 mo., no utilies

APT FOR RENT
2 BR, 1 BA, new kit., lge. liv. rm.,
nr. hospital & shopping mall,
elev., gar. $1200
Call (426) 933-4800

1. How many bedrooms are there in the apartment?
A. one
B. two
C. three
D. four

2. How much is the rent?
A. one apartment
B. (426) 933-4800
C. 2 BR
D. $1200

3. Tell about the living room.
A. It's new.
B. There's an elevator.
C. It's large.
D. There's a garage.

4. Where is this apartment?
A. in a hospital
B. in an elevator
C. near a living room
D. near a shopping mall

Choose the correct answer.

1. There's a laundromat in my
___.
A. closet
B. neighborhood
C. apartment
D. bathroom

2. There's ___ in the kitchen.
A. a jacuzzi
B. an elevator
C. a sidewalk
D. a refrigerator

3. There's ___ in the bedroom.
A. a closet
B. a clinic
C. a stove
D. an apartment

4. Our apartment building is in
a convenient place. There's
___ near the building.
A. an air conditioner
B. an elevator
C. a bus stop
D. a satellite dish

5. The ___ is fixing the stove.
A. superintendent
B. supermarket
C. refrigerator
D. kitchen

6. There are four ___ in my
apartment.
A. streets
B. sidewalks
C. buildings
D. rooms

7. Our neighborhood is noisy
because there are a lot of ___.
A. floors
B. cars
C. walls
D. landlords

8. There's a ___ on the roof of
our apartment building.
A. bathroom
B. mailbox
C. satellite dish
D. bus stop

Mark your answers in the answer box.

Answers
1 Ⓐ Ⓑ Ⓒ Ⓓ
2 Ⓐ Ⓑ Ⓒ Ⓓ
3 Ⓐ Ⓑ Ⓒ Ⓓ
4 Ⓐ Ⓑ Ⓒ Ⓓ
5 Ⓐ Ⓑ Ⓒ Ⓓ
6 Ⓐ Ⓑ Ⓒ Ⓓ
7 Ⓐ Ⓑ Ⓒ Ⓓ
8 Ⓐ Ⓑ Ⓒ Ⓓ
9 Ⓐ Ⓑ Ⓒ Ⓓ
10 Ⓐ Ⓑ Ⓒ Ⓓ

Look at the map. Choose the correct answer.

9. The bakery is ___.
A. on Main Street
B. next to the drug store
C. across from the post office
D. between the post office and
the drug store

10. The book store is ___.
A. across from the clinic
B. between the post office
and the drug store
C. next to the post office
D. next to the bakery

POST OFFICE	BANK	DRUG STORE
	Pine Street	
BAKERY	BOOK STORE	CLINIC

SKILLS CHECK ✓

Words:
- ☐ airport
- ☐ bakery
- ☐ bank
- ☐ barber shop
- ☐ book store
- ☐ bus station
- ☐ cafeteria
- ☐ church
- ☐ clinic
- ☐ clothing store
- ☐ department store

- ☐ drug store
- ☐ fire station
- ☐ gas station
- ☐ hair salon
- ☐ health club
- ☐ hospital
- ☐ hotel
- ☐ laundromat
- ☐ library
- ☐ movie theater
- ☐ park
- ☐ police station

- ☐ post office
- ☐ restaurant
- ☐ school
- ☐ shopping mall
- ☐ supermarket
- ☐ train station
- ☐ video store
- ☐ zoo

- ☐ air conditioner
- ☐ apartment
- ☐ building

- ☐ bus stop
- ☐ closet
- ☐ elevator
- ☐ fire escape
- ☐ floor
- ☐ jacuzzi
- ☐ mailbox
- ☐ refrigerator
- ☐ stove
- ☐ superintendent
- ☐ washing machine

I can ask & answer:
- ☐ Where's the *restaurant*?
- ☐ Is there a *laundromat* in this neighborhood?
- ☐ Excuse me. I'm looking for a *post office*.
- ☐ Is there a *stove* in the *kitchen*?
- ☐ How many *bedrooms* are there in the *apartment*?
- ☐ Are there any *children* in the *building*?

I can read:
- ☐ a map
- ☐ housing ad abbreviations
- ☐ a classified ad

I can write about:
- ☐ my home and my neighborhood

8

Singular/Plural
Adjectives
This/That/These/Those

- Clothing
- Colors
- Shopping for Clothing
- Money

- Price Tags
- Clothing Sizes
- Clothing Ads
- Store Receipts

VOCABULARY PREVIEW

1. shirt
2. coat
3. dress
4. skirt
5. blouse

6. jacket
7. suit
8. tie
9. belt
10. sweater

11. pants
12. jeans
13. pajamas
14. shoes
15. socks

Clothing

1. shirt
2. tie
3. jacket
4. belt
5. pants
6. sock
7. shoe

8. earring
9. necklace
10. blouse
11. bracelet
12. skirt
13. briefcase
14. stocking

15. hat
16. coat
17. glove
18. purse/
   pocketbook
19. dress
20. glasses

21. suit
22. watch
23. umbrella
24. sweater
25. mitten
26. jeans
27. boot

Shirts Are Over There

SINGULAR/PLURAL*

a shirt – shirt**s**
a coat – coat**s**
a hat – hat**s**
a belt – belt**s**

a tie – tie**s**
an umbrella – umbrella**s**
a sweater – sweater**s**

a dress – dress**es**
a watch – watch**es**
a blouse – blous**es**
a necklace – necklac**es**

A. Excuse me.
   I'm looking for **a shirt**.
B. **Shirts** are over there.
A. Thanks.

A. Excuse me.
   I'm looking for **a tie**.
B. **Ties** are over there.
A. Thanks.

A. Excuse me.
   I'm looking for **a dress**.
B. **Dresses** are over there.
A. Thanks.

1.

2.

3.

4.

5.

6.

7.

8.

Put these words in the correct column.

| boots | briefcases | earrings | glasses | gloves | pants | purses | shoes | socks |

 S

boots

_____

_____

_____

 Z

_____

_____

_____

 IZ

_____

_____

_____

* Some irregular plurals you know are:

a man – men
a woman – women
a child – children
a person – people
a tooth – teeth
a mouse – mice

I'm Looking for a Jacket

COLORS

red   orange   yellow   green   blue   purple   black   silver

pink   gray   white   gold   brown

A. May I help you?

B. Yes, please. I'm looking for a jacket.

A. Here's a nice jacket.

B. But this is a PURPLE jacket!

A. That's okay. Purple jackets are very POPULAR this year.

A. May I help you?

B. Yes, please. I'm looking for a _____.

A. Here's a nice _____.

B. But this is a _____ _____!

A. That's okay. _____ _____s are very POPULAR this year.

1. *red*

2. *white*

3. *pink*

4. *orange*

5. *yellow*

6. *green and purple*

7. *striped*

8. *polka dot*

I'm Looking for a Pair of Gloves

pair of shoes/socks . . .

A. Can I help you?

B. Yes, please. I'm looking for a pair of gloves.

A. Here's a nice pair of gloves.

B. But these are GREEN gloves!

A. That's okay. Green gloves are very POPULAR this year.

A. Can I help you?

B. Yes, please. I'm looking for a pair of _____.

A. Here's a nice pair of _____.

B. But these are _____ _____s!

A. That's okay. _____ _____s are very POPULAR this year.

1. *yellow*

2. *blue*

3. *pink*

4. *orange*

5. *striped*

6. *green*

7. *red, white, and blue*

8. *polka dot*

How About You?

What are you wearing today?
What are the students in your class wearing today?
What's your favorite color?

NOTHING TO WEAR

Fred is upset this morning. He's looking for something to wear to work, but there's nothing in his closet.

He's looking for a clean shirt, but all his shirts are dirty. He's looking for a sports jacket, but all his sports jackets are at the dry cleaner's. He's looking for a pair of pants, but all the pants in his closet are ripped. And he's looking for a pair of socks, but all his socks are on the clothesline, and it's raining!

Fred is having a difficult time this morning. He's getting dressed for work, but his closet is empty, and there's nothing to wear.

✔ READING CHECK-UP

CHOOSE

1. Fred's closet is _____.
   a. upset
   b. empty

2. Fred is _____.
   a. at home
   b. at work

3. Fred's shirts are _____.
   a. dirty
   b. clean

4. He's looking for a pair of _____.
   a. jackets
   b. pants

5. The weather is _____.
   a. not very good
   b. beautiful

6. Fred is upset because _____.
   a. he's getting dressed
   b. there's nothing to wear

WHICH WORD DOESN'T BELONG?

Example:	a. socks	b. stockings	c. jeans	d. shoes
1.	a. sweater	b. jacket	c. briefcase	d. coat
2.	a. necklace	b. belt	c. bracelet	d. earrings
3.	a. blouse	b. skirt	c. dress	d. tie
4.	a. clean	b. green	c. gray	d. blue
5.	a. pants	b. shoes	c. earrings	d. blouse

Excuse Me. I Think That's My Jacket.

This/That is   These/Those are

1. hat

2. boots

3. coat

4. pen

5. pencils

6. umbrella

7. sunglasses

8.

Lost and Found

A. Is this your umbrella?

B. No, it isn't.

A. Are you sure?

B. Yes. THAT umbrella is BROWN, and MY umbrella is BLACK.

A. Are these your boots?

B. No, they aren't.

A. Are you sure?

B. Yes. THOSE boots are DIRTY, and MY boots are CLEAN.

Make up conversations, using colors and other adjectives you know.

1. *watch*   **2.** *gloves*   **3.** *briefcase*   **4.** *mittens*   **5.** _____

How to Say It!

Complimenting

A. That's a very nice *hat*!
B. Thank you.

A. Those are very nice *boots*!
B. Thank you.

Practice conversations with other students.

READING

HOLIDAY SHOPPING

Mrs. Miller is doing her holiday shopping. She's looking for gifts for her family, but she's having a lot of trouble.

She's looking for a brown umbrella for her son, but all the umbrellas are black. She's looking for a gray raincoat for her daughter, but all the raincoats are yellow. She's looking for a cotton sweater for her husband, but all the sweaters are wool.

She's looking for an inexpensive bracelet for her sister, but all the bracelets are expensive. She's looking for a leather purse for her mother, but all the purses are vinyl. And she's looking for a polka dot tie for her father, but all the ties are striped.

Poor Mrs. Miller is very frustrated. She's looking for special gifts for all the special people in her family, but she's having a lot of trouble.

✔ READING *CHECK-UP*

Q & A

Mrs. Miller is in the department store. Using this model, create dialogs based on the story.

A. Excuse me. I'm looking for *a brown umbrella* for my *son*.
B. I'm sorry. All our *umbrellas* are *black*.

LISTENING

WHAT'S THE WORD?

Listen and choose the correct answer.

1. a. blouse   b. dress
2. a. shoes   b. boots
3. a. necklace   b. bracelet
4. a. coat   b. raincoat
5. a. socks   b. stockings
6. a. shirt   b. skirt

WHICH WORD DO YOU HEAR?

Listen and choose the correct answer.

1. a. jacket   b. jackets
2. a. belt   b. belts
3. a. sweater   b. sweaters
4. a. suit   b. suits
5. a. shoe   b. shoes
6. a. tie   b. ties

PRONUNCIATION Emphasized Words

Listen. Then say it.

But this is a PURPLE jacket!

Green gloves are very POPULAR this year.

I think this is MY jacket.

THAT umbrella is BROWN, and
    MY umbrella is BLACK.

Say it. Then listen.

But these are YELLOW shoes!

Striped socks are very POPULAR this year.

I think these are MY glasses.

THOSE boots are DIRTY, and
    MY boots are CLEAN.

What are you wearing today? Tell about the clothing and the colors. Write about it in your journal.

GRAMMAR FOCUS

SINGULAR/PLURAL

[s]
I'm looking for **a** coat.
Coat**s** are over there.

[z]
I'm looking for **an** umbrella.
Umbrella**s** are over there.

[IZ]
I'm looking for **a** dress.
Dress**es** are over there.

THIS/THAT/THESE/THOSE

Is **this** your umbrella?
That umbrella is brown.

Are **these** your boots?
Those boots are dirty.

ADJECTIVES

This is a **purple** jacket.
These are **green** gloves.

Choose the correct word.

1. A. May I help you?
   B. Yes. I'm looking for a (shirt   shirts).

2. A. Pants (is   are) over there.
   B. Thank you.

3. A. Can I help you?
   B. Yes. I'm looking for a (necklace   jeans).

4. A. May I help you?
   B. Yes. I'm looking for an (hat   umbrella).

5. A. (Blouse   Blouses) are over there.
   B. Thanks.

6. A. Can I help you?
   B. I'm looking for a pair of (gloves   earring).

7. A. Here's a nice (socks   dress).
   B. But this (socks   dress) (is   are) orange!

8. Is (this   these) your jacket?

9. (That   Those) are my gloves.

10. This isn't my coat. (That's   This) my coat

11. (These   This) briefcase is black.

12. (Those are   That's) yellow ties.

13. (That's   Those are) my purse.

14. (This   These) are my (mitten   mittens)

76

1 MONEY COINS

Practice.

a penny
1¢ $.01
one cent

a nickel
5¢ $.05
five cents

a dime
10¢ $.10
ten cents

a quarter
25¢ $.25
twenty-five cents

a half dollar
50¢ $.50
fifty cents

Write the amount two ways.

1. _____ 25¢ _____ $.25 _____

2. _____

3. _____

4. _____

5. _____

6. _____

2 MONEY CURRENCY

Practice.

a dollar bill
$1.00
one dollar

a 5-dollar bill
$5.00
five dollars

a 10-dollar bill
$10.00
ten dollars

a 20-dollar bill
$20.00
twenty dollars

Write the amount.

1. _____

2. _____

3. _____

4. _____

3 TEAMWORK MATH: ADDITION PROBLEMS

Walk around the room.
Ask students addition
problems with money.

(a dime and a nickel) (15 cents) (a 5-dollar bill and a quarter) (5 dollars and 25 cents)

76a

4 CONVERSATION ASKING ABOUT PRICES IN A STORE

WOMEN'S
100% COTTON
CLR: PINK
SIZE: L
PRICE:
$21.00

A. How much is this blouse?

B. It's twenty-one dollars.

A. Thank you.

MEN'S
100% POLYESTER
CLR: BLUE
SIZE: W 32 L 34
PRICE:
$34.99

A. How much are these pants?

B. They're thirty-four ninety-nine.

A. Thank you.

Practice conversations with a classmate.

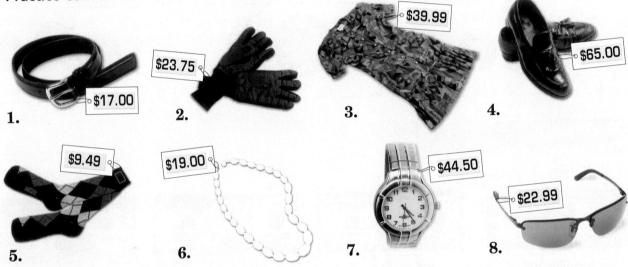

$23.75

$39.99

$65.00

1. $17.00   2.   3.   4.

$9.49 $19.00 $44.50 $22.99

5.   6.   7.   8.

5 CONVERSATION STATING CLOTHING NEEDS

Practice conversations about these clothing items.

A. What color _____ are you looking for?

B. _____.

A. And what size?

B. _____.

	Sizes
S	Small
M	Medium
L	Large
XL	Extra-Large

1. S   2. L   3. 9   4. M

Look at the clothing tags and answer the questions.

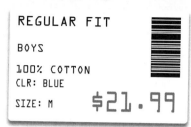

REGULAR FIT

BOYS

100% COTTON

CLR: BLUE

SIZE: M $21.99

```
107883
H4001
WHITE
———SIZE———
      32
   $22.00
   $36.00
```

1. What size is this? _____

2. How much is it? _____

3. What color is it? _____

4. What size is this? _____

5. It's on sale. What's the old price? _____

6. What's the sale price? _____

Look at the store receipt and answer the questions.

CLYDE'S CLOTHING

BLOUSE	16.95
SKIRT	24.95
SUBTOTAL	41.90
SALES TAX	2.10
TOTAL	44.00

Thank you for shopping at Clyde's Clothing!

7. How much is the skirt? _____

8. How much is the blouse? _____

9. How much is the tax? _____

10. How much is the person paying? _____

Look at the ad and answer the questions.

SALE
19.99

9⁹⁹ Reg. 14.99
Blouses
S, M, L

24⁹⁹ Reg. 39.99
Misses' Jeans
Sizes 6–16

Reg. $25.00
Men's Shirts Sizes S, M, L, XL

11. What sizes are the men's shirts?

_____

12. What's the regular price of the blouses?

_____

13. What's the sale price of the blouses?

_____

14. How much are the jeans?

_____

Choose the correct answer.

1. My favorite color is _____.
   A. dress
   B. striped
   C. purple
   D. clean

2. It's raining. Where's my _____?
   A. briefcase
   B. umbrella
   C. watch
   D. bracelet

3. My children are sleeping. They're wearing _____.
   A. suits
   B. ties
   C. glasses
   D. pajamas

4. It's cold today. Where are my _____?
   A. gloves
   B. glasses
   C. earrings
   D. watches

5. My brother is wearing a blue suit, a red tie, and a white _____.
   A. dress
   B. shirt
   C. skirt
   D. briefcase

6. It's snowing. Where are my _____?
   A. pajamas
   B. belts
   C. boots
   D. earrings

Mark your answers in the answer box.

Answers
1 Ⓐ Ⓑ Ⓒ Ⓓ
2 Ⓐ Ⓑ Ⓒ Ⓓ
3 Ⓐ Ⓑ Ⓒ Ⓓ
4 Ⓐ Ⓑ Ⓒ Ⓓ
5 Ⓐ Ⓑ Ⓒ Ⓓ
6 Ⓐ Ⓑ Ⓒ Ⓓ
7 Ⓐ Ⓑ Ⓒ Ⓓ
8 Ⓐ Ⓑ Ⓒ Ⓓ
9 Ⓐ Ⓑ Ⓒ Ⓓ
10 Ⓐ Ⓑ Ⓒ Ⓓ

Look at the clothing tag and answer the questions.

7. What size is this item?
   A. blue
   B. large
   C. a men's shirt
   D. $24.99

8. What color is it?
   A. black
   B. large
   C. $19.99
   D. blue

9. How much is this item?
   A. $19.99
   B. $24.99
   C. large
   D. 428765-53

10. Where is this item in the store?
    A. Women's Clothing
    B. Children's Clothing
    C. Men's Clothing
    D. Large Blue Clothing

```
428765-53

|| ||| | || |||| |

MEN'S SHIRT
CLR: BLUE
------------------
SIZE: L

$24.99
$19.99
```

SKILLS CHECK ✓

Words:

□ belt	□ jeans	□ sports jacket	□ brown
□ blouse	□ mittens	□ stocking	□ gold
□ boots	□ necklace	□ suit	□ gray
□ bracelet	□ pajamas	□ sunglasses	□ green
□ briefcase	□ pants	□ sweater	□ orange
□ coat	□ pocketbook	□ tie	□ pink
□ dress	□ purse	□ umbrella	□ purple
□ earring	□ raincoat	□ watch	□ red
□ glasses	□ shirt		□ silver
□ glove	□ shoe		□ white
□ hat	□ skirt	□ black	□ yellow
□ jacket	□ sock	□ blue	

I can express clothing needs:
□ I'm looking for a *shirt*.
□ How much is this *blouse*?
□ How much are these *pants*?
□ What color *shirt* are you looking for?
   Red.
And what size?
   Medium.

I can:
□ identify money
□ read clothing tags (size, price)
□ identify regular prices & sale prices
□ read a store receipt

Clothing, Colors, and Cultures

Blue and pink aren't children's clothing colors all around the world

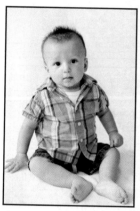 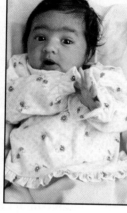 

The meanings of colors are sometimes very different in different cultures. For example, in some cultures, blue is a common clothing color for little boys, and pink is a common clothing color for little girls. In other cultures, other colors are common for boys and girls.

There are also different colors for special days in different cultures. For example, white is the traditional color of a wedding dress in some cultures, but other colors are traditional in other cultures.

For some people, white is a happy color. For others, it's a sad color. For some people, red is a beautiful and lucky color. For others, it's a very sad color.

What are the meanings of different colors in YOUR culture?

LISTENING

Attention, J-Mart Shoppers!

_c_	**1** jackets	**a.**	Aisle 1
___	**2** gloves	**b.**	Aisle 7
___	**3** blouses	**c.**	Aisle 9
___	**4** bracelets	**d.**	Aisle 11
___	**5** ties	**e.**	Aisle 5

That's a very nice _____ .

 ■ bathrobe

 ■ tee shirt

 ■ scarf

 ■ wallet

 ■ ring

Those are very nice _____ .

 ■ sandals

 ■ slippers

 ■ sneakers

 ■ shorts

 ■ sweat pants

AROUND THE WORLD

People's Homes

Homes are different all around the world.

This family is living in a farmhouse.

This family is living in a hut.

This family is living in a houseboat.

These people are living in a mobile home (a trailer).

What different kinds of homes are there in your country?

FACT FILE

Urban, Suburban, and Rural

urban areas	=	cities
suburban areas	=	places near cities
rural areas	=	places in the countryside, far from cities

About 50% (percent) of the world's population is in urban and suburban areas.

About 50% (percent) of the world's population is in rural areas.

urban and suburban / rural

Global Exchange

RosieM: My apartment is in a wonderful neighborhood. There's a big, beautiful park across from my apartment building. Around the corner, there's a bank, a post office, and a laundromat. There are also many restaurants and stores in my neighborhood. It's a noisy place, but it's a very interesting place. There are a lot of people on the sidewalks all day and all night. How about your neighborhood? Tell me about it.

Send a message to a keypal. Tell about your neighborhood.

What Are They Saying?

He's tall.
Is he tall?

There's a park on Main Street.
Is there a park on Main Street?

Practice these conversations with a classmate.

Your computer is new.

A. What's the sentence?

B. *Your computer is new.*

A. What kind of sentence is it?

B. It's **a statement.**

A. Can you change it to a question?

B. Yes. *Is your computer new?*

Are your neighbors noisy?

A. What's the sentence?

B. *Are your neighbors noisy?*

A. What kind of sentence is it?

B. It's **a question.**

A. Can you change it to a statement?

B. Yes. *Your neighbors are noisy.*

There's a dishwasher in the kitchen.

A. What's the sentence?

B. *There's a dishwasher in the kitchen.*

A. What kind of sentence is it?

B. It's **a statement.**

A. Can you change it to a question?

B. Yes. *Is there a dishwasher in the kitchen?*

Are there mice in the apartment?

A. What's the sentence?

B. *Are there mice in the apartment?*

A. What kind of sentence is it?

B. It's **a question.**

A. Can you change it to a statement?

B. Yes. *There are mice in the apartment.*

Rewrite these sentences. *Capitalize* the first letter of the first word in each sentence. Put the correct *punctuation mark* at the end of each sentence. Then practice new conversations about these sentences.

1. his car is old

2. are your brothers tall

3. there's a bank on Main Street

4. are there closets in the bedrooms

5. your parents are at home

6. there are many stores in the mall

7. is this restaurant expensive

8. there's a bus stop near the building

9. is there a window in the bathroom

10. are purple jackets popular this year

Urban and Rural Areas

Around the world, there are many big cities and suburban areas. There are also many rural areas. Millions of people are in cities and the suburban areas near those cities. There are not many people in rural areas.

Cities are busy, with many different places. In cities, there are bus stations, train stations, department stores, factories, and large streets. There are also many apartments, houses, schools, and hospitals. Cities are noisy, but they are very convenient because everything is nearby. There are also many different types of jobs in cities.

Rural areas are very different. Rural areas are quiet. People are in small towns or on farms. Schools are small. In many towns, there isn't a hospital or a department store. Houses and apartments are inexpensive, but in many rural areas, there are not many good jobs. Some rural areas are very poor.

Cities are convenient, but there are also many problems. Some urban areas are expensive, and many people are poor. Some schools aren't good, and many families are in small apartments. Streets are sometimes dirty, and some people in cities are not happy.

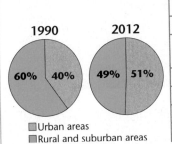

1990   2012

60%   40%   49%   51%

☐ Urban areas
☐ Rural and suburban areas

Percentage of People in Urban Areas	
Brazil	62%
Canada	81%
Guatemala	49%
India	31%
Mexico	78%
People's Republic of China	51%
South Korea	83%
Thailand	34%
United States	82%
Vietnam	31%

1. Around the world, _____ people live in cities.
   - A. all
   - B. many
   - C. not many
   - D. one million

2. There are many _____ in cities.
   - A. rural areas
   - B. inexpensive houses
   - C. farms
   - D. apartments

3. In rural areas, _____.
   - A. some people are poor
   - B. houses are expensive
   - C. there are many good jobs
   - D. there are many hospitals

4. According to the World Population graph, the percentage of people in urban areas in 2012 is _____.
   - A. 60%
   - B. 51%
   - C. 49%
   - D. 40%

5. According to the chart, 83% of the people in _____ are in urban areas.
   - A. India
   - B. Thailand
   - C. South Korea
   - D. the United States

6. This passage is about _____.
   - A. urban areas around the world
   - B. urban areas in the United States
   - C. suburban areas in the United States
   - d. urban and rural areas around the world

APPLY YOUR KNOWLEDGE
1. Is your area urban, suburban, or rural?
2. What are some problems in your area?

Simple Present Tense

- **Languages and Nationalities**
- **Everyday Activities**

- **Civics: Staying Informed**

VOCABULARY PREVIEW

1. call
2. cook
3. drive
4. eat
5. listen to music

6. paint
7. play
8. read
9. sell
10. shop

11. sing
12. speak
13. visit
14. watch TV
15. work

Interviews Around the World

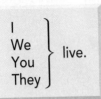

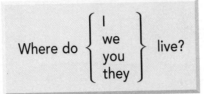

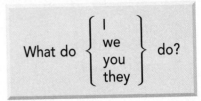

A. What's your name?

B. My name is Antonio.

A. Where do you live?

B. I live in Rome.

A. What language do you speak?

B. I speak Italian.

A. Tell me, what do you do every day?

B. I eat Italian food,
I sing Italian songs,
and I watch Italian TV shows!

Interview these people.

What's your name?
Where do you live?
What language do you speak?
What do you do every day?

1. Carmen — Spanish — MADRID

2. Kenji — Japanese — TOKYO

3. Nicole — French — PARIS

4. Erik and Monika — German — BERLIN

5. Jae Hee — Korean — SEOUL

6. Boris and Natasha — Russian — MOSCOW

People Around the World

He
She > lives.
It

Where does { he she it } live?

What does { he she it } do?

MEXICO CITY

A. What's his name?

B. His name is Miguel.

A. Where does he live?

B. He lives in Mexico City.

A. What language does he speak?

B. He speaks Spanish.

A. What does he do every day?

B. He eats Mexican food,
he reads Mexican newspapers,
and he listens to Mexican music.

Ask and answer questions about these people.

What's his/her name?
Where does he/she live?
What language does he/she speak?
What does he/she do every day?

English
Canadian
TORONTO

1. Kate

Spanish
Puerto Rican
SAN JUAN

2. Carlos

Greek
ATHENS

3. Anna

Chinese
HONG KONG

4. Ming

Portuguese
Brazilian
RIO de JANEIRO

5. Sonia

Arabic
Egyptian
CAIRO

6. Omar

TALK ABOUT IT! *Where Do They Live, and What Do They Do?*

I We You They } live.	He She It } lives.

Where do { I
we
you
they } live?
does { he
she
it }

What do { I
we
you
they } do?
does { he
she
it }

My name is Linda.
I live in London.
I work in a library.

My name is Brian.
I live in Boston.
I work in a bank.

We're Walter and Wendy.
We live in Washington, D.C.
We work in an office.

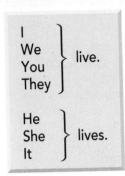 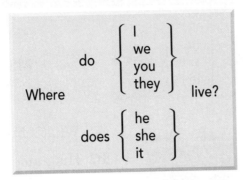 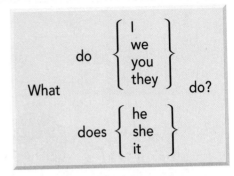

My name is Bob.
I live in Buffalo.
I drive a bus.

We're Howard and Henry.
We live in Honolulu.
We paint houses.

My name is Tina.
I live in Tampa.
I drive a taxi.

 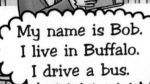 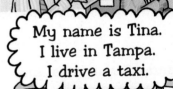

We're Carol and Ray.
We live in Cleveland.
We cook in a restaurant.

My name is Susan.
I live in San Diego.
I sell cars.

My name is Victor.
I live in Vancouver.
I play the violin.

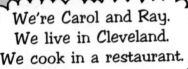  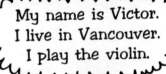

Use these models to talk with other students about the people above.

A. Where does *Linda* live?

B. *She* lives in *London*.

A. What does *she* do?

B. *She works in a library*.

A. Where do *Walter* and *Wendy* live?

B. They live in *Washington, D.C.*

A. What do they do?

B. They *work in an office*.

How About You?

Where do you live?
What do you do?

82

MR. AND MRS. DiCARLO

Mr. and Mrs. DiCarlo live in an old Italian neighborhood in New York City. They speak a little English, but usually they speak Italian.

They read the Italian newspaper. They listen to Italian radio programs. They shop at the Italian grocery store around the corner from their apartment building. And every day they visit their friends and neighbors and talk about life back in "the old country."

Mr. and Mrs. DiCarlo are upset about their son, Joe. He lives in a small suburb outside the city. He speaks a little Italian, but usually he speaks English. He reads American newspapers. He listens to American radio programs. He shops at big suburban supermarkets and shopping malls. And when he visits his friends and neighbors, he always speaks English.

In fact, Joe speaks Italian only when he calls his parents on the telephone, or when he visits them every weekend.

Mr. and Mrs. DiCarlo are sad because their son speaks so little Italian. They're afraid he's forgetting his language, his culture, and his country.

✓ READING CHECK-UP

WHAT'S THE ANSWER?

1. Where do Mr. and Mrs. DiCarlo live?
2. Where does Joe live?
3. What language do Mr. and Mrs. DiCarlo usually speak?
4. What language does Joe usually speak?
5. What do Mr. and Mrs. DiCarlo read?
6. What does Joe read?

7. What do Mr. and Mrs. DiCarlo listen to?
8. What does Joe listen to?
9. Where do Mr. and Mrs. DiCarlo shop?
10. Where does Joe shop?

WHICH WORD IS CORRECT?

1. Mrs. DiCarlo (read   reads) the Italian newspaper.
2. Mr. DiCarlo (shop   shops) at the Italian grocery store.
3. They (live   lives) in New York City.
4. Joe (live   lives) outside the city.
5. He (speak   speaks) English.
6. Mr. and Mrs. DiCarlo (listen   listens) to the radio.
7. They (visit   visits) their friends every day.
8. Their friends (talk   talks) about life back in "the old country."
9. Joe (call   calls) his parents on the telephone.
10. Joe's friends (speak   speaks) English.

LISTENING

Listen and choose the correct answer.

1. a. live   b. lives
2. a. work   b. works
3. a. speak   b. speaks
4. a. drive   b. drives
5. a. read   b. reads

6. a. visit   b. visits
7. a. cook   b. cooks
8. a. paint   b. paints
9. a. call   b. calls
10. a. shop   b. shops

How to Say It!

Hesitating

A. What do you do every day?
B. Hmm. Well . . .
   I *work*, I *read the newspaper*, and I *visit my friends*.

Practice conversations with other students. Hesitate while you're thinking of your answer.

IN YOUR OWN WORDS

MRS. KOWALSKI

Mrs. Kowalski lives in an old Polish neighborhood in Chicago. She's upset about her son, Michael, and his wife, Kathy. Using the story on page 83 as a model, tell a story about Mrs. Kowalski.

INTERVIEW

Where do you live?
What language do you speak?
What do you do every day?

Interview another student.   Then tell the class about that person.

I live in an apartment in the city.
I speak Spanish and a little English.
I go to school and visit my friends.

She lives in an apartment in the city.
She speaks Spanish and a little English.
She goes to school and visits her friends.

PRONUNCIATION Blending with *does*

Listen. Then say it.

Where does he work?

Where does she live?

What does he do?

What does she read?

Say it. Then listen.

Where does he shop?

Where does she eat?

What does he cook?

What does she talk about?

Where do you live? What language do you speak? What do you do every day? Write a paragraph about it in your journal.

GRAMMAR FOCUS

SIMPLE PRESENT TENSE

Where	do	I we you they	live?
	does	he she it	

I We You They	live	in Rome.
He She It	lives	

Match the questions and answers.

____ 1. Where do you and your wife live?

____ 2. Where does your brother live?

____ 3. Where do your parents live?

____ 4. Where does your sister live?

____ 5. Where do you live?

a. They live in Mexico City.

b. I live in Chicago.

c. She lives in Los Angeles.

d. We live in Dallas.

e. He lives in London.

Choose the correct word.

6. He (drive   drives) a truck.

7. We (speak   speaks) Portuguese.

8. I (sell   sells) cars.

9. They (read   reads) every day.

10. Where (do   does) they live?

11. Where (do   does) she work?

12. You (speak   speaks) Arabic.

13. She (listen   listens) to the radio.

14. Where (do   does) you work?

15. What language (do   does) you and your wife speak?

1 CONVERSATION INTERVIEWS

Practice these interviews with other students.

— How do you stay informed? —

Eduardo
I watch the news on TV.

Sonia
I read the newspaper.

Rodney
I listen to the news on the radio.

Herman
I read magazines.

Kate
I get the news online on the Internet.

Carmen
I go to community meetings.

2 CLOZE READING STAYING INFORMED

Complete the story about the people above.

Eduardo ___watches___ ¹ the news on TV. Sonia _____ ² the newspaper. Rodney _____ ³ to the news on the radio. Herman _____ ⁴ magazines. Kate _____ ⁵ the news online on the Internet. Carmen _____ ⁶ to community meetings.

3 TEAMWORK CLASSROOM INTERVIEWS

Interview five students. Write the information on the chart.

NAME	ACTIVITY
Tuan	reads the newspaper

Now write a story about the students you interviewed.

SHARE & SOLVE Are there books, newspapers, and magazines in your language at the library in your community? Is this a problem? Discuss in class. Then talk with someone in your library.

86a

Choose the correct answer.

1. They live in _____.
  A. Puerto Rican
  B. Chinese
  C. Spanish
  D. San Juan

2. I read the _____ every day.
  A. food
  B. newspaper
  C. TV show
  D. neighborhood

3. I'm from Canada. I speak _____.
  A. Canadian
  B. Toronto
  C. English and French
  D. language

4. My wife _____ in a bank.
  A. works
  B. lives
  C. visits
  D. shops

5. We eat Mexican _____ every day.
  A. music
  B. food
  C. shopping malls
  D. songs

6. I _____ my grandparents every weekend.
  A. visit
  B. listen
  C. paint
  D. play

7. They usually shop at Italian _____.
  A. apartment buildings
  B. houses
  C. grocery stores
  D. radio programs

8. My sister _____ a bus.
  A. works
  B. talks
  C. calls
  D. drives

9. My husband _____ cars.
  A. plays
  B. sells
  C. speaks
  D. reads

10. I get the news online _____.
  A. on the radio
  B. on TV
  C. on the Internet
  D. at community meetings

Mark your answers in the answer box.

	Answers			
1	A	B	C	D
2	A	B	C	D
3	A	B	C	D
4	A	B	C	D
5	A	B	C	D
6	A	B	C	D
7	A	B	C	D
8	A	B	C	D
9	A	B	C	D
10	A	B	C	D

SKILLS CHECK ✓

Words:
- ☐ call
- ☐ cook
- ☐ drive
- ☐ eat
- ☐ listen
- ☐ paint
- ☐ play
- ☐ read
- ☐ sell
- ☐ shop
- ☐ sing
- ☐ speak
- ☐ visit
- ☐ watch TV
- ☐ work

Nationalities:
- ☐ Brazilian
- ☐ Canadian
- ☐ Chinese
- ☐ Egyptian
- ☐ French
- ☐ German
- ☐ Greek
- ☐ Italian
- ☐ Japanese
- ☐ Korean
- ☐ Mexican
- ☐ Polish
- ☐ Puerto Rican
- ☐ Russian
- ☐ Spanish

Languages:
Portuguese
English, French
Chinese
Arabic
French
German
Greek
Italian
Japanese
Korean
Spanish
Polish
Spanish
Russian
Spanish

I can ask & answer:
- ☐ What's your/his/her name?
- ☐ What are their names?
- ☐ Where do you/they live?
- ☐ Where does he/she live?
- ☐ What language do you/they speak?
- ☐ What language does he/she speak?
- ☐ What do you/they do every day?
- ☐ What does he/she do every day?
- ☐ How do you stay informed?

I can write about:
- ☐ my everyday activities
- ☐ how students stay informed

10

Simple Present Tense: Yes/No Questions
Negatives
Short Answers

- **Days of the Week**
- **Habitual Actions**
- **People's Interests and Activities**
- **Work Schedules**
- **Bus Destination Signs**

VOCABULARY PREVIEW

①	②	③	④	⑤	⑥	⑦
SUN	**MON**	**TUE**	**WED**	**THU**	**FRI**	**SAT**
1	2	3	4	5	6	7
8	9	10	11	12	13	14
15	16	17	18	19	20	21
22	23	24	25	26	27	28
29	30	31				

1. Sunday
2. Monday
3. Tuesday
4. Wednesday
5. Thursday
6. Friday
7. Saturday

8. baby-sit
9. clean
10. do yoga
11. go dancing
12. jog

13. play volleyball
14. ride
15. see a movie
16. see a play

87

Stanley's International Restaurant

He cooks.
He doesn't cook.
(does not)

Does he cook?
Yes, he does.
No, he doesn't.

What kind of food
When } does he cook?

MONDAY	TUESDAY	WEDNESDAY	THURSDAY	FRIDAY	SATURDAY	SUNDAY
Italian	Greek	Chinese	Puerto Rican	Japanese	Mexican	American

Stanley's International Restaurant is a very special place. Every day Stanley cooks a different kind of food. On Monday he cooks Italian food. On Tuesday he cooks Greek food. On Wednesday he cooks Chinese food. On Thursday he cooks Puerto Rican food. On Friday he cooks Japanese food. On Saturday he cooks Mexican food. And on Sunday he cooks American food.

A. What kind of food does Stanley cook on **Monday**?

B. On **Monday** he cooks **Italian** food.

Ask and answer questions about the other days of the week.

A. Does Stanley cook **Greek** food on **Tuesday**?

B. Yes, he does.

Ask six questions with "yes" answers.

A. Does Stanley cook **Japanese** food on **Sunday**?

B. No, he doesn't.

A. When does he cook **Japanese** food?

B. He cooks **Japanese** food on **Friday**.

Ask six questions with "no" answers.

A. Do you go to Stanley's Restaurant on **Wednesday**?

B. Yes, I do.

A. Why?

B. Because I like **Chinese** food.

Ask these people.

1. *Monday?*

2. *Thursday?*

3. *Saturday?*

4. *Sunday?*

A. Do you go to Stanley's Restaurant on **Sunday**?

B. No, I don't.

A. Why not?

B. Because I don't like **American** food.

Ask these people.

5. *Tuesday?*

6. *Wednesday?*

7. *Friday?*

8. *Monday?*

A. What kind of food do you like?

B. I like **Russian** food.

A. When do you go to Stanley's Restaurant?

B. I don't go there.

A. Why not?

B. Because Stanley doesn't cook **Russian** food.

Ask these people.

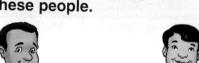

9. *French*

10. *Ethiopian*

11. *Thai*

12. *Vietnamese*

89

Busy People!

| MONDAY | TUESDAY | WEDNESDAY | THURSDAY | FRIDAY | SATURDAY | SUNDAY |

Jeff is a very athletic person. He does a different kind of exercise or sport every day. On Monday he jogs. On Tuesday he plays tennis. On Wednesday he does yoga. On Thursday he swims. On Friday he goes to a health club. On Saturday he plays basketball. And on Sunday he rides his bike.

| MONDAY | TUESDAY | WEDNESDAY | THURSDAY | FRIDAY | SATURDAY | SUNDAY |

Julie is a very busy student. She does a different activity every day. On Monday she sings in the choir. On Tuesday she plays in the orchestra. On Wednesday she writes for the school newspaper. On Thursday she plays volleyball. On Friday she baby-sits for her neighbors. On Saturday she works at the mall. And on Sunday she visits her grandparents.

| MONDAY | TUESDAY | WEDNESDAY | THURSDAY | FRIDAY | SATURDAY | SUNDAY |

Mr. and Mrs. Baker are very active people. They do something different every day of the week. On Monday they go to a museum. On Tuesday they see a play. On Wednesday they go to a concert. On Thursday they take a karate lesson. On Friday they go dancing. On Saturday they see a movie. And on Sunday they play cards with their friends.

Yes,
$\begin{Bmatrix} I \\ we \\ you \\ they \end{Bmatrix}$ do.

$\begin{Bmatrix} he \\ she \\ it \end{Bmatrix}$ does.

No,
$\begin{Bmatrix} I \\ we \\ you \\ they \end{Bmatrix}$ don't.

$\begin{Bmatrix} he \\ she \\ it \end{Bmatrix}$ doesn't.

A. Does Jeff play tennis on Tuesday?

B. Yes, he does.

A. Does Julie work at the mall on Saturday?

B. Yes, she does.

A. Do Mr. and Mrs. Baker go dancing on Friday?

B. Yes, they do.

Ask other questions with "yes" answers.

A. Does Jeff do yoga on Sunday?

B. No, he doesn't.

A. Does Julie sing in the choir on Thursday?

B. No, she doesn't.

A. Do Mr. and Mrs. Baker see a movie on Monday?

B. No, they don't.

Ask other questions with "no" answers.

Do you swim on Thursday?

Yes, I do.

Do you play volleyball on Sunday?

No, I don't.

Do you go dancing on Friday?

Yes, we do.

Do you see a play on Monday?

No, we don't.

Now interview Jeff, Julie, and Mr. and Mrs. Baker. Practice conversations with other students.

EVERY WEEKEND IS IMPORTANT TO THE GARCIA FAMILY

Every weekend is important to the Garcia family. During the week they don't have very much time together, but they spend a LOT of time together on the weekend.

Mr. Garcia works at the post office during the week, but he doesn't work there on the weekend. Mrs. Garcia works at the bank during the week, but she doesn't work there on the weekend. Jennifer and Jonathan Garcia go to school during the week, but they don't go to school on the weekend. And the Garcias' dog, Max, stays home alone during the week, but he doesn't stay home alone on the weekend.

On Saturday and Sunday the Garcias spend time together. On Saturday morning they clean the house together. On Saturday afternoon they work in the garden together. And on Saturday evening they watch videos together. On Sunday morning they go to church together. On Sunday afternoon they have a big dinner together. And on Sunday evening they play their musical instruments together.

As you can see, every weekend is special to the Garcias. It's their only time together as a family.

✓ READING CHECK-UP

Q & A

Using these models, make questions and answers based on the story on page 92.

A. What *does Mr. Garcia* do during the week?
B. *He works at the post office.*

A. What do the Garcias do on *Saturday morning*?
B. They *clean the house* together.

DO OR DOES?

1. _____ Mr. Garcia work on the weekend?
2. _____ Jennifer and Jonathan go to school during the week?
3. When _____ they watch videos?
4. Where _____ Mrs. Garcia work?
5. _____ you speak Spanish?
6. What _____ Mr. Garcia do during the week?

WHAT'S THE ANSWER?

1. Does Mr. Garcia work at the post office?
2. Do Jennifer and Jonathan go to school during the week?
3. Does Mrs. Garcia work at the post office?
4. Do Mr. and Mrs. Garcia have much time together during the week?
5. Does Jennifer watch videos on Saturday evening?
6. Do Jennifer and her brother clean the house on Saturday morning?
7. Does Mr. Garcia work in the garden on Saturday evening?

DON'T OR DOESN'T?

1. Mr. and Mrs. Garcia _____ work on the weekend.
2. Jennifer _____ work at the bank.
3. We _____ watch videos during the week.
4. My son _____ play a musical instrument.
5. My sister and I _____ eat at Stanley's Restaurant.
6. Our dog _____ like our neighbor's dog.

LISTENING

WHAT'S THE WORD?

Listen and choose the word you hear.

1. a. do   b. does
2. a. do   b. does
3. a. Sunday   b. Monday
4. a. don't   b. doesn't
5. a. don't   b. doesn't
6. a. does   b. goes
7. a. Tuesday   b. Thursday
8. a. go   b. don't

WHAT'S THE ANSWER?

Listen and choose the correct response.

1. a. Yes, I do.   b. Yes, he does.
2. a. Yes, they do.   b. Yes, she does.
3. a. No, she doesn't.   b. No, we don't.
4. a. No, he doesn't.   b. No, we don't.
5. a. No, I don't.   b. No, he doesn't.
6. a. No, I don't.   b. No, they don't.
7. a. Yes, we do.   b. Yes, they do.
8. a. Yes, they do.   b. Yes, he does.

How About You?

Tell about yourself:
What do you do during the week?
What do you do on the weekend?

Now tell about another person—a friend, someone in your family, or another student:
What does he/she do during the week?
What does he/she do on the weekend?

READING

A VERY OUTGOING PERSON

Alice is a very outgoing person. She spends a lot of time with her friends. She goes to parties, she goes to movies, and she goes to concerts. She's very popular.

She also likes sports very much. She plays basketball, she plays baseball, and she plays volleyball. She's very athletic.

Alice doesn't stay home alone very often. She doesn't read many books, she doesn't watch TV, and she doesn't listen to music. She's very active.

As you can see, Alice is a very outgoing person.

IN YOUR OWN WORDS

FOR WRITING AND DISCUSSION

A VERY SHY PERSON

Using the story about Alice as a model, tell a story about Sheldon. Begin your story:

Sheldon is a very shy person. He doesn't spend a lot of time with his friends. He doesn't go . . .

How About You?

Tell about yourself:
What kind of person are you?
Are you outgoing? shy? active? athletic?
Tell how you spend your time.

How to Say It!

Starting a Conversation

A. Tell me, what kind of *movies* do you like?
B. I like *comedies*.
A. Who's your favorite *movie star*?
B. *Tim Kelly*.

Practice the interviews on this page, using "Tell me" to start the conversations.

INTERVIEW

First, answer these questions about yourself. Next, interview another student.
Then, tell the class about yourself and the other student.

1. What kind of movies do you like?

   Who's your favorite movie star?

   comedies   dramas   westerns   adventure movies   science fiction movies   cartoons

2. What kind of books do you like?

   Who's your favorite author?

   novels   poetry   short stories   non-fiction   biographies

3. What kind of TV programs do you like?

   Who's your favorite TV star?

   comedies   dramas   cartoons   game shows   news programs

4. What kind of music do you like?

   Who's your favorite performer?

   classical music   popular music   jazz   rock music   country music

5. What kind of sports do you like?

   Who's your favorite athlete? What's your favorite team?

   football   baseball   soccer   golf   hockey   tennis

PRONUNCIATION Reduced of

Listen. Then say it.

What kind of movies do you like?

What kind of books do you like?

She spends a lot of time with her friends.

Say it. Then listen.

What kind of music do you like?

What kind of TV programs do you like?

I read a lot of books.

 SIDE by SIDE JOURNAL

What do you do during the week?
What do you do on the weekend?
Write about it in your journal.

GRAMMAR FOCUS

SIMPLE PRESENT TENSE: YES/NO QUESTIONS

Do	I we you they	work?
Does	he she it	

SHORT ANSWERS

Yes,	I we you they	do.
	he she it	does.

No,	I we you they	don't.
	he she it	doesn't.

Complete the sentences.

1. A. _____ you and your wife like Italian food?
   B. Yes, we _____.

2. A. _____ your brother work at the mall?
   B. Yes, he _____.

3. A. _____ your friends play cards?
   B. No, they _____.

4. A. _____ you play a musical instrument?
   B. Yes, I _____.

5. A. _____ your sister take karate lessons?
   B. No, she _____.

6. A. _____ I ask a lot of questions?
   B. Yes, you _____.

7. A. _____ you and your husband play golf?
   B. No, _____ _____.

8. A. _____ your uncle speak French?
   B. No, _____ _____.

9. A. Do your neighbors make a lot of noise?
   B. Yes, _____ _____.

10. A. _____ your daughter speak Chinese?
    B. Yes, _____ _____.

SIMPLE PRESENT TENSE: NEGATIVES

I We You They	don't	work.
He She It	doesn't	

Complete the sentences with *don't* or *doesn't*.

11. I _____ work on Sunday.

12. My husband _____ play tennis.

13. My parents _____ go dancing.

14. My sister and I _____ sing in the choir.

15. My wife _____ watch TV.

16. You _____ like hockey.

1 CONVERSATION WORK SCHEDULES

Look at the work schedules and practice conversations. Fill in the days of the week.

A. When do you work this week?
B. I work on _____, _____, _____, _____, and _____.
A. When are your days off?
B. I don't work on _____ and _____.

S	M	T	W	T	F	S
	✓	✓	✓	✓	✓	

1.

S	M	T	W	T	F	S
✓		✓	✓		✓	✓

2.

S	M	T	W	T	F	S
✓	✓	✓		✓		✓

3.

2 WRITING YOUR SCHEDULE

When do you go to school this week? Check the days on this schedule. Then write about it.

S	M	T	W	T	F	S

I go to school on _____.

I don't go to school on _____.

3 CONVERSATION ASKING ABOUT BUS DESTINATIONS

Look at the bus signs and practice conversations. Ask some questions with "Yes" answers and some questions with "No" answers.

A. Excuse me. Does this bus go to the _____?
B. { Yes, it does.
    { No, it doesn't.

1.

2.

3.

4.

4 CONVERSATION ASKING ABOUT BUS ROUTES

Look at the bus signs above and practice conversations.

A. Excuse me. How do I get to the _____?
B. Take Bus Number ____.
A. Bus Number ____? Thank you.

Choose the correct answer.

1. My husband cooks _____.
   A. videos
   B. books
   C. Greek food
   D. yoga

2. I ride _____ every day.
   A. American food
   B. a different kind of sport
   C. books
   D. my bicycle

3. My daughter plays _____.
   A. a musical instrument
   B. karate
   C. dinner
   D. novels

4. I work during the week. I don't work on the weekend. I don't work on _____.
   A. Tuesday
   B. Sunday
   C. Thursday
   D. Monday

5. My favorite kind of music is _____.
   A. poetry
   B. jazz
   C. golf
   D. science fiction

6. Wanda writes for her school _____.
   A. orchestra
   B. choir
   C. newspaper
   D. concert

7. Janet is very athletic. She _____ every weekend.
   A. sings
   B. plays in the orchestra
   C. sees a play
   D. plays tennis

8. I read every day. I usually read _____.
   A. short stories
   B. videos
   C. game shows
   D. classical music

Mark your answers in the answer box.

Answers
1 (A) (B) (C) (D)
2 (A) (B) (C) (D)
3 (A) (B) (C) (D)
4 (A) (B) (C) (D)
5 (A) (B) (C) (D)
6 (A) (B) (C) (D)
7 (A) (B) (C) (D)
8 (A) (B) (C) (D)
9 (A) (B) (C) (D)
10 (A) (B) (C) (D)

Emma works five days a week. This is her work schedule. Choose the correct answer.

9. She doesn't work on _____.
   A. Sunday
   B. Monday
   C. Thursday
   D. Saturday

10. She works on _____.
   A. Saturday and Sunday
   B. Tuesday and Thursday
   C. Monday and Wednesday
   D. Sunday and Tuesday

S	M	T	W	T	F	S
	✓		✓	✓	✓	✓

SKILLS CHECK ✓

Words:
- ☐ Sunday
- ☐ Monday
- ☐ Tuesday
- ☐ Wednesday
- ☐ Thursday
- ☐ Friday
- ☐ Saturday
- ☐ baby-sit
- ☐ clean
- ☐ do yoga
- ☐ go dancing
- ☐ jog
- ☐ play volleyball
- ☐ ride a bicycle
- ☐ see a movie
- ☐ see a play

I can ask & answer:
- ☐ Do you/they *work* on *Sunday*?
- ☐ Does he/she *work* on *Saturday*?

- ☐ What kind of *food* do you like?
- ☐ When do you *go to Stanley's Restaurant*?
- ☐ Who's your favorite *author*?

- ☐ When do you work this week?
- ☐ When are your days off?

- ☐ Excuse me. Does this bus go to the *mall*?
- ☐ Excuse me. How do I get to the *airport*?

I can start a conversation:
- ☐ Tell me, _____?

I can read:
- ☐ simple work schedules
- ☐ bus destination signs

I can write about:
- ☐ things I do during the week
- ☐ things I do on the weekend

Language

Millions speak Chinese. Only hundreds speak Bahinemo.

There are over 20,000 languages in the world. Some of these languages are very common. For example, millions of people speak Chinese, Spanish, English, Arabic, Portuguese, and Japanese. On the other hand, some languages are very rare. For example, only 500 people in Papua, New Guinea speak the language Bahinemo.

Languages grow and change. They borrow words from other languages. For example, in the English language, the word *rodeo* is from Spanish, *cafe* comes from French, *ketchup* is from Chinese, *sofa* is from Arabic, and *potato* comes from Haitian Kreyol. New words also come from technology. For example, *cyberspace*, *website*, and *e-mail* are recent words that relate to the Internet.

FACT FILE

Common Languages

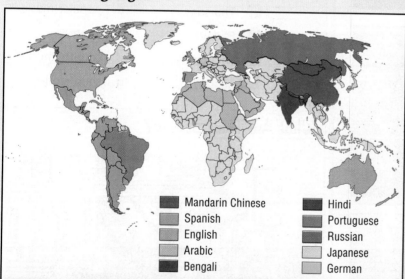

Mandarin Chinese
Spanish
English
Arabic
Bengali

Hindi
Portuguese
Russian
Japanese
German

Language	Number of Speakers	Language	Number of Speakers
Mandarin Chinese	885 million	Hindi	182 million
Spanish	332 million	Portuguese	170 million
English	322 million	Russian	170 million
Arabic	268 million	Japanese	125 million
Bengali	189 million	German	98 million

Every day I _____ .

 ▪ get up

 ▪ take a shower

 ▪ brush my teeth

 ▪ comb my hair

 ▪ get dressed

 ▪ go to school

 ▪ go to work

 ▪ eat

 ▪ take a bath

 ▪ go to bed

AROUND THE WORLD

Exercising

People around the world exercise in different ways.

Some people exercise in health clubs.

Some people exercise at the beach.

Some people go hiking.

And some people exercise together outdoors.

How do people exercise in your country?

Global Exchange

Jogger9: I'm a very active person. I jog and I swim. I go to a lot of movies and concerts. I sing in a choir. I play basketball with my friends every weekend. I like rock music and jazz. I don't watch TV very often. I only watch news programs. I read a lot of books. I like novels. My favorite author is Tom Clancy. How about you? Tell me about your activities and interests.

Send a message to a keypal. Tell about your activities and interests.

LISTENING

Hello! This Is the International Cafe!

_c_	**1** Monday	**a.**	jazz
___	**2** Tuesday	**b.**	rock music
___	**3** Wednesday	**c.**	classical music
___	**4** Thursday	**d.**	popular music
___	**5** Friday	**e.**	poetry
___	**6** Saturday	**f.**	country music
___	**7** Sunday	**g.**	short stories

What Are They Saying?

In every sentence there is a **subject** and there is a **verb**.
The subject is a person or a thing.
The verb is an action.
The subject is **singular** or **plural**.
The verb agrees with the subject.

Rosa speaks English.

singular verb
subject

The students speak English.

plural verb
subject

Practice these conversations with a classmate.

Helen (work   works) in a bank.

A. What's the subject?
B. *Helen.*
A. Is the subject singular or plural?
B. *Singular.*
A. Which verb agrees with the subject—
   work or *works*?
B. *Works.*
A. So, what's the sentence?
B. *Helen works in a bank.*

We (study   studies) English every day.

A. What's the subject?
B. *We.*
A. Is the subject singular or plural?
B. *Plural.*
A. Which verb agrees with the subject—
   study or *studies*?
B. *Study.*
A. So, what's the sentence?
B. *We study English every day.*

Choose the correct word to complete each sentence. Then practice new conversations about these sentences.

1. Marco (read   reads) Mexican newspapers.
2. Milton and Paula (live   lives) in Los Angeles.
3. They (go   goes) to Stanley's Restaurant every Saturday.
4. My son (play   plays) basketball every day.
5. We (clean   cleans) our apartment every Saturday morning.
6. Amir (call   calls) his parents in Egypt every Sunday.
7. My sister and I (sing   sings) in the choir at our church.
8. Our daughter (work   works) at the post office.

TELECOMMUTING

Rita Carranza and her family get up early every morning during the week. They get dressed and have breakfast. Then Rita and her children go to the school bus stop on the corner. After that, Rita goes to work. She's in her office in five minutes. Why? Because Rita works at home. Rita's company office building is far from her house, but Rita doesn't work in the office building. She is a telecommuter. She doesn't commute by car or by bus. She "commutes" to work by telephone and the Internet.

Rita is a computer specialist, and she usually works 40 hours a week. She works in the morning and after lunch. Then she meets her children at the bus stop. Rita's children do their homework when they get home, and then they all have dinner together. After her children are in bed, Rita sits at her computer and works in the evening. Rita doesn't work in an office building, but she works very hard.

Rita likes telecommuting. She doesn't drive two hours to and from work, and she's at home with her children every day after school. She doesn't need expensive work clothes, so she and her children have more money in the bank

Rita's boss likes telecommuters because they don't usually need offices or furniture in the company building.

Also, when people work at home, their homes are usually quiet and they work hard. And that's good for companies.

In the United States, there are over 2.4 million telecommuters. Some telecommuters work at home full-time. Others work part-time. Fifty-three percent of telecommuters are men, and forty-seven percent are women. There are many different telecommuter jobs. Telecommuters are computer engineers, bookkeepers, administrators, typists, lawyers, and technology specialists.

Sometimes, however, telecommuters have problems. They don't see other workers. They are home alone and their house is quiet. They're very busy, but it isn't easy. They aren't in an office with other people. They don't see other people at work every day.

1. Rita's office is ____.
   - (A) in her home
   - (B) in an office building
   - (C) five minutes from her home
   - (D) near her children's school

2. Rita is a ____.
   - (A) boss
   - (B) bookkeeper
   - (C) lawyer
   - (D) computer specialist

3. Rita is happy because she ____.
   - (A) drives her car to the company office every day
   - (B) needs expensive work clothes
   - (C) is at home with her children every afternoon
   - (D) sees other people at work every day

4. Telecommuting is ____ for companies.
   - (A) bad
   - (B) good
   - (C) hard
   - (D) expensive

5. In the United States, ____ percent of telecommuters are men.
   - (A) 24
   - (B) 40
   - (C) 47
   - (D) 53

6. This passage is about ____.
   - (A) Rita's children
   - (B) Rita's office building
   - (C) telecommuting in the United States
   - (D) problems with telecommuting

What do YOU think?

1. Why is telecommuting good for people in rural and suburban areas?
2. What does a telecommuter usually have in a home office?
3. What kind of job is good for telecommuting?
4. Do you like to work alone or with other people? Is telecommuting good for you?

11

Object Pronouns
Simple Present Tense:
  -s vs. non-s Endings

Have/Has
Adverbs of Frequency

- **Calendar**
- **Describing Frequency of Actions**

- **Describing People**
- **Family Responsibilities**

VOCABULARY PREVIEW

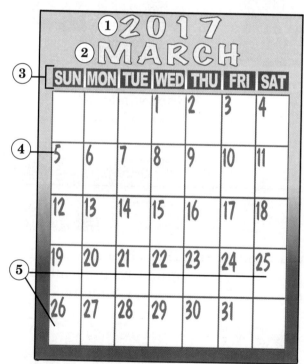

1. year
2. month
3. week
4. day
5. weekend

6. morning
7. afternoon
8. evening
9. night

How Often?

I	me
he	him
she	her
it	it
we	us
you	you
they	them

A. How often does your boyfriend call you?

B. He calls me every night.

1. How often do you use your computer?
every day

2. How often do you write to your son?
every week

3. How often do you clean your windows?
every month

4. How often do you visit your aunt in Minnesota?
every year

5. How often do you wash your car?
every weekend

6. How often do your grandchildren call you?
every Sunday

7. How often does your boss say "hello" to you?
every morning

8. How often do you feed the animals?
every afternoon

9. How often do you think about me?
all the time

She Usually Studies in the Library

[s]	
eat	eats
write	writes
bark	barks
speak	speaks

[z]	
read	reads
jog	jogs
call	calls
clean	cleans

[ɪz]	
wash	washes
watch	watches
dance	dances
fix	fixes

always	100%
usually	90%
sometimes	50%
rarely	10%
never	0%

A. Does Carmen usually study in her room?

B. No. She rarely studies in her room. She usually studies in the library.

1. Does Linda usually eat lunch in her office?
   rarely
   in the cafeteria

2. Does Alan always watch the news after dinner?
   never
   game shows

3. Does Diane sometimes read *The National Star*?
   never
   Time magazine

4. Does Henry usually wash his car on Sunday?
   rarely
   on Saturday

5. Does your girlfriend usually jog in the evening?
   sometimes
   in the afternoon

6. Does your neighbor's dog always bark during the day?
   never
   at night

We Have Noisy Neighbors

I We You They } have	brown eyes.
He She It } has	

A. Do you have quiet neighbors?

B. No. We have noisy neighbors.

1. Do you have a sister?
   a brother

2. Does this store have an elevator?
   an escalator

3. Does your daughter have straight hair?
   curly hair

4. Does your son have brown hair?
   blond hair

5. Do you and your husband have a dog?
   a cat

6. Does your baby boy have blue eyes?
   brown eyes

7. Do Mr. and Mrs. Hill have a satellite dish?
   an old TV antenna

8. Does your grandmother have a car?
   a motorcycle

9.

My brother and I look very different. I have brown eyes and he has blue eyes. We both have brown hair, but I have short, curly hair and he has long, straight hair. I'm tall and thin. He's short and heavy.

As you can see, I don't look like my brother. We look very different.

Who in your family do you look like? Who DON'T you look like? Tell about it.

My sister and I are very different. I'm a teacher. She's a journalist. I live in Miami. She lives in London. I have a large house in the suburbs. She has a small apartment in the city.

I'm married. She's single. I play golf. She plays tennis. I play the piano. She doesn't play a musical instrument. On the weekend I usually watch videos and rarely go out. She never watches videos and always goes to parties.

As you can see, we're very different. But we're sisters . . . and we're friends.

Compare yourself with a member of your family, another student in your class, or a famous person. Tell how you and this person are different.

How to Say It!

Reacting to Information

A. Tell me about *your sister.*
B. *She's a journalist. She lives in London.*
A. Oh, really? That's interesting.

Practice conversations with other students. Talk about people you know.

CLOSE FRIENDS

My husband and I are very lucky. We have many close friends in this city, and they're all interesting people.

Our friend Greta is an actress. We see her when she isn't making a movie in Hollywood. When we get together with her, she always tells us about her life in Hollywood as a movie star. Greta is a very close friend. We like her very much.

Our friend Dan is a scientist. We see him when he isn't busy in his laboratory. When we get together with him, he always tells us about his new experiments. Dan is a very close friend. We like him very much.

Our friends Bob and Carol are famous television news reporters. We see them when they aren't traveling around the world. When we get together with them, they always tell us about their conversations with presidents and prime ministers. Bob and Carol are very close friends. We like them very much.

Unfortunately, we don't see Greta, Dan, Bob, or Carol very often. In fact, we rarely see them because they're usually so busy. But we think about them all the time.

✓ READING CHECK-UP

WHAT'S THE WORD?

Greta is a famous actress. _____**1** lives in Hollywood. _____**2** movies are very popular. When _____**3** walks down the street, people always say "hello" to _____**4** and tell _____**5** how much they like _____**6** movies.

Dan is always busy. _____**7** works in _____**8** laboratory every day. Dan's friends rarely see _____**9**. When they see _____**10**, _____**11** usually talks about _____**12** experiments. Everybody likes _____**13** very much. _____**14** is a very nice person.

Bob and Carol are television news reporters. _____**15** friends don't see _____**16** very often because _____**17** travel around the world all the time. Presidents and prime ministers often call _____**18** on the telephone. _____**19** like _____**20** work very much.

LISTENING

Listen to the conversations. Who and what are they talking about?

1. a. grandfather
   b. grandmother
2. a. window
   b. windows
3. a. brother
   b. sister

4. a. sink
   b. cars
5. a. neighbor
   b. neighbors
6. a. computer
   b. news reporter

7. a. game show
   b. car
8. a. Ms. Brown
   b. Mr. Wong
9. a. Ken
   b. Jim and Karen

IN YOUR OWN WORDS

FOR WRITING AND DISCUSSION

MY CLOSE FRIENDS

Tell about your close friends.

What are their names?
Where do they live?
What do they do?
When do you get together with them?
What do you talk about?

Listen. Then say it.

I visit her every year.

I write to him every week.

We see her very often.

She calls him every month.

Say it. Then listen.

I visit him every year.

I write to her every week.

We see him very often.

He calls her every month.

SIDE by SIDE JOURNAL

Write in your journal about your daily activities.

I always _____. I usually _____.

I sometimes _____. I rarely _____. I never _____.

GRAMMAR FOCUS

OBJECT PRONOUNS

He calls	me him her it us you them	every night.

Complete the sentences.

1. A. How often do you and your wife read the newspaper?
   B. We read _____ every morning.
2. A. How often do you write to your grandmother?
   B. I write to _____ every week.
3. A. How often do you call your brother in Miami?
   B. I call _____ every Sunday.
4. A. How often do the Baxters play cards with their friends?
   B. They play cards with _____ every Saturday night.
5. A. How often does your uncle call you and your sister?
   B. He calls _____ every weekend.

HAVE/HAS

I We You They	have	brown eyes.
He She It	has	

Complete the sentences with *have* or *has*.

6. We _____ noisy neighbors.
7. My son _____ brown eyes.
8. I _____ curly black hair.
9. My sister _____ a new car.
10. You _____ a very nice apartment.
11. My parents _____ a new cat.
12. The new mall _____ more than fifty stores.

SIMPLE PRESENT TENSE: *s* VS. NON-*s* ENDINGS

He She It	eats. reads. washes.	[s] [z] [ɪz]	I We You They	eat. read. wash.

Complete the sentences with the correct form of the verb.

13. (like) I _____ jazz. My brother _____ rock music.
14. (jog) My wife _____ in the morning. I _____ in the afternoon.
15. (study) I _____ in my room. My sister _____ in the library.
16. (watch) Our son _____ game shows after dinner. My wife and I _____ the news.

1 CONVERSATION DESCRIBING PEOPLE AT WORK

Practice conversations about these people.

A. Please give this to _____.
B. What does he/she look like?
A. He's/She's _____, and he/she has _____.

1.

Mr. Clark
short
short gray hair

2.

Ms. Diaz
average height
long brown hair

3.

Mrs. Bell
tall
short blond hair

Now practice more conversations. Describe students in your class.

2 CONVERSATION INTERVIEWS

Practice these interviews with other students.

How do you help at home?

Linda
I make breakfast.

Miguel
I sweep the floor.

Ronald
I buy groceries.

Emma
I vacuum.

Joy
I do the laundry.

Quan
I fix things.

Kelly
I pay the bills.

Armando
I help my children
with their homework.

3 CLOZE READING FAMILY RESPONSIBILITIES

Complete the story about the people above.

Linda ___makes___ [1] breakfast. Miguel _____ [2] the floor. Ronald _____ [3] groceries. Emma _____ [4]. Joy _____ [5] the laundry. Quan _____ [6] things. Kelly _____ [7] the bills. Armando _____ [8] his children with _____ [9] homework.

ASK & SHARE How do students in your class help at home? Interview them. Then discuss in class.

106a

Choose the correct answer.

1. Marie ___ her computer every day.

A. writes
B. reads
C. uses
D. makes

2. I usually take the bus to work. I ___.

A. always drive
B. usually drive
C. drive every day
D. rarely drive

3. My brother and I look very different. I'm tall and thin. He's ___.

A. short and heavy
B. a teacher
C. curly hair
D. thin and tall

4. I wash my car every Sunday. I wash it ___.

A. once a day
B. once a week
C. once a month
D. once a year

5. My son has ___ eyes.

A. curly
B. blue
C. blond
D. tall

6. We never go out on the weekend. We always ___.

A. go to the movies
B. go to parties
C. go dancing
D. watch videos at home

	Answers			
1	A	B	C	D
2	A	B	C	D
3	A	B	C	D
4	A	B	C	D
5	A	B	C	D
6	A	B	C	D
7	A	B	C	D
8	A	B	C	D
9	A	B	C	D
10	A	B	C	D

Fernando has three jobs. Look at his schedule and answer the questions.

MON	TUE	WED	THU	FRI	SAT	SUN
drug store	drug store	supermarket	drug store	supermarket	bakery	bakery

7. He works at the drug store ___.

A. once (one time) a week
B. twice (two times) a week
C. three times a week
D. every day

8. He works at the supermarket ___.

A. once a week
B. twice a week
C. three times a week
D. every day

9. On the weekend he ___.

A. works at the drug store
B. works at the supermarket
C. doesn't work
D. works at the bakery

10. According to the schedule, he ___ works seven days a week.

A. always
B. rarely
C. never
D. sometimes

SKILLS CHECK ✓

Words:

☐ day
☐ week
☐ month
☐ year
☐ weekend

☐ morning
☐ afternoon
☐ evening
☐ night

☐ brown eyes
☐ blue eyes

☐ long hair
☐ short hair
☐ straight hair
☐ curly hair
☐ blond hair
☐ brown hair
☐ black hair
☐ gray hair

☐ short
☐ average height
☐ tall

☐ buy groceries
☐ do the laundry
☐ fix things
☐ help my children with their homework
☐ make breakfast
☐ pay the bills
☐ sweep the floor
☐ vacuum

I can ask & answer:

☐ How often do you *use your computer?*
☐ Does he/she usually *watch the news?*
☐ Does he/she have *curly hair?*
☐ Do you have *a brother?*
☐ What does he/she look like?
☐ How do you help at home?

I can react to information:

☐ Oh, really? That's interesting.

I can write about:

☐ my daily activities
☐ my close friends

12

Contrast: Simple Present and Present Continuous Tenses
Adjectives

- **Feelings and Emotions**
- **Describing Usual and Unusual Activities**
- **The Education System**
- **School Personnel and Locations**

VOCABULARY PREVIEW

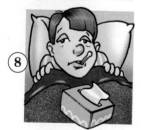

1. happy
2. sad
3. hungry
4. thirsty

5. hot
6. cold
7. tired
8. sick

9. angry
10. nervous
11. scared
12. embarrassed

I Always Cry When I'm Sad

smile
smiling

A. Why are you crying?

B. I'm crying because I'm sad.
I ALWAYS cry when I'm sad.

A. Why is she smiling?

B. She's smiling because she's happy.
She ALWAYS smiles when she's happy.

shout
shouting

1. A. Why are you shouting?

B. _____ angry.

I ALWAYS _____.

bite
biting

2. A. Why is he biting his nails?

B. _____ nervous.

He ALWAYS _____.

drink
drinking

3. A. Why is the bird drinking?

B. _____ thirsty.

It ALWAYS _____.

shiver
shivering

4. A. Why are they shivering?

B. _____ cold.

They ALWAYS _____.

go
going

5. A. Why are they going to
Stanley's Restaurant?

B. _____ hungry.

They ALWAYS _____.

go
going

6. A. Why is she going to
the doctor?

B. _____ sick.

She ALWAYS _____.

perspire
perspiring

blush
blushing

7. A. Why are you perspiring?
   B. _____ hot.
      I ALWAYS _____.

8. A. Why is he blushing?
   B. _____ embarrassed.
      He ALWAYS _____.

yawn
yawning

cover
covering

9. A. Why is she yawning?
   B. _____ tired.
      She ALWAYS _____.

10. A. Why is he covering his eyes?
    B. _____ scared.
       He ALWAYS _____.

ON YOUR OWN   *What Do You Do When You're Nervous?*

What do you do when you're nervous?

When I'm nervous, I perspire.

When I'm nervous, I bite my nails.

When I'm nervous, I walk back and forth.

Answer these questions.

What do you do when you're . . .

1. nervous?

2. sad?

3. happy?

4. tired?

5. sick?

6. cold?

7. hot?

8. hungry?

9. thirsty?

10. angry?

11. embarrassed?

12. scared?

Now ask another student in your class.

I'm Washing the Dishes in the Bathtub

A. What are you doing?!

B. I'm washing the dishes in the bathtub.

A. That's strange! Do you USUALLY wash the dishes in the bathtub?

B. No. I NEVER wash the dishes in the bathtub, but I'm washing the dishes in the bathtub TODAY.

A. Why are you doing THAT?!

B. Because my sink is broken.

A. I'm sorry to hear that.

A. What are you doing?!

B. I'm _____.

A. That's strange! Do you USUALLY _____?

B. No. I NEVER _____, but I'm _____ TODAY.

A. Why are you doing THAT?!

B. Because my _____ is broken.

A. I'm sorry to hear that.

1. sleep
   sleeping } on the floor
   bed

2. study
   studying } with a flashlight
   lamp

3. walk
   walking } to work
   car

4. use
   using } a typewriter
   computer

5. sweep
   sweeping } the carpet
   vacuum

6.

How to Say It!

Reacting to Bad News

A. My sink is broken.

B. { I'm sorry to hear that.
     That's too bad!
     What a shame!

Practice conversations with other students. Share some bad news and react to it.

READING

A BAD DAY AT THE OFFICE

Mr. Blaine is the president of the Acme Internet Company. The company has a staff of energetic employees. Unfortunately, all of the employees are out today. Nobody is there. As a result, Mr. Blaine is doing everybody's job, and he's having a VERY bad day at the office!

He's answering the telephone because the receptionist who usually answers it is at the dentist's office. He's typing letters because the secretary who usually types them is at home in bed with the flu. He's sorting the mail because the office assistant who usually sorts it is on vacation. And he's even cleaning the office because the custodian who usually cleans it is on strike.

Poor Mr. Blaine! It's a very busy day at the Acme Internet Company, and nobody is there to help him. He's having a VERY bad day at the office!

✔ READING CHECK-UP

TRUE OR FALSE?

1. Mr. Blaine is the president of the Ajax Internet Company.
2. Mr. Blaine is out today.
3. The secretary is sick.
4. The office assistant is on strike.
5. The custodian isn't cleaning the office today.
6. The receptionist usually answers the phone at the dentist's office.

LISTENING

Listen and choose the correct answer.

1. a. I clean my house.
   b. I'm cleaning my house.
2. a. He sorts the mail.
   b. He's sorting the mail.
3. a. She answers the telephone.
   b. She's answering the telephone.
4. a. Yes. He yawns.
   b. Yes. He's yawning.
5. a. I'm covering my eyes.
   b. I cover my eyes.
6. a. I study in the library.
   b. I'm studying in the library.

EARLY MONDAY MORNING IN CENTERVILLE

Early Monday morning is usually a very busy time in Centerville. Men and women usually rush to their jobs. Some people walk to work, some people drive, and others take the bus. Children usually go to school. Some children walk to school, some children take the school bus, and others ride their bicycles. The city is usually very busy. Trucks deliver food to supermarkets, mail carriers deliver mail to homes and businesses, and police officers direct traffic at every corner. Yes, early Monday morning is usually a very busy time in Centerville.

✔ READING *CHECK-UP*

Using the story above as a guide, complete the following:

THE SNOWSTORM

Today isn't a typical early Monday morning in Centerville. In fact, it's a very unusual morning. It's snowing very hard there. All the people are at home. The streets are empty, and the city is quiet. The men and women who usually rush to their jobs aren't rushing to their jobs today. The people

who usually walk to work aren't walking, the people who usually drive aren't _____1, and the people who usually take the bus aren't _____2 the bus. The children who usually go to school aren't _____3 to school today. The children who usually walk to school aren't _____4 today. The children who usually _____5 the school bus aren't _____6 it today. And the children who usually _____7 their bicycles aren't _____8 them this morning.

The city is very quiet. The trucks that usually _____9 food aren't _____10 it today. The mail carriers who usually _____11 mail aren't _____12 it this morning. And the police officers who usually_____13 traffic aren't _____14 it today. Yes, it's a very unusual Monday morning in Centerville.

PRONUNCIATION Reduced *to*

Listen. Then say it.

I'm sorry to hear that.

We go to school.

He listens to the radio.

Mail carriers deliver mail to homes.

Say it. Then listen.

I'm happy to hear that.

They're going to the doctor.

She listens to music.

Trucks deliver food to supermarkets.

Describe a typical day in your city or town. What do people usually do? Write about it in your journal.

GRAMMAR FOCUS

SIMPLE PRESENT TENSE

I always **cry** when I'm sad.
I never **wash** the dishes in the bathtub.

PRESENT CONTINUOUS TENSE

I'm **crying** because I'm sad.
I'm **washing** the dishes in the bathtub today.

Complete the sentences with the correct form of the verb.

bite	clean	shiver	smile	walk
biting	cleaning	shivering	smiling	walking
blush	cry	shout	use	yawn
blushing	crying	shouting	using	yawning

1. I often _____ when I'm sad.

2. Why are you _____? Are you angry?

3. Carol is _____. She's very tired.

4. He's _____ because he's happy.

5. I'm _____ my office today because the people who usually _____ it are on strike.

6. When I'm nervous, I _____ my nails.

7. I _____ when I'm embarrassed.

8. Why are you _____ a typewriter today?

9. I usually _____ when I'm very cold.

10. I don't usually _____ to work, but I'm _____ to work today.

Read the news article and answer the questions.

A School and Its Employees

There are three schools in Lincolnville. There's an elementary school for young children in kindergarten and grades one through five. There's a middle school for children in grades six, seven, and eight. There's a high school for students in grades nine through twelve.

More than twenty people work at Lincolnville Elementary School. There are twelve classroom teachers, a music teacher, and other employees. Mrs. Teng, the principal, manages the school. When teachers and students have problems, they go to the principal's office and talk to her. The secretary, Mr. Shaw, and the office assistant, Ms. Jenkins, work in the school office. Mr. Shaw answers the telephone and types letters to parents. Ms. Jenkins sorts the mail and calls the homes of students who are absent.

The librarian, Mr. Velasco, manages the school library. He buys books, magazines, and CDs for the library and organizes them on the shelves. He teaches students how to use the library. Sometimes he reads to the children in

kindergarten and grade one. When students are sick, they go to the nurse's office. Ms. Hasan, the school nurse, takes care of them.

At lunchtime, the cafeteria workers serve lunch to the students in the cafeteria. After lunch, Mr. Harper, the custodian, cleans the cafeteria. When school is finished, the school bus drivers take students home. Then Mr. Harper cleans all the classrooms and the offices. He washes the blackboards, sweeps the floors, and vacuums the carpets. He's a very busy person!

1. Children in grade _____ go to Lincolnville Elementary School.
   A. four
   B. six
   C. eight
   D. ten

2. The _____ takes care of sick students.
   A. principal
   B. school nurse
   C. custodian
   D. bus driver

3. The secretary _____.
   A. sorts the mail
   B. buys books for the library
   C. serves lunch
   D. types letters to parents

4. Mr. Velasco works in _____.
   A. the principal's office
   B. the cafeteria
   C. the school library
   D. the nurse's office

5. _____ cleans the cafeteria.
   A. A cafeteria worker
   B. Mrs. Teng
   C. Ms. Jenkins
   D. The custodian

6. The librarian DOESN'T _____.
   A. buy magazines and CDs
   B. read to the children
   C. manage the school
   D. organize books on shelves

Choose the correct answer.

1. I usually go to the doctor when I'm ____.
   A. happy
   B. hungry
   C. sick
   D. angry

2. I'm ____ because I'm tired.
   A. biting my nails
   B. yawning
   C. smiling
   D. perspiring

3. She's walking to school today because her ____ is broken.
   A. computer
   B. sink
   C. lamp
   D. bicycle

4. The receptionist at our office ____ the telephone.
   A. types
   B. answers
   C. rushes
   D. takes

5. I'm a police officer. Every morning I ____ traffic on Main Street.
   A. deliver
   B. walk
   C. direct
   D. make

6. The office assistant is ____ the mail.
   A. sorting
   B. helping
   C. typing
   D. driving

7. I'm a custodian at the Bay Company. Every day I ____ the office.
   A. watch
   B. study
   C. use
   D. clean

8. Mail carriers ____ mail.
   A. write
   B. deliver
   C. direct
   D. answer

9. The students eat lunch in ____.
   A. the cafeteria
   B. the principal's office
   C. the library
   D. the school office

10. Our son is in middle school. He's in ____.
   A. kindergarten
   B. grade two
   C. grade seven
   D. grade twelve

Mark your answers in the answer box.

Answers

1 (A) (B) (C) (D)
2 (A) (B) (C) (D)
3 (A) (B) (C) (D)
4 (A) (B) (C) (D)
5 (A) (B) (C) (D)
6 (A) (B) (C) (D)
7 (A) (B) (C) (D)
8 (A) (B) (C) (D)
9 (A) (B) (C) (D)
10 (A) (B) (C) (D)

SKILLS CHECK ☑

Words:
angry, cold, embarrassed, happy, hot, hungry, nervous, sad, scared, sick, thirsty, tired, answer the telephone, bite my nails, blush, buy, call, clean, cover my eyes, cry, deliver, drive, manage, perspire, ride a bicycle, serve, shiver, shout, sleep, smile, sort the mail, study, sweep, take care of, take the bus, type, use, vacuum, walk, walk back and forth, wash, yawn, elementary school, middle school, high school, cafeteria worker, custodian, librarian, music teacher, office assistant, principal, school bus driver, school nurse, secretary, teacher, cafeteria, nurse's office, principal's office, school library, school office

I can ask & answer:
Why are you *crying*?
What do you do when you're *sick*?
What are you doing?!
Why are you doing THAT?!
Do you usually *walk to work*?

I can:
identify schools in the education system (elementary, middle school, high school)
identify school personnel & locations

I can write about:
a typical day in my city or town

Traffic: A Global Problem

There are more and more people and more and more cars

Traffic is a big problem in many cities around the world. Traffic is especially bad during *rush hour*—the time when people go to work or school and the time when they go home. Many people take buses, subways, or trains to work, but many other people drive their cars. As a result, the streets are very busy, and traffic is very bad.

Many cities are trying to solve their traffic problems. Some cities are building more roads. Other cities are expanding their bus and subway systems.

Many cities are trying to reduce the number of cars on their roads. Some highways have *carpool lanes*—special lanes for cars with two, three, or more people. In some cities, people drive their cars only on certain days of the week. For example, in Athens, people with license plate numbers ending in 0 through 4 drive on some days, and people with numbers ending in 5 through 9 drive on other days.

Every day around the world, more and more people drive to and from work in more and more cars. As a result, traffic is a global problem.

LISTENING

And Now, Here's Today's News!

TODAY'S NEWS

_b_	❶	There's a subway problem in . . .	**a.** Toronto
___	❷	Police officers are on strike in . . .	**b.** Boston
___	❸	It's snowing very hard in . . .	**c.** Miami
___	❹	There aren't any problems in . . .	**d.** Sacramento
___	❺	Children aren't going to school in . . .	**e.** Chicago

BUILD YOUR VOCABULARY!

How Do You Get to Work?

I _____ .

 ■ walk

 ■ drive

 ■ take the bus

 ■ take the train

 ■ take the subway

 ■ take a taxi

 ■ ride a bicycle

 ■ ride a motor scooter

 ■ ride a motorcycle

Getting Places

People around the world go to work or school in many different ways.

Some people take the subway.

Some people ride a motor scooter.

Some people even roller-blade!

Some people ride a bicycle.

How do people go to work or school in different countries you know?

FACT FILE

World's Largest Subway Systems

City	Number of Riders in a Year (in millions)	City	Number of Riders in a Year (in millions)
Moscow	3,160	Paris	1,120
Tokyo	2,740	Osaka	1,000
Mexico City	1,420	Hong Kong	779
Seoul	1,390	London	770
New York	1,130	Sao Paulo	701

Global Exchange

JeffZ: I live in a small apartment in the center of our city. I have a brother and two sisters. My brother's name is Kevin, and my sisters' names are Emily and Melissa. Our family has a dog and a bird. Our dog's name is Buster, and our bird's name is Lulu. I'm tall, and I have brown eyes. My hair is short and curly. It's usually black, but this week it's red. How about you? Where do you live? Do you have brothers or sisters? What are their names? Do you have a dog or a cat or another pet? What do you look like?

Send a message to a keypal. Tell about yourself.

What Are They Saying?

She lives in London.
Does she live in London?

Your neighbors have a dog.
Do your neighbors have a dog?

Practice these conversations with a classmate.

Their son always walks to school.

A. What's the sentence?
B. *Their son always walks to school.*
A. What kind of sentence is it?
B. It's a statement.
A. Can you change it to a question?
B. Yes. *Does their son always walk to school?*

Does he usually watch TV at night?

A. What's the sentence?
B. *Does he usually watch TV at night?*
A. What kind of sentence is it?
B. It's a question.
A. Can you change it to a statement?
B. Yes. *He usually watches TV at night.*

Many people ride bicycles to work.

A. What's the sentence?
B. *Many people ride bicycles to work.*
A. What kind of sentence is it?
B. It's a statement.
A. Can you change it to a question?
B. Yes. *Do many people ride bicycles to work?*

Do her parents like classical music?

A. What's the sentence?
B. *Do her parents like classical music?*
A. What kind of sentence is it?
B. It's a question.
A. Can you change it to a statement?
B. Yes. *Her parents like classical music.*

Rewrite these sentences. *Capitalize* the first letter of the first word in each sentence. Put the correct *punctuation mark* at the end of each sentence. Then practice new conversations about these sentences.

1. rita sometimes works on the weekend
2. does Stanley cook Italian food
3. the students eat lunch in the cafeteria
4. do some highways have carpool lanes
5. does the office assistant sort the mail
6. the apartment building has an elevator
7. your parents have a cat
8. does she have a new computer
9. our boss takes the subway to work
10. do they visit their grandparents often

Public Schools

Public schools are open to all students. There are three kinds of public schools: elementary schools, middle schools, and high schools. However, there are many different kinds of elementary, middle, and high schools. Different cities, towns, and states have different schools.

PRE-SCHOOL Children 3 to 5 years old often go to pre-school. In pre-school, students play games, sing songs, and do things together. Teachers teach children about books, numbers, language, and the classroom. Some elementary schools have pre-schools, but some do not.

KINDERGARTEN AND ELEMENTARY SCHOOL All elementary schools have kindergarten classes.

Children are 5 to 6 years old in kindergarten. Some kindergartens are all-day. Others are half-day—in the morning or in the afternoon. Some elementary schools go from kindergarten to grade four. Others go to grade five or six.

MIDDLE SCHOOL Middle schools, or junior high schools, are different in each city, town, or state. Some middle schools have grades six to eight. Others have grades seven to nine.

HIGH SCHOOL Most high schools are very large. They go from grade nine or ten to grade twelve. In high schools, students study for college and for jobs.

CHARTER SCHOOLS A charter school is a different kind of school. It is a public school, but it is not a traditional school. Teachers teach in different ways and usually use new technology. Often, charter schools are small. Charter schools are for elementary, middle, or high school students.

SPECIALTY SCHOOLS Some schools have special programs for music, painting, acting, or subjects such as math or science. A vocational high school is a kind of specialty school. In a vocational school, students study school subjects and also prepare for jobs.

1. Children 3 years old go to ____.
- A. grade one
- B. pre-school
- C. kindergarten
- D. middle school

2. In kindergarten, children are ____.
- A. 3 to 5 years old
- B. 3 to 6 years old
- C. 4 to 6 years old
- D. 5 to 6 years old

3. Some elementary schools go from kindergarten to grade ____.
- A. six
- B. eight
- C. ten
- D. twelve

4. Charter schools and specialty schools are ____.
- A. very large
- B. high schools
- C. public schools
- D. traditional schools

5. A vocational school prepares students for ____.
- A. jobs
- B. college
- C. high school
- D. charter schools

6. This passage is about ____.
- A. children in grades one to twelve
- B. high schools and middle schools
- C. different kinds of public schools
- D. different schools in different areas

APPLY YOUR KNOWLEDGE
1. What are the names of some public schools in your city or town?
2. In your area, what grades are in the elementary schools?
3. Is there a charter school or specialty school in your area? Tell about the school.

13

Can

Have to

- **Occupations**
- **Expressing Ability**
- **Looking for a Job**
- **Help Wanted Signs and Want Ads**

- **Job Interview**
- **Filling Out a Job Application**
- **Asking Permission at Work**
- **Safety Signs**

VOCABULARY PREVIEW

1. actor
2. actress
3. baker
4. chef
5. construction worker

6. dancer
7. mechanic
8. salesperson
9. secretary

10. singer
11. superintendent
12. teacher
13. truck driver

Can You?

I	
He	
She	
It	can / can't sing.
We	(cannot)
You	
They	

Can you sing?
Yes, I can.
No, I can't.

Can you speak Hungarian?

No, I can't. But I can speak Romanian.

1. Can Betty drive a bus?

2. Can Fred cook Italian food?

3. Can they ski?

4. Can you skate?

5. Can Roger use a cash register?

6. Can Judy and Donna play baseball?

7. Can Rita play the trumpet?

8. Can Marvin paint pictures?

Ask another student in your class: "Can you _____?"

Of Course They Can

A. Can Jack fix cars?

B. Of course he can.
He fixes cars every day. He's a mechanic.

1. Can Michael type?
secretary

2. Can Barbara teach?
teacher

3. Can Oscar bake pies and cakes?
baker

4. Can Jane drive a truck?
truck driver

5. Can Stanley cook?
chef

6. Can Claudia sing?
singer

7. Can Bruce and Helen dance?
dancers

8. Can Arthur act?
actor

9. Can Elizabeth and Katherine act?
actresses

THE ACE EMPLOYMENT SERVICE

Many people are sitting in the reception room at the Ace Employment Service. They're all looking for work, and they're hoping they can find jobs today.

Natalie is looking for a job as a secretary. She can type, she can file, and she can use business software on the computer. William is looking for a job as a building superintendent. He can paint walls, he can repair locks, and he can fix stoves and refrigerators.

Sandra is looking for a job as a construction worker. She can use tools, she can operate equipment, and she can build things. Nick is looking for a job as a salesperson. He can talk to customers, he can use a cash register, and he can take inventory. Stephanie and Tiffany are looking for jobs as actresses. They can sing, they can dance, and they can act.

Good luck, everybody! We hope you find the jobs you're looking for!

✓ READING *CHECK-UP*

Q & A

Natalie, William, Sandra, Nick, Stephanie, and Tiffany are having their interviews at the Ace Employment Service. Using this model, create dialogs based on the story.

A. What's your name?
B. *Natalie Kramer.*
A. Nice to meet you. Tell me, *Natalie*, what kind of job are you looking for?
B. I'm looking for a job as *a secretary*.
A. Tell me about your skills. What can you do?
B. I can *type*, I can *file*, and I can *use business software on the computer*.

LISTENING

CAN OR CAN'T?

Listen and choose the word you hear.

1. a. can   b. can't
2. a. can   b. can't
3. a. can   b. can't
4. a. can   b. can't
5. a. can   b. can't
6. a. can   b. can't

WHAT CAN THEY DO?

Listen and choose what each person can do.

1. a. file   b. type
2. a. cook   b. bake
3. a. repair locks   b. repair stoves
4. a. drive a truck   b. drive a bus
5. a. teach French   b. teach English
6. a. take inventory   b. paint

ON YOUR OWN *Your Skills*

Think about your skills. What can you do? What CAN'T you do? Make two lists. Then talk about your lists with other students.

Things I Can Do	Things I Can't Do
....	....
....	....
....	....
....	....
....	....

They Can't Go to Herbert's Party

I		
We	have to	
You		work.
They		
He		
She	has to	
It		

Herbert is depressed. He's having a party today, but his friends can't go to his party. They're all busy.

A. Can you go to Herbert's party?

B. No, I can't. I have to work.

A. Can Michael go to Herbert's party?

B. No, he can't. He has to go to the doctor.

1. *you and Tom?*
fix our car

2. *Susan?*
go to the dentist

3. *your children?*
do their homework

4. *John?*
wash his clothes

5. *your parents?*
clean their apartment

6. Can YOU go to Herbert's party?

How to Say It!

Apologizing

A. Can you *go to a movie* with me on *Saturday*?
B. I'm sorry. I can't. I have to *clean my apartment*.

Practice the interactions on this page, using "I'm sorry" to apologize.

INTERACTIONS

A. Can you _____ with me on _____?
B. I'm sorry. I can't. I have to _____.

Practice conversations with other students. Practice inviting, apologizing, and giving reasons.

go to a soccer game

have lunch

have dinner

go swimming

go shopping

go dancing

go skating

go skiing

go bowling

123

APPLYING FOR A DRIVER'S LICENSE

Henry is annoyed. He's applying for a driver's license, and he's upset about all the things he has to do.

First, he has to go to the Motor Vehicles Department and pick up an application form. He can't ask for the form on the telephone, and he can't ask for it by mail. He has to go downtown and pick up the form in person.

He has to fill out the form in duplicate. He can't use a pencil. He has to use a pen. He can't use blue ink. He has to use black ink. And he can't write in script. He has to print.

He also has to attach two photographs to the application. They can't be old photographs. They have to be new. They can't be large. They have to be small. And they can't be black and white. They have to be color.

Then he has to submit his application. He has to wait in a long line to pay his application fee. He has to wait in another long line to have an eye examination. And believe it or not, he has to wait in ANOTHER long line to take a written test!

Finally, he has to take a road test. He has to start the car. He has to make a right turn, a left turn, and a U-turn. And he even has to park his car on a crowded city street.

No wonder Henry is annoyed! He's applying for his driver's license, and he can't believe all the things he has to do.

✔ READING CHECK-UP

WHAT'S THE ANSWER?

1. Can Henry apply for a driver's license on the telephone?
2. Where does he have to go to apply for a license?
3. How does he have to fill out the form?
4. How many photographs does he have to attach to the application?
5. What kind of photographs do they have to be?
6. What does Henry have to do during the road test?

FIX THIS SIGN!

This sign at the Motor Vehicles Department is wrong. The things people have to do are in the wrong order. On a separate sheet of paper, fix the sign based on the story.

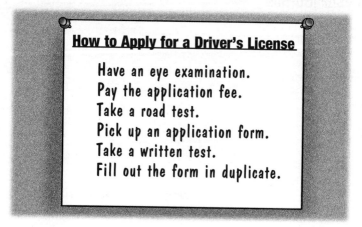

How to Apply for a Driver's License

Have an eye examination.
Pay the application fee.
Take a road test.
Pick up an application form.
Take a written test.
Fill out the form in duplicate.

IN YOUR OWN WORDS

FOR WRITING AND DISCUSSION

Explain how to apply for one of the following: a passport, a marriage license, a loan, or something else. In your explanation, use "You have to."*

* "You have to" = "A person has to"

Listen. Then say it.

I cán type.

She cán teach.

Yes, I can.

No, he can't.

Say it. Then listen.

We cán dance.

He cán sing.

Yes, they can.

No, she can't.

SIDE *by* **SIDE JOURNAL**

What do you have to do this week? Write about it in your journal.

GRAMMAR FOCUS

CAN

Can	I he she it we you they	sing?

I He She It We You They	can / can't	sing.

Yes,	I he she it we you they	can.

No,	I he she it we you they	can't.

Complete the sentences with *can* or *can't*.

1. I _____ bake. I'm a very good baker.

2. Gregory is a very bad singer. He _____ sing.

3. Maria can't ski, but she _____ skate.

4. We _____ dance. We aren't good dancers.

5. They can play baseball, but they _____ play tennis.

6. A. _____ you drive a truck?
   B. Yes, I _____.

7. A. _____ your brother fix cars?
   B. No, he _____.

8. A. _____ she repair stoves?
   B. No, she _____, but she _____ repair locks.

HAVE TO

I We You They	have to	work.
He She It	has to	

Complete the sentences with *have to* or *has to*.

9. I can't go to your party. I _____ work.

10. Beth _____ go to the dentist today.

11. Mr. and Mrs. Shen _____ clean their apartment today.

12. Ruben _____ wash his clothes today.

13. We can't go swimming. We _____ fix our car.

14. Bobby, you can't go skating. You _____ do your homework.

1 CONVERSATION STATING JOB INTEREST & WORK SKILLS

Practice conversations about these people.

A. What kind of job are you looking for?

B. I'm looking for a job as _____.

A. Tell me about your skills.

B. I can _____, and I can _____.

a secretary
type
file

1.

a cashier
use a cash
register
handle
money

2.

a waiter
take orders
serve
customers

3.

a construction
worker
use tools
operate
equipment

4.

a cook
use cooking
equipment
prepare
meals

5.

a security
guard
guard
buildings
inspect bags
and packages

6.

2 TEAMWORK SKILLS INTERVIEW

Using the conversation above, interview four classmates.
Write their information on the chart.

NAME	JOB	SKILLS

3 CONVERSATION ASKING PERMISSION TO LEAVE WORK EARLY

Practice the conversation with a classmate.

A. Excuse me, *Mr. Cooper*.
Can I possibly leave work early today?
I have to *take my daughter to the doctor*.

B. Yes. That's okay.

A. Thanks very much.

With your classmate, make a list of *good* reasons to ask to leave work early.
Practice new conversations with these reasons.

THINK & SHARE What are *bad* reasons to ask to leave work early?
Discuss as a class.

126a

READING A HELP WANTED SIGN

Look at the help wanted sign and answer the questions.

1. They need people who can _____.
   A. use tools
   B. operate equipment
   C. sell things
   D. type

2. The job is for _____ a week.
   A. 10 hours
   B. 15 hours
   C. 25 hours
   D. 40 hours

3. They need people with work experience in _____.
   A. a library
   B. a store
   C. an office
   D. a restaurant

4. To apply for this job, _____.
   A. get an application form from the manager
   B. send a letter to the manager
   C. send your resume to the manager
   D. call the manager on the telephone

Help Wanted

- Now hiring full-time salespeople
- $10 an hour
- Sales experience required
- Ask manager for application form

ABBREVIATIONS IN WANT ADS

Match the words and abbreviations.

_____ 1. eves.   a. experience
_____ 2. excel.   b. full-time
_____ 3. exper.   c. evenings
_____ 4. FT   d. excellent

_____ 5. hr.   e. part-time
_____ 6. M-F   f. hour
_____ 7. PT   g. required
_____ 8. req.   h. Monday to Friday

READING WANT ADS

Look at the ads and answer the questions.

Mechanics Wanted
FT & PT positions. Days or eves. Excel. salary. 1 year exper. req. Call George at 803-246-9763.

Cashier
Small store needs FT cashier. M–F. No exper. req. $9/hr. Apply in person. 146 Main St.

1. The mechanic has to _____.
   A. apply for the job in person
   B. work full-time
   C. work evenings
   D. have experience

2. The ad for a mechanic doesn't have _____.
   A. the salary
   B. the telephone number
   C. the experience required
   D. the name of the person to call

3. The cashier has to _____.
   A. work on the weekend
   B. work 9 hours a day
   C. work 5 days a week
   D. know how to use a cash register

4. The ad for a cashier doesn't have _____.
   A. the store's address
   B. the store's telephone number
   C. the salary
   D. the work days

READING SAFETY SIGNS

For each warning, choose the correct sign.

A   B   C   D

E   F   G   H

1. Wear a helmet. _____

2. The floor is wet. _____

3. Don't smoke. _____

4. Wear gloves. _____

5. Don't touch that. _____

6. Wear safety glasses. _____

7. Don't stand there. _____

8. Don't go that way. _____

COMMUNITY CONNECTIONS What other safety signs are there at school, at work, and in the community? Draw three signs, bring them to class, and share with other students.

WRITING   FILLING OUT A JOB APPLICATION

Fill out the application form with your information.

NAME:		SOCIAL SECURITY NO.	
LAST	FIRST		

ADDRESS: | | | APT. #
NUMBER   STREET

CITY | STATE | ZIP CODE

TELEPHONE: |
DAY | EVE. | CELL

AVAILABILITY: CHECK ONE:

☐ FULL-TIME   ☐ PART-TIME

DAYS AVAILABLE (CIRCLE):

S   M   T   W   T   F   S

SKILLS AND ABILITIES:

WHAT CAN YOU DO? DESCRIBE YOUR SKILLS AND ABILITIES:

Choose the correct answer.

1. Ramon can _____. He's looking for a job as a secretary.
   A. bake
   B. paint
   C. type
   D. ski

2. Ann can _____. She's looking for a job as a mechanic.
   A. repair cars
   B. fix stoves
   C. skate
   D. paint pictures

3. Ivan can _____. He's looking for a job as a salesperson.
   A. file
   B. operate equipment
   C. use tools
   D. take inventory

4. I'm a construction worker. I can _____.
   A. use business software
   B. build things
   C. take inventory
   D. use a cash register

5. _____ come to your party on Saturday. I have to work.
   A. I have to
   B. I can
   C. I can't
   D. You can't

6. I'm sick. I can't go to work today. _____ go to the doctor.
   A. I have
   B. I have to
   C. You have to
   D. You have

Mark your answers in the answer box.

Answers
1 (A) (B) (C) (D)
2 (A) (B) (C) (D)
3 (A) (B) (C) (D)
4 (A) (B) (C) (D)
5 (A) (B) (C) (D)
6 (A) (B) (C) (D)
7 (A) (B) (C) (D)
8 (A) (B) (C) (D)
9 (A) (B) (C) (D)
10 (A) (B) (C) (D)

Look at the classified ads. Answer the questions.

7. Lynn can cook. She's applying for the job as _____.
   A. a construction worker
   B. a superintendent
   C. a restaurant
   D. a chef

8. Lynn has to _____.
   A. work full-time
   B. work evenings
   C. call Eve
   D. apply in person

9. Ahmed can manage a building. He has experience for the job _____.
   A. as a chef
   B. at Capital Construction
   C. at 947 Franklin Street
   D. at 1400 Central Avenue

10. To apply, Ahmed has to _____.
    A. call 377-2560
    B. ask for Frank
    C. call 930-7432
    D. go to 947 Franklin Street

Help Wanted

Chef PT. Eves. Small restaurant. Call Mario at 930-7432.

Construction Workers
Capital Construction Company. M–F. Apply in person. 1400 Central Ave. Ask for Frank.

Superintendent
Large apartment building. 947 Franklin St. Exper. req. Call Ms. Wong at 377-2560.

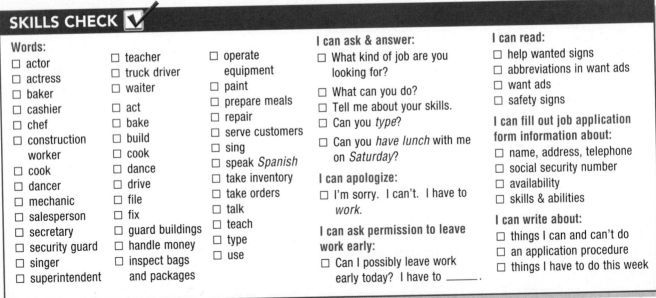

SKILLS CHECK ✓

Words:
- ☐ actor
- ☐ actress
- ☐ baker
- ☐ cashier
- ☐ chef
- ☐ construction worker
- ☐ cook
- ☐ dancer
- ☐ mechanic
- ☐ salesperson
- ☐ secretary
- ☐ security guard
- ☐ singer
- ☐ superintendent

- ☐ teacher
- ☐ truck driver
- ☐ waiter
- ☐ act
- ☐ bake
- ☐ build
- ☐ cook
- ☐ dance
- ☐ drive
- ☐ file
- ☐ fix
- ☐ guard buildings
- ☐ handle money
- ☐ inspect bags and packages

- ☐ operate equipment
- ☐ paint
- ☐ prepare meals
- ☐ repair
- ☐ serve customers
- ☐ sing
- ☐ speak Spanish
- ☐ take inventory
- ☐ take orders
- ☐ talk
- ☐ teach
- ☐ type
- ☐ use

I can ask & answer:
- ☐ What kind of job are you looking for?
- ☐ What can you do?
- ☐ Tell me about your skills.
- ☐ Can you *type*?
- ☐ Can you *have lunch* with me on *Saturday*?

I can apologize:
- ☐ I'm sorry. I can't. I have to *work*.

I can ask permission to leave work early:
- ☐ Can I possibly leave work early today? I have to _____.

I can read:
- ☐ help wanted signs
- ☐ abbreviations in want ads
- ☐ want ads
- ☐ safety signs

I can fill out job application form information about:
- ☐ name, address, telephone
- ☐ social security number
- ☐ availability
- ☐ skills & abilities

I can write about:
- ☐ things I can and can't do
- ☐ an application procedure
- ☐ things I have to do this week

Future: Going to

Want to

Time Expressions

- **Describing Future Plans and Intentions**
- **Weather Forecasts**
- **Telling Time**
- **Months of the Year**

- **Ordinal Numbers**
- **Dates**
- **Schedules**
- **Job Application Forms**

VOCABULARY PREVIEW

Time

2:00
It's two o'clock.

2:15
It's two fifteen.
It's a quarter after two.

2:30
It's two thirty.
It's half past two.

2:45
It's two forty-five.
It's a quarter to three.

Months of the Year

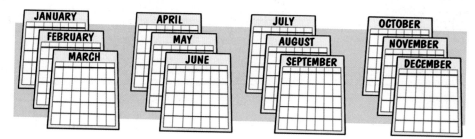

Seasons

spring

summer

fall / autumn

winter

What Are They Going to Do Tomorrow?

What	am I is { he she it } are { we you they }	going to do?

(I am)	I'm	
(He is)	He's	
(She is)	She's	
(It is)	It's	going to read.
(We are)	We're	
(You are)	You're	
(They are)	They're	

A. What's Fred going to do tomorrow?

B. He's going to fix his car.

1. *Jenny?*

2. *Cathy and Dave?*

3. *Tony?*

4. *you and your brother?*

5. *Andrew?*

6. *Ashley?*

128

They're Going to the Beach

They're going (to go) to the beach.	=	They're going to the beach. They're going to go to the beach.
We're going (to go) swimming.	=	We're going swimming. We're going to go swimming.

today	tomorrow
this morning	tomorrow morning
this afternoon	tomorrow afternoon
this evening	tomorrow evening
tonight	tomorrow night

A. What are Mr. and Mrs. Brown going to do tomorrow?

B. They're going (to go) to the beach.

1. What's Anita going to do this morning?

2. What are Steve and Brenda going to do tonight?

3. What's Fernando going to do tomorrow evening?

4. What are you and your friends going to do tomorrow afternoon?

What are YOU going to do tomorrow?

129

When Are You Going to . . . ?

Time Expressions

this _____
next _____

{
week / month / year
Sunday / Monday / Tuesday / Wednesday / Thursday /
Friday / Saturday
January / February / March / April / May / June /
July / August / September / October /
November / December
spring / summer / fall (autumn) / winter
}

right now
right away
immediately
at once

Practice conversations with other students. Use any of the time expressions on page 130.

1. When are you going to clean your garage?

2. When are you going to call your grandmother?

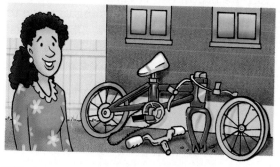

3. When are you going to fix your bicycle?

4. When are you going to visit us?

5. When are you going to wash your car?

6. When are you going to plant flowers this year?

7. When are you going to write to your Aunt Martha?

8. Mr. Smith! When are you going to iron those pants?

Now ask another student: "When are you going to _____?"

READING

HAPPY NEW YEAR!

It's December thirty-first, New Year's Eve. Ruth and Larry Carter are celebrating the holiday with their children, Nicole and Jonathan. The Carters are a very happy family this New Year's Eve. Next year is going to be a very good year for the entire family.

Next year, Ruth and Larry are going to take a long vacation. They're going to visit Larry's brother in Alaska. Nicole is going to finish high school. She's going to move to San Francisco and begin college. Jonathan is going to get his driver's license. He's going to save a lot of money and buy a used car.

As you can see, the Carters are really looking forward to next year. It's going to be a very happy year for all of them.

Happy New Year!

✓ READING *CHECK-UP*

COMPUTER CHAT

Fill in the missing words. Then practice this computer chat with another student.

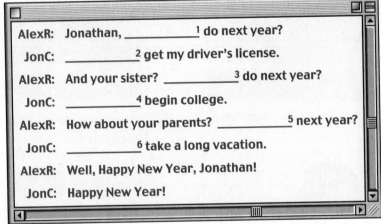

AlexR: Jonathan, _____¹ do next year?

JonC: _____² get my driver's license.

AlexR: And your sister? _____³ do next year?

JonC: _____⁴ begin college.

AlexR: How about your parents? _____⁵ next year?

JonC: _____⁶ take a long vacation.

AlexR: Well, Happy New Year, Jonathan!

JonC: Happy New Year!

LISTENING

Listen and choose the words you hear.

1. a. Tomorrow.   b. This March.
2. a. Next December.   b. Next November.
3. a. Next month.   b. Next Monday.
4. a. This evening.   b. This morning.
5. a. This summer.   b. This Sunday.

6. a. This Tuesday.   b. This Thursday.
7. a. This afternoon.   b. Tomorrow afternoon.
8. a. Next year.   b. Next week.
9. a. Next winter.   b. Next summer.
10. a. This month.   b. At once.

What's the Forecast?

I We You They } want to	study.
He She It } wants to	

A. What are you going to do tomorrow?

B. I don't know. I want to **go swimming**, but I think the weather is going to be bad.

A. Really? What's the forecast?

B. The radio says it's going to **rain**.

A. That's strange! According to the newspaper, it's going to **be sunny**.

B. I hope you're right. I REALLY want to **go swimming**.

1. *have a picnic*
rain
be nice

2. *go to the beach*
be cloudy
be sunny

3. *go sailing*
be foggy
be clear

4. *go skiing*
be warm
snow

5. *work in my garden*
be very hot
be cool

6. *take my children to the zoo*
be cold
be warm

Discuss in class: What's the weather today?
What's the weather forecast for tomorrow?

What Time Is It?

2:00

It's two o'clock.

2:15

It's two fifteen.
It's a quarter after two.

2:30

It's two thirty.
It's half past two.

2:45

It's two forty-five.
It's a quarter to three.

It's noon.
It's twelve noon.

It's midnight.
It's twelve midnight.

A. What time does the movie begin?

B. It begins at 8:00.

A. At 8:00?! Oh no! We're going to be late!

B. Why? What time is it?

A. It's 7:30! We have to leave RIGHT NOW!

B. I can't leave now. I'm SHAVING!

A. Please try to hurry! I don't want to be late for the movie.

A. What time does _____?

B. It _____ at _____.

A. At _____?! Oh no! We're going to be late!

B. Why? What time is it?

A. It's _____! We have to leave RIGHT NOW!

B. I can't leave now. I'm _____!

A. Please try to hurry! I don't want to be late for the _____.

1. What time does the football game begin?
3:00 / 2:30
taking a bath

2. What time does the bus leave?
7:15 / 6:45
packing my suitcase

3. What time does the train leave?
5:30 / 5:15
taking a shower

4. What time does the concert begin?
8:00 / 7:45
looking for my pants

How to Say It!

Asking the Time

A. { What time is it?
{ What's the time?

B. It's 4:00.

A. { Can you tell me the time?
{ Do you know the time?

B. Yes. It's 4:00.

Practice conversations with other students. Ask the time in different ways.

THE FORTUNE TELLER

Walter is visiting Madame Sophia, the famous fortune teller. He's wondering about his future, and Madame Sophia is telling him what is going to happen next year. According to Madame Sophia, next year is going to be a very interesting year in Walter's life.

In January he's going to meet a very nice woman and fall in love.

In February he's going to get married.

In March he's going to take a trip to a warm, sunny place.

In April he's going to have a bad cold.

In May his parents are going to move to a beautiful city in California.

In June there's going to be a fire in his apartment building, and he's going to have to find a new place to live.

In July his friends are going to give him a DVD player for his birthday.

In August his boss is going to fire him.

In September he's going to start a new job with a very big salary.

In October he's going to be in a car accident, but he isn't going to be hurt.

In November he's going to be on a television game show and win a million dollars.

And in December he's going to become a father!

According to Madame Sophia, a lot is going to happen in Walter's life next year. But Walter isn't sure he believes any of this. He doesn't believe in fortunes or fortune tellers. But in January he's going to get a haircut and buy a lot of new clothes, just in case Madame Sophia is right and he meets a wonderful woman and falls in love!

✔ READING *CHECK-UP*

Q & A

Walter is talking to Madame Sophia. Using these models, create dialogs based on the story.

A. Tell me, what's going to happen in *January*?
B. In *January*? Oh! *January* is going to be a very good month!
A. Really? What's going to happen?
B. *You're going to meet a very nice woman and fall in love.*
A. Oh! That's wonderful!

A. Tell me, what's going to happen in *April*?
B. In *April*? Oh! *April* is going to be a very bad month!
A. Really? What's going to happen?
B. *You're going to have a bad cold.*
A. Oh! That's terrible!

PRONUNCIATION *Going to & Want to*

> going to = gonna
> want to = wanna

Listen. Then say it.

I'm going to study.

It's going to rain.

We want to go swimming.

They want to leave.

Say it. Then listen.

He's going to cook.

They're going to paint.

I want to read.

We want to go to the beach.

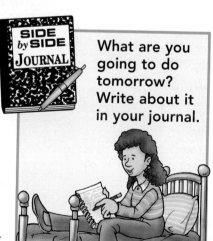

SIDE by SIDE JOURNAL

What are you going to do tomorrow? Write about it in your journal.

GRAMMAR FOCUS

FUTURE: GOING TO

What	am	I	going to do?
	is	he she it	
	are	we you they	

(I am)	I'm	going to read.
(He is)	He's	
(She is)	She's	
(It is)	It's	
(We are)	We're	
(You are)	You're	
(They are)	They're	

Complete the sentences using *going to* and the correct verb.

go	read	wash	watch	write

1. A. What's your husband going to do this afternoon?
   B. _____ _____ _____ _____ a book.

2. A. What are you going to do this morning?
   B. _____ _____ _____ _____ a letter to my aunt.

3. A. What are Sally and Paul going to do tonight?
   B. _____ _____ _____ _____ TV.

4. A. What are you and your wife going to do this Saturday?
   B. _____ _____ _____ _____ our windows.

5. A. What's your sister going to do this Sunday?
   B. _____ _____ _____ _____ to the beach.

TIME EXPRESSIONS

I'm going to call	today. this morning. this afternoon. this evening. tonight.	tomorrow. tomorrow morning. tomorrow afternoon. tomorrow evening. tomorrow night.	right now. right away. immediately. at once.

I'm going to fix my car	this next	week / month / year. Sunday / Monday / Tuesday / . . . / Saturday. January / February / March / . . . / December. spring / summer / fall (autumn) / winter.

Number the following from the present (1) to the future (12).

____ next Saturday
____ tomorrow afternoon
____ next year
____ this Friday
_1_ immediately
____ this Wednesday
____ next month
____ tomorrow night
____ tonight
____ this evening
____ next Tuesday
____ this afternoon

It's	eleven o'clock.		11:00
	eleven fifteen.	a quarter after eleven.	11:15
	eleven thirty.	half past eleven.	11:30
	eleven forty-five.	a quarter to twelve.	11:45

Match the times.

____ 1. 3:15   a. three forty-five
____ 2. 2:45   b. half past two
____ 3. 2:30   c. a quarter after three
____ 4. 3:45   d. a quarter to three

WANT TO

I We You They	want to	study.
He She It	wants to	

Choose the correct word.

1. I (want to   wants to) go to a movie tomorrow night.
2. My husband (want to   wants to) go to the beach tomorrow.
3. My sister and I (want to   wants to) go swimming today.
4. My parents (want to   wants to) buy a new car.
5. Do you (want to   wants to) have a picnic this afternoon?
6. My grandmother (want to   wants to) work in her garden today.

1 MONTHS OF THE YEAR RECOGNIZING ABBREVIATIONS

Look at the abbreviation and write the month.

OCT _____   MAY _____   FEB _____

JUL _____   AUG _____   MAR _____

APR _____   DEC _____   JAN _____

JUN _____   NOV _____   SEP _____

2 CONVERSATION ORDINAL NUMBERS & DATES

Practice the ordinal numbers.

1st	first	11th	eleventh	21st	twenty-first
2nd	second	12th	twelfth	22nd	twenty-second
3rd	third	13th	thirteenth	30th	thirtieth
4th	fourth	14th	fourteenth	40th	fortieth
5th	fifth	15th	fifteenth	50th	fiftieth
6th	sixth	16th	sixteenth	60th	sixtieth
7th	seventh	17th	seventeenth	70th	seventieth
8th	eighth	18th	eighteenth	80th	eightieth
9th	ninth	19th	nineteenth	90th	ninetieth
10th	tenth	20th	twentieth	100th	one hundredth

Practice with a classmate.

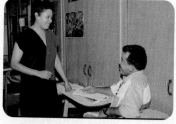

A. When's your birthday?

B. My birthday is *April third*.

Look at the calendars and practice conversations.

1. AUG 7   2. NOV 1   3. JUN 19   4. FEB 12   5. SEP 22

3 TEAMWORK ORDINAL NUMBERS & MONTHS

Practice conversations with a classmate.

What's the third month of the year?

March.

4 PROJECT CLASS BIRTHDAYS

As a class project, make a calendar with the birthdays of all the students in your class.

5 READING & WRITING DATES DATES WRITTEN IN NUMBERS

4/25/18 } April 25, 2018
|0|4| |2|5| |1|8|
Month Day Year

7/12/94 } July 12, 1994
|0|7| |1|2| |9|4|
Month Day Year

Write out these dates.

1. 2/10/19 ___February 10, 2019___

2. 5/30/18 _____

3. 3/7/20 _____

4. 9/28/17 _____

5. 10/30/21 _____

6. 4/20/19 _____

Write these dates in numbers two ways.

7. November 6, 2001 ___11/6/01___ |1|1| |0|6| |0|1|
Month Day Year

8. January 27, 2021 _____ |_|_| |_|_| |_|_|
Month Day Year

9. June 1, 1999 _____ |_|_| |_|_| |_|_|
Month Day Year

10. December 19, 2019 _____ |_|_| |_|_| |_|_|
Month Day Year

11. September 6, 2002 _____ |_|_| |_|_| |_|_|
Month Day Year

12. February 4, 2010 _____ |_|_| |_|_| |_|_|
Month Day Year

6 CONVERSATION SAYING COMPLETE DATES (MONTH, DAY, & YEAR)

Practice the conversations.

3/10/20

A. What's today's date?

B. March tenth, two thousand twenty.

|0|8| |1|1| |9|4|
Month Day Year

A. What's your date of birth?

B. August eleventh, nineteen ninety-four.

Walk around the classroom and practice conversations. Use today's date and your date of birth.

7 WRITING FILLING OUT A FORM

Fill out the form with your personal information.

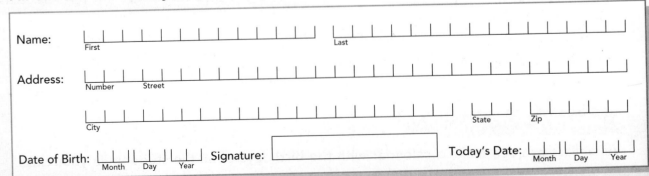

138b

READING A SCHEDULE

This sign shows the hours a library is open. Look at the sign and answer the questions.

CENTRAL LIBRARY

Summer Hours				
	Monday	10:00 – 5:30	Friday	10:00 – 4:30
	Tuesday	10:00 – 5:30	Saturday	10:00 – 3:00
	Wednesday	12:00 – 8:00	Sunday	closed
	Thursday	10:00 – 7:00		

1. The library opens at noon on ____.
   A. Monday
   B. Wednesday
   C. Friday
   D. Saturday

2. The library closes at half past four on ____.
   A. Tuesday
   B. Wednesday
   C. Friday
   D. Saturday

3. The library is open for five hours on ____.
   A. Monday
   B. Friday
   C. Saturday
   D. Sunday

4. The library is open ____.
   A. all day on Sunday
   B. on Wednesday morning
   C. on Saturday evening
   D. on Thursday afternoon

5. The library is open for the most hours on ____.
   A. Wednesday
   B. Thursday
   C. Friday
   D. Saturday

6. The library hours on the sign are for ____.
   A. July and August
   B. April and May
   C. January and February
   D. October and November

COMMUNITY CONNECTIONS What are the hours of these places in your community: library? post office? bank? supermarket? Make a sign for each place.

READING A JOB APPLICATION FORM

Look at the application and answer the questions.

EMPLOYMENT APPLICATION

NAME: (first, last) Alex Ramirez		SOC. SEC. NO. 225-66-2278				TEL. NO. 305-578-3457		

WHAT HOURS ARE YOU AVAILABLE TO WORK? FILL IN CHART BELOW.

	MON	TUE	WED	THU	FRI	SAT	SUN	CHECK ONE
FROM	7:00 A.M.	5:00 P.M.			7:00 A.M.	1:00 P.M.	1:00 P.M.	____ FULL TIME
TO	12:00 P.M.	9:00 P.M.			12:00 P.M.	7:00 P.M.	7:00 P.M.	✓ PART TIME

1. Alex can work ____.
   A. full time
   B. five hours on Tuesday
   C. six hours on Friday
   D. six hours on Saturday

2. He can work on Monday ____.
   A. morning
   B. afternoon
   C. evening
   D. night

3. He can begin work at ____.
   A. 12 noon on Monday
   B. 5:00 P.M. on Thursday
   C. 1:00 in the afternoon on Sunday
   D. 5:00 in the morning on Tuesday

4. He CAN'T work at ____.
   A. 10 A.M. on Monday
   B. noon on Saturday
   C. 11 A.M. on Friday
   D. 7 P.M. on Tuesday

Choose the correct answer.

Mark your answers in the answer box.

1. The plumber is going to fix our _____ tomorrow morning.
   A. bicycle
   B. doorbell
   C. sink
   D. flowers

2. We're going to the beach tomorrow. It's going to _____.
   A. rain
   B. snow
   C. be cold and cloudy
   D. be warm and sunny

3. My father and I are going to a baseball game at two o'clock _____.
   A. tomorrow afternoon
   B. this morning
   C. this evening
   D. tonight

4. June is my favorite _____.
   A. week of the year
   B. month of the year
   C. day of the week
   D. holiday

5. I'm going to save a lot of money. I want to _____.
   A. go to the library
   B. see a movie
   C. buy a car
   D. have a picnic

6. I'm going to iron my _____ this afternoon.
   A. windows
   B. flowers
   C. bicycle
   D. shirts

7. My family and I are going to take a vacation. We're going to _____.
   A. go to college
   B. go to Hawaii
   C. see a play
   D. go to the laundromat

8. We're having breakfast now. We're going to have lunch _____.
   A. at noon
   B. at midnight
   C. tonight
   D. tomorrow morning

	Answers			
1	A	B	C	D
2	A	B	C	D
3	A	B	C	D
4	A	B	C	D
5	A	B	C	D
6	A	B	C	D
7	A	B	C	D
8	A	B	C	D
9	A	B	C	D
10	A	B	C	D

Look at the bank sign. Answer the questions.

9. During the week, the bank opens at _____.
   A. a quarter after eight
   B. four thirty
   C. a quarter to eight
   D. a quarter to nine

10. The bank is open for four hours on _____.
   A. Wednesday
   B. Friday
   C. Saturday
   D. Sunday

National Bank NB

MON	8:45 – 4:30	FRI	8:45 – 6:00
TUE	8:45 – 4:30	SAT	9:00 – 1:00
WED	8:45 – 4:30	SUN	closed
THU	8:45 – 7:30		

SKILLS CHECK ✓

Words:
- ☐ January
- ☐ February
- ☐ March
- ☐ April
- ☐ May
- ☐ June
- ☐ July
- ☐ August
- ☐ September
- ☐ October
- ☐ November
- ☐ December

- ☐ Sunday
- ☐ Monday
- ☐ Tuesday
- ☐ Wednesday
- ☐ Thursday
- ☐ Friday
- ☐ Saturday
- ☐ spring
- ☐ summer
- ☐ fall/autumn
- ☐ winter

I can ask & answer:
- ☐ What are you going to do tomorrow?
- ☐ What's going to happen in *January*?
- ☐ What's the forecast?
- ☐ What time is it?/What's the time?
- ☐ What time does the *movie* begin?
- ☐ What's today's date?
- ☐ What's your date of birth?
- ☐ When's your birthday?
- ☐ When are you going to *visit us*?

I can read:
- ☐ abbreviations for months of the year
- ☐ schedule signs on public buildings
- ☐ schedule information on a job application form

I can write:
- ☐ dates
- ☐ dates in number form
- ☐ personal information on a form

I can write about:
- ☐ what I'm going to do tomorrow

SIDE by SIDE Gazette

A. What do you do?
B. I'm a / an _____ .

Time Zones

What time is it right now? What time is it in other parts of the world? How do you know?

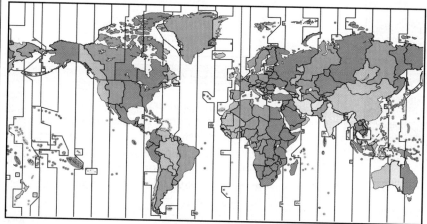

There are 24 time zones around the world. In each time zone, it is a different hour of the day. The time zone that is east of your time zone is one hour ahead. The time zone to your west is one hour behind. So, for example, when it's 10:00 in Chicago, it's 11:00 in New York, it's 9:00 in Denver, and it's 8:00 in Los Angeles.

New Zealand is 12 time zones to the east of London. Therefore, when it's midnight in London and people are sleeping, it's noon the next day in New Zealand and people are eating lunch!

 architect

 carpenter

 cashier

 farmer

 lawyer

 painter

 pilot

 translator

 waiter

 waitress

FACT FILE

A Moment in the Life of the World

TIME AND DAY	PLACE
5:00 A.M.* Monday morning	Los Angeles, USA
7:00 A.M. Monday morning	Mexico City, Mexico
8:00 A.M. Monday morning	New York City, USA; Toronto, Canada
9:00 A.M. Monday morning	Caracas, Venezuela
10:00 A.M. Monday morning	Rio de Janeiro, Brazil; Buenos Aires, Argentina
1:00 P.M.* Monday afternoon	London, England; Lisbon, Portugal
2:00 P.M. Monday afternoon	Paris, France; Madrid, Spain; Rome, Italy
3:00 P.M. Monday afternoon	Athens, Greece; Istanbul, Turkey
4:00 P.M. Monday afternoon	Moscow, Russia
9:00 P.M. Monday night	Hong Kong, China
10:00 P.M. Monday night	Seoul, Korea; Tokyo, Japan
12:00 A.M. Tuesday morning	Sydney, Australia

*A.M. = 12:00 midnight to 11:59 in the morning   P.M. = 12:00 noon to 11:59 at night

AROUND THE WORLD

Time and Culture

People in different cultures think of time in different ways.

In your culture, do people arrive on time for work? Do people arrive on time for appointments? Do people arrive on time for parties? Tell about time in your culture.

Thank You for Calling the Multiplex Cinema!

_c_ **①**

___ **②**

___ **③**

___ **④**

___ **⑤**

a. _The Fortune Teller_

b. _Tomorrow Is Right Now_

c. _The Spanish Dancer_

d. _The Time Zone Machine_

e. _When Are You Going to Call the Plumber?_

Global Exchange

JulieP: I'm going to be very busy this weekend. On Friday evening, I'm going to get together with my friends from college. We're going to have dinner, and then we're going to a concert. On Saturday morning, I have to clean my apartment because my parents are going to visit me in the afternoon. In the evening, we're going to go bowling. On Sunday I'm going to teach my Sunday school class in the morning, I'm going to a soccer game in the afternoon, and I'm going to wash my clothes in the evening. How about you? What are you going to do this weekend?

Send a message to a keypal. Tell about your plans for the weekend.

What Are They Saying?

Word order is different in statements and questions with *can*.

The students can use computers.

Can the students use computers?

subject — auxiliary verb — base form of the verb

auxiliary verb — subject — base form of the verb

Practice these conversations with a classmate.

Sandra can use business software.

A. What's the sentence?
B. *Sandra can use business software.*
A. What kind of sentence is it?
B. It's a statement.
A. How do you change it to a question?
B. Put the auxiliary verb "can" before the subject *Sandra*.
A. So, what is the question?
B. *Can Sandra use business software?*

Can the mechanic fix large trucks?

A. What's the sentence?
B. *Can the mechanic fix large trucks?*
A. What kind of sentence is it?
B. It's a question.
A. How do you change it to a statement?
B. Put the auxiliary verb "can" after the subject *the mechanic*.
A. So, what is the statement?
B. *The mechanic can fix large trucks.*

Use a capital letter to begin . . .

the first word of a sentence: **H**e fixes cars every day.
the names of people: Where is **W**endy?
the names of streets: I live on **C**entral **A**venue.
people's titles: Where are **M**r. and **M**rs. Hendrix?
days and months: They're going to get married on a **S**unday in **J**une.
names of languages: I can speak **A**rabic.
the word "I": Can **I** park my car here?

Rewrite these sentences. *Capitalize* the words that need capitalization. **Put the correct** *punctuation mark* **at the end of each sentence. Then practice new conversations about these sentences.**

1. they can speak spanish and english
2. can mr. and mrs. park ski
3. my daughter anna can sing and dance
4. can i park my car on main street
5. can you have lunch with me on friday
6. monica can take a vacation in august
7. he can get his license next april
8. can ms. paterson work on saturday

PART-TIME WORKERS

In the United States, there are more and more part-time workers every year. Some people work part-time because they can't find full-time jobs. Others work part-time because they need the extra money and like the flexible hours. With flexible hours, people can work in the morning, afternoon, evening, or at night.

Today's part-time workers are young and old, men and women, married and single—from fast-food workers and store employees to teachers and doctors. Let's meet a few of these part-time workers.

Mai Nguyen is a high school student. She wants money for college, so she works part-time at her uncle's grocery store. "I'm happy with my job, but sometimes I'm very tired. I do homework until midnight every night." She can't do school sports because she works nights and weekends. But Nguyen is learning important things about business and customers.

Ron Thurman, a 70-year-old senior, works part-time at a movie theater. He greets customers and takes their tickets. "I enjoy people and I want to stay busy. My job makes me feel young. And I like the extra money."

Carlos Santos, a father of three children, is a part-time hospital nurse. He works a total of 24 hours a week—eight-hour shifts, three nights a week. When he works, his wife is at home with the children. During the day, he takes care of the children while his wife is at her full-time job. "I love my work, and I love my children. I like the flexible hours. I can be with my sons, but I can also have my job. When my sons are teenagers, I'm going to work full-time again."

Kim Chung has a two-year college degree, but she can't find a full-time job. She works part-time at a department store. She wants to take more college classes and get a 4-year college degree. With more education, she hopes she can find a full-time job in the future.

1. Part-time workers _____.
   - Ⓐ can't find full-time jobs
   - Ⓑ want to get college degrees
   - Ⓒ usually work in the evening and at night
   - Ⓓ often have jobs with flexible hours

2. Mai Nguyen's job is difficult because _____.
   - Ⓐ she can't go to school
   - Ⓑ she's sometimes very tired
   - Ⓒ she doesn't like her uncle
   - Ⓓ she can't finish her homework

3. Carlos Santos works _____.
   - Ⓐ every weekend
   - Ⓑ 24 hours a month
   - Ⓒ three nights a week
   - Ⓓ eight hours a week

4. Kim Chung _____.
   - Ⓐ is a college student
   - Ⓑ can't find a full-time job
   - Ⓒ works at a grocery store
   - Ⓓ works eight-hour shifts

5. Ron Thurman works part-time because _____.
   - Ⓐ he likes his job
   - Ⓑ he likes movies
   - Ⓒ he's young
   - Ⓓ he can't find a full-time job

6. This passage is about _____.
   - Ⓐ part-time workers around the world
   - Ⓑ four part-time workers
   - Ⓒ people who can't find full-time jobs
   - Ⓓ problems with part-time jobs

Think & Share
1. Why do people work part-time?
2. Do people in your family work part-time or full-time? What are their jobs and hours?
3. Do your friends have part-time jobs or full-time jobs? Where do they work?

15

Past Tense: Regular Verbs
Introduction to Irregular Verbs

- Past Actions and Activities
- Describing an Event
- Ailments
- Making a Doctor's Appointment

- A Medical Exam
- Medical Appointment Cards
- Medicine Labels
- Staying Healthy

VOCABULARY PREVIEW

1. headache
2. stomachache
3. toothache

4. backache
5. earache
6. cold

7. fever
8. cough
9. sore throat

How Do You Feel Today?

A. How do you feel today?

B. Not so good.

A. What's the matter?

B. I have a headache.

A. I'm sorry to hear that.

1. stomachache

2. toothache

3. backache

4. earache

5. cold

6. fever

7. cough

8. sore throat

How to Say It!

Saying How You Feel

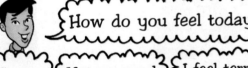

How do you feel today?

I feel great! I feel fine. I feel okay.

So-so. Not so good. I feel terrible.

I'm glad to hear that.

I'm sorry to hear that.

Practice conversations with other students.

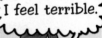

What Did You Do Yesterday?

I work   every day.
I work**ed** yesterday.

I play   the piano every day.
I play**ed** the piano yesterday.

I rest   every day.
I rest**ed** yesterday.

What did you do yesterday?   I worked.

1. *cook*

2. *wash my car*

3. *fix my bicycle*

4. *brush my teeth*

5. *watch TV*

6. *type* *

7. *dance* *

8. *bake* *

9. *clean*

10. *play the piano*

11. *yawn*

12. *listen to music*

13. *shave* *

14. *smile* *

15. *cry* †

16. *study* †

17. *shout*

18. *rest*

19. *plant flowers*

20. *wait for the bus*

* type – typed   shave – shaved   † cry – cried
  dance – danced   smile – smiled   study – studied
  bake – baked

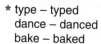
143

What's the Matter?

| I / We / You / They | work every day. |
| He / She / It | works every day. |

| I / We / You / They / He / She / It | worked yesterday. |

A. How does David feel?

B. Not so good.

A. What's the matter?

B. He has a backache.

A. A backache? How did he get it?

B. He played basketball all day.*

* Or: all morning / all afternoon / all evening / all night

1. *Brian*

2. *Linda*

3. *you*

4. *Gary*

5. *Maria*

6. *Charlie*

7. *Mrs. Clark*

8. *you*

9. *Carlos*

eat – ate	sing – sang	drink – drank	sit – sat	ride – rode

10. *Daniel*

11. *Jennifer*

12. *you*

13. *Sarah*

14. *you*

15. *Tim*

ROLE PLAY   *Do You Want to Make an Appointment?*

You don't feel very well today. Call the doctor's office and make an appointment.

A. Doctor's Office.

B. Hello. This is _____.

A. Hello, Mr./Ms./Mrs. _____.
How are you?

B. Not so good.

A. I'm sorry to hear that. What seems to be the problem?

B. I _____ all _____ yesterday, and now I have a TERRIBLE _____.

A. I see. Do you want to make an appointment?

B. Yes, please.

A. Can you come in tomorrow at _____ o'clock?

B. At _____ o'clock? Yes. That's fine. Thank you.

THE WILSONS' PARTY

Mr. and Mrs. Wilson invited all their friends and neighbors to a party last night. They stayed home all day yesterday and prepared for the party.

In the morning the Wilsons worked outside. Their daughter, Margaret, cleaned the yard. Their son, Bob, painted the fence. Mrs. Wilson planted flowers in the garden, and Mr. Wilson fixed their broken front steps.

In the afternoon the Wilsons worked inside the house. Margaret washed the floors and vacuumed the living room carpet. Bob dusted the furniture and cleaned the basement. Mr. and Mrs. Wilson stayed in the kitchen all afternoon. He cooked spaghetti for dinner, and she baked apple pies for dessert.

The Wilsons finished all their work at six o'clock. Their house looked beautiful inside and out!

The Wilsons' guests arrived at about 7:30. After they arrived, they all sat in the living room. They ate cheese and crackers, drank lemonade, and talked. Some people talked about their children. Other people talked about the weather. And EVERYBODY talked about how beautiful the Wilsons' house looked inside and out!

The Wilsons served dinner in the dining room at 9:00. Everybody enjoyed the meal very much. They liked Mr. Wilson's spaghetti and they "loved" Mrs. Wilson's apple pie. In fact, everybody asked for seconds.

After dinner everybody sat in the living room again. First, Bob Wilson played the piano and his sister, Margaret, sang. Then, Mr. and Mrs. Wilson showed a video of their trip to Hawaii. After that, they turned on the music and everybody danced.

As you can see, the Wilsons' guests enjoyed the party very much. In fact, nobody wanted to go home!

✔ READING *CHECK-UP*

WHAT'S THE ANSWER?

1. What did Margaret and Bob Wilson do in the morning?
2. How did Mr. and Mrs. Wilson prepare for the party in the afternoon?
3. When did the guests arrive?
4. Where did the guests sit after they arrived?
5. What did they eat and drink before dinner?
6. What did Margaret do after dinner?
7. What did Mr. and Mrs. Wilson do after dinner?

LISTENING

Listen and choose the word you hear.

1. a. plant   b. planted
2. a. work   b. worked
3. a. study   b. studied
4. a. sit   b. sat
5. a. drink   b. drank
6. a. wait   b. waited
7. a. finish   b. finished
8. a. invite   b. invited
9. a. eat   b. ate
10. a. clean   b. cleaned
11. a. wash   b. washed
12. a. watch   b. watched

IN YOUR OWN WORDS

FOR WRITING OR DISCUSSION

A PARTY

Tell about a party you enjoyed.

What did you eat?
What did you drink?
What did people do at the party?
   (eat, dance, talk about . . .)

PRONUNCIATION Past Tense Endings

Put these words in the correct column. Then practice saying the words in each column.

| cleaned | danced | dusted | painted | played | studied | talked | typed | waited |

{t}

_____

_____

_____

{d}

cleaned

_____

_____

_____

{ɪd}

_____

_____

_____

Listen. Then say it.

I cooked, I cleaned, and I dusted.

I worked, I played, and I planted flowers.

Say it. Then listen.

I typed, I studied, and I painted.

I talked, I cried, and I shouted.

SIDE by SIDE JOURNAL

What did you eat yesterday?
What did you drink?
Write about it in your journal.

GRAMMAR FOCUS

PAST TENSE

| I He She It We You They | worked yesterday. |

[t]
I worked.
I danced.

[d]
I cleaned.
I played.

[ɪd]
I rested.
I shouted.

IRREGULAR VERBS

eat – ate
drink – drank
ride – rode
sing – sang
sit – sat

Complete each sentence with the past tense of the correct verb.

| drink | listen | play | sing | study | wash |
| eat | plant | ride | sit | wait | watch |

1. I _____ my car yesterday.

2. I _____ TV yesterday.

3. I _____ the piano yesterday.

4. I _____ to music yesterday.

5. I _____ flowers yesterday.

6. I _____ English yesterday.

7. I _____ four cookies this afternoon.

8. I _____ milk with my lunch today.

9. I have a sore throat because I _____ all day yesterday.

10. My daughter _____ her bicycle all afternoon.

11. I _____ at my desk all day yesterday.

12. I _____ for the bus all morning.

1 A MEDICAL EXAM FOLLOWING INSTRUCTIONS

Practice with a classmate. Say these instructions and do the actions.

Stand on the scale.

I'm going to check your weight.

Let's measure your height.

I'm going to check your blood pressure.

I'm going to take your temperature.

Sit on the examination table.

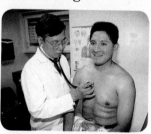
I'm going to listen to your heart.

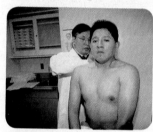
Take a deep breath.

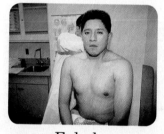
Exhale.

Open your mouth and say, "Ahh!"

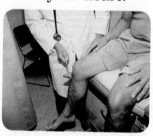
I'm going to check your reflexes.

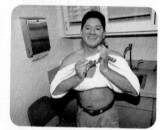
Get dressed.

2 CLOZE READING A MEDICAL EXAM

Complete the story. Fill in the past tense of the correct verb.

First, I ____stood____ ¹ on the scale. The nurse _____ ²
my weight. Then she _____ ³ my height. She
_____ ⁴ my blood pressure, and she _____ ⁵ my
temperature. Then I _____ ⁶ on the examination table.
The doctor _____ ⁷ to my heart. I _____ ⁸ a deep
breath, and then I _____ ⁹. After that, I _____ ¹⁰
my mouth and _____ ¹¹, "Ahh!" Then the doctor
_____ ¹² my reflexes. Finally, I _____ ¹³ dressed.

Irregular Verbs
get – got
say – said
sit – sat
stand – stood
take – took

THINK & SHARE Do you have a medical exam every year? Where? Is it difficult
to get a medical exam? Discuss with your classmates.

MEDICAL APPOINTMENT CARDS

Look at the medical appointment cards and answer the questions.

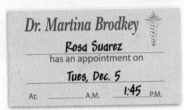

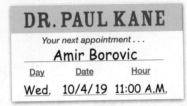

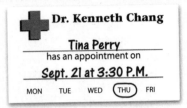

1. Rosa Suarez has an appointment ____.
   A. with Dr. Paul Kane
   B. on Thursday
   C. at 11:00 A.M.
   D. on December 5th

2. Tina Perry has an appointment ____.
   A. in October
   B. on Wednesday
   C. with Dr. Kenneth Chang
   D. at 1:45 P.M.

3. Mr. Borovic is going to see Dr. Kane ____.
   A. on October 4th
   B. in April
   C. in the afternoon
   D. on Tuesday

4. Tina is going to see Dr. Chang ____.
   A. on Tuesday
   B. at 3:30 P.M.
   C. on September 20th
   D. in the morning

MEDICINE LABELS AND DOSAGES

Look at the medicine labels and answer the questions.

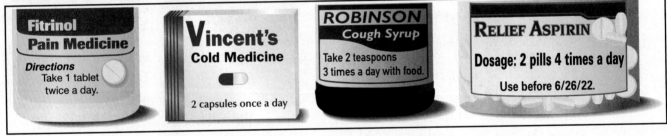

1. What's the aspirin *dosage*? (How much aspirin can you take each time?) ____
2. How often can you take the aspirin? ____
3. How often can you take the cold medicine? ____
4. How much cold medicine can you take each time? ____
5. How often can you take the cough syrup? ____
6. How many teaspoons of cough syrup can you take in a day? ____
7. How often can you take the pain medicine? ____
8. How much pain medicine can you take in a day? ____
9. When is the last day you can take the aspirin? ____
10. What do you have to take with the cough syrup? ____

Read the magazine article.

A Healthy Life

People today don't have time to live a healthy life. They don't have much time to prepare and eat healthy food at home, and they don't have time to exercise. When they have some free time at the end of a busy day, they usually just sit and watch TV. Is that how you live your life? Then it's time to change!

First, get up from the sofa and exercise! Choose something you can do often, such as jogging, swimming, or just walking. Exercise thirty minutes three days a week. When you begin to exercise, be careful. Exercise for only a short time at first. Each day do a little more. When your back or stomach hurts, it's time to stop and rest.

You don't have to join a health club to exercise. You can make exercise a part of your everyday activities. Walk or ride a bicycle when you go to school or work. Don't take the elevator. Instead, walk up and down the stairs. On weekends take long walks.

Eat the right foods. Start each day with a healthy breakfast. Find time to sit down and have a good lunch. These meals give you the energy you need to be active during the day. In the evening, eat a small dinner. Don't eat desserts like ice cream and cake. Don't go to fast-food restaurants very often. Instead, eat healthy food at home.

Yoga is good exercise, and it can help you relax. Get a good night's sleep. Men and women usually need seven to eight hours of sleep every night. Finally, have a medical checkup every year. It's your life. Be healthy!

What does the article tell you to do to live a healthy life? Choose the correct answer.

1. Exercise _____.
   A. thirty minutes every day
   B. thirty minutes a week
   C. thirty times a week
   D. three times a week

2. Eat _____.
   A. a big dinner
   B. ice cream and cake
   C. a healthy breakfast
   D. at fast-food restaurants

3. _____ once a year.
   A. Get a good night's sleep
   B. Go for a medical exam
   C. Take long walks
   D. Be healthy

4. It's important to _____.
   A. join a health club
   B. eat a good lunch
   C. take the elevator
   D. get 10 hours of sleep each night

5. Don't _____.
   A. relax
   B. have a medical checkup
   C. eat ice cream and cake
   D. ride a bicycle

6. _____ ISN'T a good way to exercise.
   A. Watching TV
   B. Jogging
   C. Swimming
   D. Walking

Choose the correct answer.

1. I _____ for the bus all morning.
  A. rode
  B. finished
  C. waited
  D. wanted

2. I _____ all afternoon, and now I have a terrible backache.
  A. sang
  B. sat
  C. talked
  D. rested

3. Amanda _____ her broken front steps.
  A. fixed
  B. worked
  C. served
  D. asked

4. I want to make an _____ to see the doctor.
  A. interview
  B. appointment
  C. afternoon
  D. application

5. Henry ate cookies all day, and now he has _____.
  A. a fever
  B. an earache
  C. a cold
  D. a stomachache

6. I _____ at work at 9:00 this morning.
  A. arrived
  B. showed
  C. rode
  D. turned

7. My son _____ his homework at 8:30.
  A. looked
  B. stayed
  C. finished
  D. watched

8. We _____ a video of our trip to Japan.
  A. asked
  B. showed
  C. sang
  D. rested

Mark your answers in the answer box.

Answers
1 (A) (B) (C) (D)
2 (A) (B) (C) (D)
3 (A) (B) (C) (D)
4 (A) (B) (C) (D)
5 (A) (B) (C) (D)
6 (A) (B) (C) (D)
7 (A) (B) (C) (D)
8 (A) (B) (C) (D)
9 (A) (B) (C) (D)
10 (A) (B) (C) (D)

Dr. Philip Johnson — Angela Ortega has an appointment on Fri., Sept. 9 At 9:30 A.M. _____ P.M.

Dr. Jennifer Wong — Appointment — Michael Silva — Day Mon. Date 9/5/19 Hour 3:45 P.M.

9. Michael Silva has an appointment _____.
  A. on May 11th
  B. with Dr. Johnson
  C. on Monday afternoon
  D. a half past nine

10. Angela is going to see Dr. Johnson _____.
  A. at 3:45
  B. on Monday
  C. in the afternoon
  D. in September

SKILLS CHECK ☑

Words:
☐ backache
☐ cold
☐ cough
☐ earache
☐ fever
☐ headache
☐ sore throat
☐ stomachache
☐ toothache

I can ask & answer:
☐ How are you?
☐ How do you feel today?
   I feel great!
   I feel fine.
   I feel okay.
   So-so.
   Not so good.
   I feel terrible.

☐ What's the matter?
☐ What seems to be the problem?
☐ What did you do yesterday?
☐ Do you want to make an appointment?
☐ Can you come in tomorrow at *two o'clock*?

I can:
☐ follow instructions during a medical exam
☐ read medical appointment cards
☐ read medicine labels & dosages
☐ identify ways to stay healthy

I can write about:
☐ a party I enjoyed
☐ food I ate and drank yesterday

16

Past Tense:
Yes/No Questions
Short Answers
Time Expressions

WH-Questions
More Irregular Verbs

- **Reporting Past Actions and Activities**
- **Giving Reasons**

- **Giving Excuses**
- **Job Applications**

VOCABULARY PREVIEW

1. got up
2. took a shower
3. had breakfast
4. read the newspaper
5. did exercises
6. ate lunch
7. drove to the supermarket
8. bought groceries
9. made dinner
10. wrote a letter
11. saw a movie
12. went to sleep

I Brushed My Teeth

I worked.	Did you work?
I didn't work.	Yes, I did.
(did not)	No, I didn't.

today	yesterday
this morning	yesterday morning
this afternoon	yesterday afternoon
this evening	yesterday evening
tonight	last night

Did you brush your hair this morning?

No, I didn't. I brushed my teeth.

1. Did he wash his windows yesterday morning?

2. Did she paint her kitchen this afternoon?

3. Did they study English last night?

4. Did you and your friends play tennis yesterday afternoon?

5. Did he bake a pie today?

6. Did you listen to the news this morning?

We Went to the Supermarket

I went.
I didn't go.
(did not)

Did you go?
Yes, I did.
No, I didn't.

Did you go to the bank this afternoon?

No, we didn't. We went to the supermarket.

go
went

take
took

1. Did you take the subway this morning?

have
had

2. Did he have a headache last night?

get
got

3. Did Wanda get up at 9:00 this morning?

make
made

4. Did your children make dinner today?

buy
bought

5. Did Michael buy a car yesterday?

do
did

6. Did they do their homework last night?

write
wrote

7. Did Tommy write to his girlfriend this week?

read
read

8. Did you read the newspaper this afternoon?

TALK ABOUT IT! *What Did They Do Yesterday?*

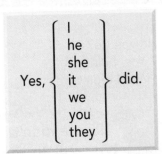

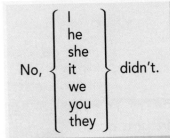

Betty fixed her car yesterday morning.
She washed her windows yesterday afternoon.
She listened to music last night.

Bob read the newspaper yesterday morning.
He went to the library yesterday afternoon.
He wrote letters last night.

Nick and Nancy went to the supermarket
   yesterday morning.
They bought a new car yesterday afternoon.
They cleaned their apartment last night.

Jennifer did her exercises yesterday
   morning.
She planted flowers yesterday afternoon.
She took a bath last night.

**Using these models, talk about the people
above with other students in your class.**

A. Did *Betty fix her car yesterday morning?*

B. Yes, *she* did.

A. Did *Bob go to the library last night?*

B. No, *he* didn't. *He went to the library
yesterday afternoon.*

How About You?

What did you do yesterday
   morning?
What did you do yesterday
   afternoon?
What did you do last night?

152

Giving an Excuse

A. I'm sorry I'm late. *I missed the bus.*
B. I see.

Practice the interactions on this page.
Apologize and give excuses.

INTERACTIONS

A. I'm sorry I'm late. _____.
B. I see.

I missed the _____.
(bus / train . . .)

I had a _____ this morning.
(headache / stomachache / . . .)

I had to go to the _____.
(doctor / dentist / . . .)

I forgot* my _____ and had to
go back home and get it.
(briefcase / backpack / . . .)

A thief stole* my _____.
(bicycle / car / . . .)

THINK ABOUT IT! *Good Excuses & Bad Excuses*

The people above have good excuses. Here are some BAD excuses:

I got up late.

I had a big breakfast today.

I met* a friend on the way to work/school.

Discuss with other students: What are some good excuses? What are some bad excuses? Why are these excuses good or bad?

* forget – forgot   steal – stole   meet – met

LATE FOR WORK

Victor usually gets up at 7 A.M. He does his morning exercises for twenty minutes, he takes a long shower, he has a big breakfast, and he leaves for work at 8:00. He usually drives his car to work and gets there at 8:30.

This morning, however, he didn't get up at 7 A.M. He got up at 6:30. He didn't do his morning exercises for twenty minutes. He did them for only five minutes. He didn't take a long shower. He took a very quick shower. He didn't have a big breakfast. He had a very small breakfast. He didn't leave for work at 8:00. He left for work at 7:00.

Victor didn't drive his car to work this morning. He drove it to the repair shop. Then he walked a mile to the train station, and he waited for the train for fifteen minutes. After he got off the train, he walked half a mile to his office.

Even though Victor got up early and rushed out of the house this morning, he didn't get to work on time. He got there forty-five minutes late. When his supervisor saw him, she got angry and she shouted at him for five minutes. Poor Victor! He really tried to get to work on time this morning.

✔ **READING** *CHECK-UP*

WHAT'S THE ANSWER?

1. Did Victor get up at 7 A.M. today?
2. What time did he get up?
3. Did he leave for work at 8:00 this morning?
4. What time did he leave for work?
5. Did he drive his car to the repair shop today?

6. How did he get to the train station?
7. Did Victor get to work on time?
8. Did his supervisor get angry at him?
9. What did she do?

WHICH IS CORRECT?

1. Victor (got up   didn't get up) at 6:30 A.M. this morning.
2. He (did   didn't do) his exercises for twenty minutes today.
3. He (took   didn't take) a very quick shower this morning.
4. He (left   didn't leave) for work at 8:00 this morning.
5. He (took   didn't take) the train to work today.
6. He (got   didn't get) to work on time this morning.

LISTENING

Listen and put a check next to all the things these people did today.

Carla's Day
— got up early
— got up late
— took a bath
— took a shower
— had breakfast
— had lunch
— took the subway
— took the bus
— met her brother
— met her mother
— had dinner
— made dinner
— saw a movie
— saw a play

Brian's Day
— fixed his car
— fixed his bicycle
— cleaned his garage
— cleaned his yard
— painted his bedroom
— planted flowers
— washed his windows
— watched TV
— read the newspaper
— read a magazine
— rode his bicycle
— wrote to his brother
— took a shower
— took a bath

COMPLETE THE STORY

Complete the story with the correct forms of the verbs.

buy	eat	get	go	make	see	sit	take

SHIRLEY'S DAY OFF

Shirley enjoyed her day off yesterday. She
_____¹ up late, _____² jogging in the park,
_____³ a long shower, and _____⁴ a big breakfast.
In the afternoon, she _____⁵ a movie with her sister.
Then she _____⁶ groceries at the supermarket, and
she _____⁷ a big dinner for her parents. After dinner,
Shirley and her parents _____⁸ in the living room and
talked. Shirley had a very nice day off yesterday.

How About You?

Tell about a day off YOU enjoyed. What did you do in the morning? in the afternoon? in the evening?

PRONUNCIATION *Did you*

Listen. Then say it.

Did you go to the bank?

Did you brush your hair?

Did you listen to the news?

Did you take the subway?

Say it. Then listen.

Did you go to the supermarket?

Did you play tennis?

Did you read the newspaper?

Did you see a movie?

SIDE *by* SIDE JOURNAL

What did you do yesterday? Write in your journal about all the things you did.

GRAMMAR FOCUS

PAST TENSE: YES/NO QUESTIONS

Did	I he she it we you they	work?

SHORT ANSWERS

Yes,	I he she it we you they	did.

No,	I he she it we you they	didn't.

PAST TENSE: WH-QUESTIONS

What did	I he she it we you they	do?

TIME EXPRESSIONS

Did you study English	yesterday? yesterday morning? yesterday afternoon? yesterday evening? last night?

Complete the conversations with the correct forms of these verbs.

do	go	have	listen	study	take	wash	watch

1. A. Did you _____ the bus this morning?
   B. No, I didn't. I _____ the train.

2. A. Did your children _____ last night?
   B. Yes, they did. They _____ English.

3. A. Did you _____ your windows yesterday?
   B. No, we didn't. We _____ our car.

4. A. Did you _____ to the bank this morning?
   B. No, I didn't. I _____ to the post office.

5. A. Did you _____ a stomachache yesterday?
   B. Yes, I _____. I also _____ a headache.

6. A. _____ Stella _____ TV last night?
   B. No, she didn't. She _____ to music.

1 READING A JOB APPLICATION

Look at this section of Linda Wang's job application and complete the story.

EDUCATION

Name of School	Location	Dates Attended
High School: Laguna Beach High School	Laguna Beach, CA	9/09 – 6/13
College: Mission College	Los Angeles, CA	9/13 – 6/15
Other: Liberty Auto Mechanics Institute	Los Angeles, CA	9/15 – 6/16

EMPLOYMENT RECORD (LIST MOST RECENT EMPLOYMENT FIRST)

Date	Name & Address of Employer	Position	Salary	Name of Supervisor	Reason for Leaving
From: 7/16 To: 2/18	All-Star Repair Shop 1240 Carter Ave., Los Angeles, CA	mechanic	$550/wk	Don Clementi	moved to Dallas
From: 7/13 To: 7/15	Ellen's Family Restaurant 420 West Third St., Los Angeles, CA	dishwasher	$8.00/hr	Ellen Miller	went back to school

Linda went to high school from <u>September</u>[1] 2009 to <u>June</u>[2] 2013. She went to college from September _____[3] to June _____[4]. She studied at Liberty Auto Mechanics Institute for ten _____[5]. She worked as a _____[6] at Ellen's Family Restaurant for _____[7] years. Her salary there was _____[8] an hour. After that, she worked as a _____[9] at an auto repair shop in _____[10]. She made $550 a _____[11]. Why did she leave her last job? Because she moved to _____[12].

2 TEAMWORK YOUR EDUCATION & EMPLOYMENT RECORD

Practice a job interview with a classmate. Ask each other these questions.

1. Did you go to high school? Where? When?

2. Did you go to college or another school? Where? When?

3. Are you going to school now? What are you studying?

4. Are you working now? Where? What's your job? When did you start to work there?

5. Where did you work before that? How long? Why did you leave that job?

3 WRITING FILL OUT THE JOB APPLICATION FORM

NAME _____ SOC. SEC. NO. _____ TEL. _____
        Last   First

EDUCATION

Name of School	Location	Dates Attended
High School:		
College:		
Other:		

EMPLOYMENT RECORD (LIST MOST RECENT EMPLOYMENT FIRST)

Date	Name & Address of Employer	Position	Salary	Name of Supervisor	Reason for Leaving
From: To:					
From: To:					

Choose the correct answer.

1. Susan arrived late for work because she missed the _____.
   A. apartment
   B. office
   C. bus
   D. newspaper

2. I met a _____ on the way to work today.
   A. bus
   B. friend
   C. bank
   D. book

3. After he _____ the train, Omar walked to his office.
   A. got off
   B. got up
   C. had
   D. went

4. I _____ my house at 7:45 to go to school.
   A. arrived
   B. took
   C. saw
   D. left

5. Roger didn't get to the meeting on time. He got there _____ late.
   A. a mile
   B. an hour
   C. half a mile
   D. a morning

6. Pamela rode _____ this morning.
   A. her bicycle
   B. a letter
   C. a magazine
   D. the newspaper

7. Justin forgot his _____ and had to go back home to get it.
   A. office
   B. bus
   C. house
   D. briefcase

8. After work today, I _____ some groceries.
   A. ate
   B. had
   C. bought
   D. made

Mark your answers in the answer box.

Answers				
1	Ⓐ	Ⓑ	Ⓒ	Ⓓ
2	Ⓐ	Ⓑ	Ⓒ	Ⓓ
3	Ⓐ	Ⓑ	Ⓒ	Ⓓ
4	Ⓐ	Ⓑ	Ⓒ	Ⓓ
5	Ⓐ	Ⓑ	Ⓒ	Ⓓ
6	Ⓐ	Ⓑ	Ⓒ	Ⓓ
7	Ⓐ	Ⓑ	Ⓒ	Ⓓ
8	Ⓐ	Ⓑ	Ⓒ	Ⓓ
9	Ⓐ	Ⓑ	Ⓒ	Ⓓ
10	Ⓐ	Ⓑ	Ⓒ	Ⓓ

Date From–To	Employer	Position	Salary
9/06–12/07	Ajax Department Store 199 Ocean Ave., Miami, FL	salesperson	$750/wk
10/04–8/06	Stop 'n Save Supermarket 110 Bay Street, Houston, TX	cashier	$10.00/hr

Eduardo filled out a job application form. Look at his Employment Record. Choose the correct answer.

9. Eduardo worked as a cashier _____.
   A. in Miami
   B. in 2007
   C. at Ajax Department Store
   D. from 2004 to 2006

10. Eduardo _____ in 2007.
    A. made $10.00 an hour
    B. worked in Miami
    C. worked in a supermarket
    D. made $750 a month

SKILLS CHECK ✔

Words:
- ☐ buy – bought
- ☐ do – did
- ☐ drive – drove
- ☐ eat – ate
- ☐ forget – forgot
- ☐ get – got
- ☐ go – went
- ☐ have – had

- ☐ leave – left
- ☐ make – made
- ☐ meet – met
- ☐ read – read
- ☐ see – saw
- ☐ steal – stole
- ☐ take – took
- ☐ write – wrote

- ☐ this afternoon
- ☐ this evening
- ☐ tonight
- ☐ yesterday
- ☐ yesterday morning
- ☐ yesterday afternoon
- ☐ yesterday evening
- ☐ today
- ☐ this morning
- ☐ last night

I can ask & answer:
- ☐ Did you *go to the bank*? Yes, I did. No, I didn't.
- ☐ Did you go to high school?/ college? Where? When?
- ☐ Are you going to school now?
- ☐ What are you studying?
- ☐ Are you working now? Where?
- ☐ What's your job?

- ☐ When did you start to work there?
- ☐ Where did you work before that? How long?
- ☐ Why did you leave that job?

I can fill out a job application form:
- ☐ education
- ☐ employment record

I can write about:
- ☐ what I did yesterday

To Be: Past Tense

- **Television Commercials**
- **Describing Physical States and Emotions**
- **Biographies and Autobiographies**
- **Basic Foods and Food Groups**

- **Making a Shopping List**
- **Ordering a Meal**
- **Reading a Simple Menu**
- **Supermarket Ads**
- **Food Labels**

VOCABULARY PREVIEW

  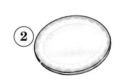  

1. sad – happy
2. clean – dirty
3. heavy – thin
4. hungry – full
5. sick – healthy
6. tiny – enormous
7. dull – shiny
8. comfortable – uncomfortable
9. tired – energetic

PRESTO Commercials

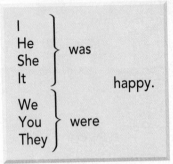

I			
He			
She	was		
It		happy.	
We			
You	were		
They			

Before our family bought PRESTO Vitamins, we were always tired.
I was tired.
My wife was tired.
My children were tired, too.
Now we're energetic, because WE bought PRESTO Vitamins. How about you?

Before our family bought _____, we were always _____.
I was _____.
My wife/husband was _____.
My children were _____, too.
Now we're _____ because WE bought _____. How about you?

Using the above script, prepare commercials for these other fine PRESTO products.

1. *sad* *happy*

2. *hungry* *full*

3. *dirty* *clean*

4. *sick* *healthy*

5. *heavy* *thin*

6. _____ _____

Before I Bought PRESTO Shampoo

Before I bought PRESTO Shampoo, my hair **was** always dirty. Now **it's** clean!

1. Before we bought PRESTO Toothpaste, our teeth _____ yellow. Now _____ white!

2. Before we bought PRESTO Paint, our house _____ ugly. Now _____ beautiful!

3. Before I bought a PRESTO armchair, I _____ uncomfortable. Now _____ very comfortable!

4. Before we bought PRESTO Dog Food, our dog _____ tiny. Now _____ enormous!

5. Before I bought PRESTO Window Cleaner, my windows _____ dirty. Now _____ clean!

6. Before we bought PRESTO Floor Wax, our kitchen floor _____ dull. Now _____ shiny!

How to Say It!

Recommending Products

A. Can you recommend a good *toothpaste*?
B. Yes. I recommend PRESTO *Toothpaste*. It's very good.
A. Thanks for the recommendation.

Practice conversations with other students. Make recommendations about real products.

Were You at the Ballgame Last Night?

| I He She It | wasn't (was not) |
| We You They | weren't (were not) |

A. Were you at the ballgame last night?

B. No, I wasn't. I was at the movies.

1. Was Albert happy yesterday?

2. Were they at home this morning?

3. Was it cold yesterday?

4. Was your grandfather a doctor?

5. Was I a quiet baby?

6. Were you at home last weekend?

7. Was Gloria on time for her plane?

8. Were your children late for the school bus?

9. Was the food good at the restaurant?

Did You Sleep Well Last Night?

| I He She We You They | did / didn't | I He She | was / wasn't |
| | | We You They | were / weren't |

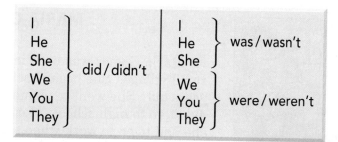

A. Did you sleep well last night?
B. Yes, I did. I was tired.

A. Did Roger sleep well last night?
B. No, he didn't. He wasn't tired.

1. Did Frank have a big breakfast today?
Yes, _____. _____ hungry.

2. Did Thelma have a big breakfast today?
No, _____. _____ hungry.

3. Did Mr. Chen go to the doctor yesterday?
Yes, _____. _____ sick.

4. Did Mrs. Chen go to the doctor yesterday?
No, _____. _____ sick.

5. Did Billy finish his milk?
Yes, _____. _____ thirsty.

6. Did Katie finish her milk?
No, _____. _____ thirsty.

7. Did Sonia miss the train?
Yes, _____. _____ late.

8. Did Stuart miss the train?
No , _____. _____ late.

161

READING

MARIA GOMEZ

Maria Gomez was born in Peru. She grew* up in a small village. She began* school when she was six years old. She went to elementary school, but she didn't go to high school. Her family was very poor, and she had to go to work when she was thirteen years old. She worked on an assembly line in a shoe factory.

When Maria was seventeen years old, her family moved to the United States. First they lived in Los Angeles, and then they moved to San Francisco. When Maria arrived in the United States, she wasn't very happy. She missed her friends back in Peru, and she didn't speak one word of English. She began to study English at night, and she worked in a factory during the day.

Maria studied very hard. She learned English, and she got a good job as a secretary. Maria still studies at night, but now she studies advertising at a business school. She wants to work for an advertising company some day and write commercials.

Maria still misses her friends back home, but she communicates with them very often over the Internet. She's very happy now, and she's looking forward to an exciting future.

✔ READING *CHECK-UP*

WHAT'S THE ANSWER?

1. Where was Maria born?
2. Did she grow up in a large city?
3. When did she begin school?
4. What happened when Maria was seventeen years old?
5. Why was Maria unhappy when she arrived in the United States?
6. What is Maria's occupation?
7. What does she want to do in the future?
8. How does Maria communicate with her friends back home?

* grow – grew   begin – began

WHAT'S THE ORDER?

Put these sentences in the correct order based on the story.

____ Maria's family moved to the United States.
____ Maria studies advertising now.
_1_ Maria grew up in a small village.
____ Maria's family moved to San Francisco.
____ Maria worked in a shoe factory.
____ Maria began to study English at night.
____ Maria went to elementary school.
____ Maria's family lived in Los Angeles.
____ Maria got a job as a secretary.

● 162

LISTENING

Listen and choose the correct answer.

1. a. They were sick.
   b. They're sick now.
2. a. Their old chairs were comfortable.
   b. Their new chairs are comfortable.
3. a. Lucy was very thirsty.
   b. Lucy wasn't thirsty.
4. a. Fred was on time this morning.
   b. Fred wasn't on time this morning.
5. a. Peter and Mary were at work yesterday.
   b. Peter and Mary are at work today.
6. a. Their kitchen floor wasn't shiny.
   b. Their kitchen floor is dull now.

Autobiography

Tell a story about yourself. In your story, answer questions such as:

Where were you born?
Where did you grow up?
Where did you go to school?
What did you study?
When did you move? Where?

ON YOUR OWN *Do You Remember Your Childhood?*

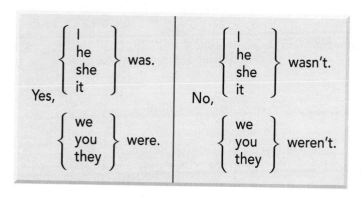

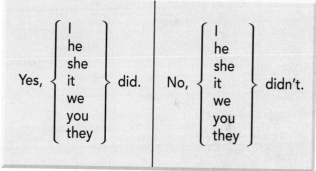

Answer these questions and then ask other students in your class.

1. What did you look like?
   Were you tall? thin? pretty? handsome? cute?
   Did you have curly hair? straight hair? long hair?
   Did you have dimples? freckles?

2. Did you have many friends?
   What did you do with your friends?
   What games did you play?

3. Did you like school?
   Who was your favorite teacher? Why?
   What was your favorite subject? Why?

4. What did you do in your spare time?
   Did you have a hobby?
   Did you play sports?

5. Who was your favorite hero?

PRONUNCIATION   Intonation of Yes/No Questions and WH-Questions

Listen. Then say it.

Were you tall?

Did you have long hair?

What did you look like?

Who was your favorite teacher?

Say it. Then listen.

Were you short?

Did you have freckles?

Where did you grow up?

When did you move?

SIDE by SIDE JOURNAL

Write in your journal about your childhood. What did you look like? What did you do with your friends? Did you like school? What did you do in your spare time?

GRAMMAR FOCUS

To Be: Past Tense

I He She It	was	happy.
We You They	were	

I He She It	wasn't	tired.
We You They	weren't	

Was	I he she it	late?
Were	we you they	

Yes,	I he she it	was.
	we you they	were.

No,	I he she it	wasn't.
	we you they	weren't.

Complete the sentences.

1. A. _____ it hot yesterday?
   B. Yes, it _____. It _____ very hot.

2. A. _____ you at home yesterday evening?
   B. No, we _____. We _____ at the movies.

3. A. _____ George on time for work today?
   B. No, he _____. He _____ late.

4. A. _____ your neighbors noisy last night?
   B. Yes, they _____. They _____ very noisy all night.

5. A. _____ your wife at the ballgame last night?
   B. Yes, _____ _____. She _____ next to me.

6. A. _____ you at work last night?
   B. No, _____ _____. I _____ at the laundromat.

7. A. _____ your homework difficult today?
   B. No, _____ _____. It _____ very easy.

8. A. _____ I a healthy baby?
   B. Yes, _____ _____. You _____ a very healthy baby.

LIFE SKILLS
• Basic foods & food groups
• Making a shopping list

1 CONVERSATION BASIC FOODS

Look at the foods and practice conversations.

A. What do we need at the supermarket?
B. We need apples.

1. apple   **2.** banana   **3.** carrot

4. cookie   **5.** egg   **6.** onion   **7.** orange   **8.** peach   **9.** potato   **10.** tomato

A. What do we need at the supermarket?
B. We need bread.

1. bread   **2.** butter   **3.** cereal   **4.** cheese

5. ice cream   **6.** lettuce   **7.** milk   **8.** soda   **9.** soup   **10.** sugar

2 CATEGORIES FOOD GROUPS

Write the foods you see in each supermarket section.

Fruits | Vegetables | Baked Goods | Dairy

bananas

3 WRITING A SHOPPING LIST

What do you need at the supermarket? Make a list. Compare lists with other students.

4 CONVERSATION ORDERING A MEAL

Practice conversations with a classmate. Look at the menu to find the prices.

A. Are you ready to order?

B. Yes. I'd like a hamburger and large fries, please.

A. Do you want anything to drink?

B. Yes. I'd like a small coffee.

A. That's a hamburger, large fries, and a small coffee. Is that for here or to go?

B. { For here.
        To go.

A. Okay. That comes to four dollars and seventy-five cents.

HAMBURGER	1.75
CHEESEBURGER	2.00
CHICKEN SANDWICH	3.50
TACO	1.50
BURRITO	2.50

FRIES	
SMALL / LARGE	1.50 / 2.00
BEANS	1.50
RICE	1.50
SALAD	1.75

SOFT DRINK / LEMONADE	
S / M / L	1.00 / 1.50 / 2.00
MILK	1.25
COFFEE	
S / M / L	1.00 / 1.25 / 1.50

1. a cheeseburger
small fries
a medium soft drink

2. a chicken sandwich
a salad
milk

3. two tacos
beans
a large lemonade

4. a burrito
rice
a small soft drink

THINK & SHARE What are some good things and bad things about fast-food restaurants? Discuss with your classmates.

READING A SUPERMARKET AD

Look at the supermarket ad and answer the questions.

1. You can buy _____ for $4.00.
   A. a quart of orange juice
   B. a gallon of milk
   C. a pound of green beans
   D. a can of peas

2. The price of Wilson Salt is
   _____.
   A. 1 for $3.00
   B. 3 for $1.00
   C. 3 for $3.00
   D. $9.00

3. Two boxes of cereal cost
   _____.
   A. $2.00
   B. $3.50
   C. $7.00
   D. $14.00

4. Four pounds of green
   beans cost _____.
   A. $1.50
   B. $3.00
   C. $4.00
   D. $6.00

5. _____ cost $10.00.
   A. Ten cans of peas
   B. Three pints of ice cream
   C. Four boxes of cereal
   D. Three gallons of milk

6. Two pints of Bob and Joe's
   ice cream cost _____.
   A. $7.00
   B. $3.50
   C. $2.00
   D. $1.00

COMPARE & SHARE Bring a supermarket ad to class. Compare ads with other students. What's the best place to buy different products?

READING FOOD LABELS

Look at the food labels and answer the questions.

Bart's Vegetable Soup

Shop & Save
Vegetable Soup

1. What four ingredients do both soups have?

   _____

2. Which soup has peas?

   _____

3. Which soup doesn't have sugar?

   _____

TEAMWORK Bring a can or package of your favorite food to class (or just the food label). Walk around the room and compare foods and ingredients with other students. Which foods have water? sugar? other ingredients?

Choose the correct answer.

1. I ate a big breakfast today because I was very ____.
- A. dull
- B. full
- C. hungry
- D. shiny

2. When I was in high school, my favorite subject was ____.
- A. basketball
- B. school
- C. my teacher
- D. English

3. We didn't like the restaurant because the food ____.
- A. was bad
- B. was sad
- C. wasn't bad
- D. was quiet

4. My best friend moved to South America. I really ____ her.
- A. look forward to
- B. meet
- C. miss
- D. see

5. I usually ____ with my friends over the Internet.
- A. grow up
- B. go
- C. see
- D. communicate

6. We cleaned our living room windows because ____.
- A. they were enormous
- B. they were dirty
- C. they weren't dirty
- D. they were clean

Answers

1	Ⓐ	Ⓑ	Ⓒ	Ⓓ
2	Ⓐ	Ⓑ	Ⓒ	Ⓓ
3	Ⓐ	Ⓑ	Ⓒ	Ⓓ
4	Ⓐ	Ⓑ	Ⓒ	Ⓓ
5	Ⓐ	Ⓑ	Ⓒ	Ⓓ
6	Ⓐ	Ⓑ	Ⓒ	Ⓓ
7	Ⓐ	Ⓑ	Ⓒ	Ⓓ
8	Ⓐ	Ⓑ	Ⓒ	Ⓓ
9	Ⓐ	Ⓑ	Ⓒ	Ⓓ
10	Ⓐ	Ⓑ	Ⓒ	Ⓓ

Look at the supermarket ad. Choose the correct answer.

7. The price of ____ is $6.00.
- A. a pound of cheese
- B. a quart of ice cream
- C. a gallon of milk
- D. a box of cookies

8. Two pounds of cheese cost ____.
- A. $2.00
- B. $6.00
- C. $8.00
- D. $12.00

9. ____ cost $14.00.
- A. Eight boxes of cookies
- B. Four boxes of cookies
- C. Two boxes of cookies
- D. One box of cookies

10. Two quarts of ice cream cost ____.
- A. $1.00
- B. $2.50
- C. $5.00
- D. $10.00

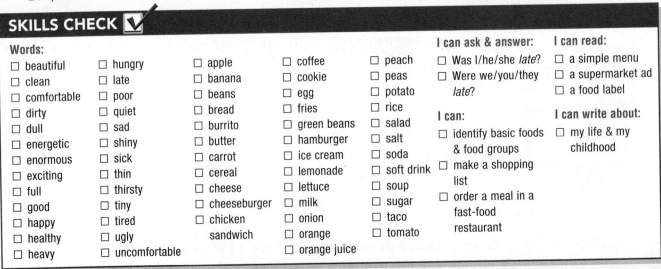

SHOP & SAVE SUPERMARKET
On Sale This Week!

Cheese $6 PER POUND

$4.00 ONE GALLON — SHOP & SAVE MILK

BEST BAKERY VANILLA COOKIES — 2 for $7

POLLY'S ICE CREAM $5.00 1 QUART — Buy 1. Get 1 free.

SKILLS CHECK ✓

Words:

☐ beautiful	☐ hungry	☐ apple	☐ coffee	☐ peach
☐ clean	☐ late	☐ banana	☐ cookie	☐ peas
☐ comfortable	☐ poor	☐ beans	☐ egg	☐ potato
☐ dirty	☐ quiet	☐ bread	☐ fries	☐ rice
☐ dull	☐ sad	☐ burrito	☐ green beans	☐ salad
☐ energetic	☐ shiny	☐ butter	☐ hamburger	☐ salt
☐ enormous	☐ sick	☐ carrot	☐ ice cream	☐ soda
☐ exciting	☐ thin	☐ cereal	☐ lemonade	☐ soft drink
☐ full	☐ thirsty	☐ cheese	☐ lettuce	☐ soup
☐ good	☐ tiny	☐ cheeseburger	☐ milk	☐ sugar
☐ happy	☐ tired	☐ chicken sandwich	☐ onion	☐ taco
☐ healthy	☐ ugly		☐ orange	☐ tomato
☐ heavy	☐ uncomfortable		☐ orange juice	

I can ask & answer:
- ☐ Was I/he/she *late*?
- ☐ Were we/you/they *late*?

I can:
- ☐ identify basic foods & food groups
- ☐ make a shopping list
- ☐ order a meal in a fast-food restaurant

I can read:
- ☐ a simple menu
- ☐ a supermarket ad
- ☐ a food label

I can write about:
- ☐ my life & my childhood

Advertisements

How do advertisers sell their products?

Advertisements are everywhere! They are on television, on the radio, and in newspapers and magazines. Ads are also on billboards, on buses and trains, and even in movie theaters. People get advertisements in their mail. There are also a lot of advertisements on the Internet.

Advertisements are sometimes in unusual places—in elevators, on top of taxis, and in public bathrooms. People sometimes carry signs with ads on the street, and small airplanes sometimes carry signs in the sky. Advertisers are always looking for new places for their ads.

FACT FILE

Countries Where Advertisers Spend the Most Money

United States	Brazil
Japan	Italy
United Kingdom	Australia
Germany	Canada
France	Korea

LISTENING

And Now a Word From Our Sponsors!

_d_	① Dazzle		a.	floor wax
___	② Shiny-Time		b.	dog shampoo
___	③ Energy Plus		c.	throat lozenges
___	④ Lucky Lemon Drops		d.	toothpaste
___	⑤ K-9 Shine		e.	vitamins

BUILD YOUR VOCABULARY!

Opposites

 dark   light

 fancy   plain

 fast   slow

 good   bad

 heavy   light

 high   low

 long   short

 neat   messy

 open   closed

 wet   dry

Shopping

People around the world buy things in different ways.

This person is shopping in a store.

These people are buying things at an outdoor market.

This person is ordering something from a catalog over the telephone.

This person is buying something from a home shopping channel on TV.

These people are looking for things at a yard sale.

This person is shopping on the Internet.

What are the ways people buy things in different countries you know?

Global Exchange

TedG: I had a very busy day today. I got up at 6:30, took a shower, ate breakfast, and went to school. In my English class this morning, I read a long story, and I wrote my autobiography. I didn't have time for lunch because I had to meet with my Spanish teacher. After I met with her, I went to math class. We had a big test today. It was very difficult! After school, I went to a basketball game. Then I went home, did some homework, had dinner, and did some more homework. How about you? What did you do today?

Send a message to a keypal. Tell about what you did today.

What Are They Saying?

SHOPPING with COUPONS

The Lopez family is at the supermarket. They're paying the cashier for their groceries. They have ten shopping bags of food for their family of five. The groceries they bought are expensive, but Ramona Lopez is smiling as she gives her money to the cashier. Why? Because she used coupons and saved more than $70!

In fact, each month the Lopez family saves hundreds of dollars with coupons. Every week Ramona Lopez cuts coupons from the newspaper. Sometimes she buys several newspapers because each one has different coupons. She also looks on her computer and finds coupons on the Internet. There are some websites with hundreds of coupons. She only prints the coupons for grocery items she needs and puts those coupons in a special notebook.

According to Lopez, "There are coupons for everything! Just find coupons for your favorite products. You can spend a lot of money when you buy things you don't need. Before you go to the supermarket, make a grocery list and take coupons for just the items on your list."

According to some shoppers, a person can save 50% on groceries with coupons. And it takes only about 30 minutes a week. Here are some tips about coupons and smart grocery shopping.

- Know your favorite store. When does that store have newspaper coupons? What day of the week are different products on sale?
- Check supermarket advertising in the Sunday newspaper. There are usually a lot of coupons on Sunday.
- Find coupons on the Internet. Only print the ones you need.
- Look at prices in several stores. Buy some things in one store and other things in a different store. You can save money when you shop at several supermarkets.
- Use a shopping list, and don't buy things that aren't on your list!

Ramona Lopez has some important advice for shoppers: "Never shop when you're hungry. People always buy more groceries when they're hungry!"

1. Ramona Lopez finds coupons _____.
   - (A) in stores
   - (B) in shopping bags
   - (C) in stores and in newspapers
   - (D) in newspapers and on the Internet

2. Every month, the Lopez family saves _____ on groceries.
   - (A) 50%
   - (B) $70.00
   - (C) hundreds of dollars
   - (D) $100.00

3. According to the passage, shoppers should _____.
   - (A) take all their coupons each time they go to the supermarket
   - (B) make a list and take coupons for just those items
   - (C) print all the coupons they find on the Internet
   - (D) always shop in the same stores

4. There are usually a lot of coupons _____.
   - (A) in Sunday newspapers
   - (B) in notebooks
   - (C) on shopping lists
   - (D) in shopping bags

5. When shoppers are hungry, they _____.
   - (A) buy only the food they need
   - (B) forget their lists
   - (C) don't use their coupons
   - (D) buy more groceries

6. This passage is about _____.
   - (A) the Lopez family
   - (B) grocery shopping
   - (C) how to save money with coupons
   - (D) coupons people find on the Internet

Your Consumer Knowledge
1. Do you use coupons? Why or why not?
2. What advice is new for you in this passage?

Hernan is preparing to write a story with the title "My Friend and I." He's going to write about how he and his friend Julio are the same and how they are different. He's brainstorming ideas for the story and writing the ideas in a Venn diagram. The diagram has three sections: one for information only about the friend, one for information only about Hernan, and a middle section for information about both of them.

Julio

from Ecuador
grew up in large city
tall
favorite subject in
  school—science
wife—librarian
two sons
auto technical school in
  U.S.
auto mechanic
favorite music—folk
favorite TV programs—
  game shows

Julio and I

language—Spanish
short, black hair
childhood—many
  friends
finished high school in
  native country
married
favorite sport—soccer
favorite movies—
  comedies

Me

from the Dominican
  Republic
grew up in small village
short
favorite subject in
  school—math
wife—music teacher
a son and a daughter
community college in
  U.S.
hospital lab technician
favorite music—rock
favorite TV programs—
  news programs

Brainstorm and write a story about yourself and a friend.

Pre-write: Make a Venn diagram. List information to show how you and your friend are the same and how you and your friend are different. Include information about your country, first language, physical description, childhood, family, education, work, and sports, music, TV shows, and other things you like.

Organize your ideas: Put together the information about your country, physical description, language, and childhood. This can be the first paragraph of your story. Put together the information about your education and your work. This can be your second paragraph. Put together the information about sports, music, TV shows, and other things you like. This can be your third paragraph.

Write a first draft: Write a story about you and your friend. Write three paragraphs with the ideas you organized. Indent the first line of each paragraph. Use this title: My Friend and I.

Listening Scripts

Unit 1 – Page 5

Listen and choose the correct answer.

1. A. What's your name?
   B. Mary Black.
2. A. What's your address?
   B. Two sixty-five Main Street.
3. A. What's your apartment number?
   B. Five C.
4. A. What's your telephone number?
   B. Two five nine – four oh eight seven.
5. A. What's your social security number?
   B. Oh three two – eight nine – six one seven nine.
6. A. What's your e-mail address?
   B. maryb-at-worldnet-dot-com.

Unit 2 – Page 15

WHAT'S THE WORD?

Listen and choose the correct answer.

1. Mr. and Mrs. Lee are in the park.
2. Jim is in the hospital.
3. She's in the living room.
4. He's in the kitchen.
5. They're in the basement.
6. We're in the yard.

WHERE ARE THEY?

Listen and choose the correct place.

1. A. Where's David?
   B. He's in the living room.
2. A. Where's Patty?
   B. She's in the bedroom.
3. A. Where are Mr. and Mrs. Kim?
   B. They're in the yard.
4. A. Where are you?
   B. I'm in the bathroom.
5. A. Where's the telephone book?
   B. It's in the kitchen.
6. A. Where are you and John?
   B. We're in the basement.

Unit 3 – Page 23

Listen and choose the correct answer.

1. What are you doing?
2. What's Mr. Carter doing?
3. What's Ms. Miller doing?
4. What are Jim and Jane doing?
5. What are you and Peter doing?
6. What am I doing?

Side by Side Gazette – Page 26

Listen to the messages on Bob's machine. Match the messages.

You have seven messages.

Message Number One: "Hello. I'm calling for Robert White. This is Henry Drake. Mr. White, please call me at 427-9168. That's 427-9168. Thank you." [*beep*]

Message Number Two: "Hi, Bob! It's Patty. How are you? Call me!" [*beep*]

Message Number Three: "Bob? Hi. This is Kevin Carter from your guitar class. My phone number is 298-4577." [*beep*]

Message Number Four: "Mr. White? This is Linda Lee, from the social security office. Please call me. My telephone number is 969-0159." [*beep*]

Message Number Five: "Hello, Bob? This is Jim. I'm in the park. We're playing baseball. Call me, okay? My cell phone number is 682-4630." [*beep*]

Message Number Six: "Hello. Mr. White? This is Mrs. Lane on River Street. Your dog is in my yard. Call me at 731-0248." [*beep*]

Message Number Seven: "Hello, Bob. This is Dad. I'm at home. I'm reading the newspaper. Mom is planting flowers in the yard. It's a beautiful day. Where are you? What are you doing? Call us." [*beep*]

Unit 4 – Page 33

Listen and choose the correct answer.

1. What are you eating?
2. What is she reading?
3. What is he playing?
4. What are they painting?
5. What are you watching?
6. What is he washing?

Unit 5 – Page 43

WHAT'S THE ANSWER?

Listen and choose the correct answer.

1. Tell me about your apartment.
2. Tell me about your new car.
3. Tell me about your neighbors.
4. How's the weather?
5. Tell me about your hotel.
6. How's the food at the restaurant?

TRUE OR FALSE?

Listen to the conversation. Then answer True or False.

A. Hello.
B. Hello. Is this Betty?
A. Yes, it is.
B. Hi, Betty. This is Louise. I'm calling from Mud Beach.
A. From Mud Beach?
B. Yes. I'm on vacation in Mud Beach for a few days.
A. How's the weather in Mud Beach?
B. It's terrible! It's cold, and it's cloudy.
A. Cold and cloudy? What a shame! How's the hotel?
B. The hotel is terrible! It's old, it's noisy, and the rooms are very small.
A. I'm sorry to hear that. Tell me about the restaurants.
B. The restaurants in Mud Beach are expensive, and the food isn't very good. In fact, I'm having problems with my stomach.
A. What a shame! So, Louise, what are you doing?
B. I'm sitting in my room, and I'm watching TV. I'm not having a very good time.
A. I'm sorry to hear that.

Unit 6 – Page 51

QUIET OR NOISY?

Listen to the sentence. Are the people quiet or noisy?

1. He's listening to loud music.
2. She's reading.
3. He's sleeping.
4. The band is playing.
5. Everybody is singing and dancing.
6. He's studying.

WHAT DO YOU HEAR?

Listen to the sound. What do you hear? Choose the correct answer.

1. [Sound: singing]
2. [Sound: crying]

3. [Sound: vacuuming]
4. [Sound: laughing]
5. [Sound: drums]

Side by Side Gazette – Page 54

Listen to the weather reports. Match the weather and the cities.

This is Robby T. with the weather report from WXBC. It's a hot day in Honolulu today. The temperature here is one hundred degrees, and everybody is swimming at the beach.

This is Annie Lu with the weather report from WCLD in Atlanta. It's snowing here in Atlanta today, and everybody is at home.

This is Herbie Ross with today's weather from KFTG radio. It's warm and sunny here in Los Angeles today. The temperature is seventy degrees. It's a beautiful day.

This is Jimmy G. with your weather on CHME radio. It's cool and sunny here in Toronto today. It's a very nice day.

This is Lisa Lee with your WQRZ weather report. It's cold and cloudy in Chicago today. The temperature here is thirty-two degrees. Yes, it's a cold and cloudy day!

Unit 7 – Page 65

WHAT PLACES DO YOU HEAR?

Listen and choose the correct places.

Ex.: My neighborhood is very nice. There's a supermarket across the street, and there's a video store around the corner.

1. My neighborhood is very convenient. There's a bank around the corner and a laundromat across the street.
2. My neighborhood is very noisy. There's a fire station next to my building, and there's a gas station across the street.
3. The sidewalks in my neighborhood are very busy. There's a school across the street and a department store around the corner.
4. There are many small stores in the center of my town. There's a bakery, a drug store, and a book store.
5. My neighborhood is very busy. There's a hotel across the street, and the hotel is between a hospital and a health club.

TRUE OR FALSE?

Listen to the conversation. Then answer True or False.

A. Tell me about the apartment.
B. There's a large living room, a large kitchen, a nice bathroom, and a very nice bedroom.
A. How many closets are there in the apartment?
B. There's a closet in the bedroom and a closet in the living room.
A. Oh, I see. And how many windows are there in the living room?
B. There are four windows in the living room.
A. Four windows?
B. Yes. That's right.
A. Tell me. Is there a superintendent in the building?
B. Yes, there is.
A. And are there washing machines in the basement?
B. Yes, there are. There are three washing machines.
A. Oh, good. Tell me, is there an elevator in the building?
B. No, there isn't. But there's a fire escape.

Unit 8 – Page 75

WHAT'S THE WORD?

Listen and choose the correct answer.

1. A. May I help you?
   B. Yes, please. I'm looking for a blouse.

2. A. Can I help you?
   B. Yes, please. I'm looking for a pair of boots.
3. A. May I help you?
   B. Yes, please. I'm looking for a necklace.
4. A. Can I help you?
   B. Yes, please. I'm looking for a raincoat.
5. A. May I help you?
   B. Yes, please. I'm looking for a pair of stockings.
6. A. Can I help you?
   B. Yes, please. I'm looking for a shirt.

WHICH WORD DO YOU HEAR?

Listen and choose the correct answer.

1. These jackets are expensive.
2. I'm looking for a leather belt.
3. I'm wearing my new wool sweater.
4. Suits are over there.
5. Is this your shoe?
6. Polka dot ties are very popular this year.

Side by Side Gazette – Page 77

Listen to these announcements in a clothing store. Match the clothing and the aisles.

Attention, J-Mart Shoppers! Are you looking for a black leather jacket? Black leather jackets are very popular this year! There are a lot of black leather jackets at J-Mart today! They're in Aisle 9, next to the coats.

Attention, J-Mart Shoppers! Are you looking for a pair of vinyl gloves? Vinyl gloves are very popular this year! Well, there are a lot of vinyl gloves at J-Mart today! They're in Aisle 5, across from the hats.

Attention, J-Mart Shoppers! Are you looking for a blouse? Is red your favorite color? Red blouses are very popular this year! There are a lot of red blouses at J-Mart today. They're in Aisle 7, next to the dresses.

Attention, J-Mart Shoppers! Are you looking for a special gift for your mother, your wife, or your sister? A silver bracelet is a special gift for that special person. All our silver bracelets are in Aisle 1, across from the earrings.

Attention, J-Mart Shoppers! Are you looking for a special gift for your father, your husband, or your brother? A polka dot tie is a special gift for that special person. All our polka dot ties are in Aisle 11, next to the belts.

Unit 9 – Page 84

Listen and choose the correct answer.

1. My brother lives in Chicago.
2. My name is Peter. I work in an office.
3. This is my friend Carla. She speaks Italian.
4. My sister drives a bus in Chicago.
5. We read the newspaper every day.
6. My parents visit their friends every weekend.
7. Charlie cooks in a Greek restaurant.
8. My brother and I paint houses.
9. My friend Betty calls me every day.
10. My parents usually shop at the mall.

Unit 10 – Page 93

WHAT'S THE WORD?

Listen and choose the word you hear.

1. Do you work on Monday?
2. Does your daughter go to this school?
3. We do a different activity every Sunday.
4. Larry doesn't play a sport.
5. We don't go to Stanley's Restaurant.
6. Sally goes to a health club every week.
7. She baby-sits for her neighbors every Thursday.
8. They go to work every morning.

Listen and choose the correct response.

1. Do you speak Korean?
2. Does Mrs. Wilson go to Stanley's Restaurant?
3. Does your sister live in Los Angeles?
4. Do you and your brother clean the house together?
5. Does your husband like American food?
6. Do you go to school on the weekend?
7. Do you and your friends play tennis?
8. Does your cousin live in this neighborhood?

Side by Side Gazette – Page 98

You're calling the International Cafe! Listen to the recorded announcement. Match the day of the week and the kind of entertainment.

Hello! This is the International Cafe—your special place for wonderful entertainment every day of the week! Every day the International Cafe presents a different kind of entertainment. On Monday, Antonio Bello plays Italian classical music. On Tuesday, Miguel Garcia reads Spanish poetry. On Wednesday, Amanda Silva sings Brazilian jazz. On Thursday, Nina Markova reads Russian short stories. On Friday, Hiroshi Tanaka plays Japanese rock music. On Saturday, Rita Rivera sings Mexican popular music. And on Sunday, Slim Wilkins sings American country music. So come to the International Cafe—your special place for wonderful entertainment . . . every day of the week!

Unit 11 – Page 105

Listen to the conversations. Who and what are they talking about?

1. A. How often do you visit him?
   B. I visit him every week.
2. A. How often do you wash them?
   B. I wash them every year.
3. A. Do you write to her very often?
   B. I write to her every month.
4. A. Is it broken?
   B. Yes. I'm fixing it now.
5. A. How often do you see them?
   B. I see them every day.
6. A. How often do you use it?
   B. I use it all the time.
7. A. When does he wash it?
   B. He washes it every Sunday.
8. A. Do you see him very often?
   B. No. I rarely see him.
9. A. Do you study with them very often?
   B. Yes. I study with them all the time.

Unit 12 – Page 112

Listen and choose the correct answer.

1. What are you doing?
2. What does the office assistant do?
3. What's the receptionist doing?
4. Is he tired?
5. What do you do when you're scared?
6. Where do you usually study?

Side by Side Gazette – Page 115

Listen to these news reports. Match the news and the city.

A. You're listening to WBOS in Boston. And now here's Randy Ryan with today's news.
B. Good morning. Well, the people in Boston who usually take the subway to work aren't taking it today. There's a big problem with the subway system in Boston.

A. You're listening to KSAC in Sacramento. And now here's Jessica Chen with the morning news.

B. Good morning. The big news here in Sacramento is the traffic! Sacramento police officers are on strike today, and nobody is directing traffic. There are traffic problems all around the city!

A. This is WCHI in Chicago. And now here's Mike Maxwell with today's news.
B. Good morning. It's snowing very hard in Chicago right now. As a result, the streets of the city are empty. People aren't walking or driving to work. There aren't any trucks or buses on the street. And mail carriers aren't delivering the mail.

A. You're listening to CTOR in Toronto. And now here's Mark Mitchell with today's news.
B. It's a quiet Tuesday morning in Toronto. There aren't any bad traffic problems right now, and there aren't any problems with the subway system or the buses.

A. You're listening to WMIA in Miami. And now here's today's news.
B. Good morning. This is Rita Rodriguez with the news. The children of Miami who usually take school buses to school aren't taking them this morning. The men and women who drive the school buses are on strike. Some children are walking to school today. Many students are staying home.

Unit 13 – Page 121

CAN OR CAN'T?

Listen and choose the word you hear.

1. I can speak Spanish.
2. He can't paint.
3. She can type.
4. We can't build things.
5. They can use tools.
6. We can't operate equipment.

WHAT CAN THEY DO?

Listen and choose what each person can do.

1. He can't file. He can type.
2. They can cook. They can't bake.
3. She can repair locks. She can't repair stoves.
4. I can't drive a truck. I can drive a bus.
5. He can teach French. He can't teach English.
6. We can take inventory. We can't paint.

Unit 14 – Page 132

Listen and choose the words you hear.

1. A. When are you going to buy a computer?
   B. Tomorrow.
2. A. When are your neighbors going to move?
   B. Next November.
3. A. When are you going to visit me?
   B. Next month.
4. A. When are you going to do your laundry?
   B. This evening.
5. A. When are you going to begin your vacation?
   B. This Sunday.
6. A. When are we going to go to the concert?
   B. This Thursday.
7. A. When are you going to wash the windows?
   B. This afternoon.
8. A. When is she going to get her driver's license?
   B. Next week.
9. A. When is your daughter going to finish college?
   B. Next winter.
10. A. When is the landlord going to fix the kitchen sink?
    B. At once.

Listen and match the theaters and the movies.

Thank you for calling the Multiplex Cinema! The Multiplex Cinema has five theaters with the best movies in town!

Now showing in Theater One: *The Spanish Dancer,* a film from Spain about the life of the famous dancer Carlos Montero. Show times are at one fifteen, three thirty, and seven o'clock.

Now showing in Theater Two: *When Are You Going to Call the Plumber?,* starring Julie Richards and Harry Grant. In this comedy, a husband and wife have a lot of problems in their new house. Show times are at two thirty, four forty-five, and seven fifteen.

Now showing in Theater Three: *The Fortune Teller.* In this film from Brazil, a woman tells people all the things that are going to happen in their lives. Show times are at five o'clock, seven forty-five, and ten fifteen.

Now showing in Theater Four: *The Time Zone Machine,* the exciting new science fiction movie. Professor Stanley Carrington's new machine can send people to different time zones around the world. Show times are at five fifteen, eight o'clock, and ten thirty. There's also a special show at midnight.

Now showing in Theater Five: *Tomorrow Is Right Now.* In this new drama, a truck driver from Australia falls in love with a businesswoman from Paris. Where are they going to live, and what are they going to tell their friends? See it and find out! Show times are at six o'clock, eight thirty, and ten forty-five.

The Multiplex Cinema is on Harrison Avenue, across from the shopping mall. So come and see a movie at the Multiplex Cinema. You're going to have a good time! Thank you, and have a nice day!

Unit 15 – Page 147

Listen and choose the word you hear.

1. We plant flowers in our garden in the spring.
2. I worked at the office all day.
3. They studied English all morning.
4. Mr. and Mrs. Jones sit in their living room all day.
5. They drank lemonade all summer.
6. I waited for the bus all morning.
7. They finish their work at five o'clock.
8. We invited our friends to the party.
9. I eat cheese and crackers.
10. She cleaned her apartment all afternoon.
11. We wash our clothes at the laundromat.
12. He watched TV all evening.

Unit 16 – Page 155

Listen and put a check next to all the things these people did today.

Carla got up early this morning. She took a shower, she had breakfast, and she took the subway to work. She didn't have lunch today. She left work at five thirty, and she met her mother at six o'clock. They had dinner at a restaurant. Then they saw a movie.

Brian had a busy day today. This morning he fixed his car. Then he cleaned his yard. This afternoon he planted flowers, and then he washed his windows. This evening he read the newspaper, and he wrote to his brother. Then he took a bath.

Unit 17 – Page 163

Listen and choose the correct answer.

1. Before we bought Captain Crispy Cereal, we were always sick. Now we're always healthy.
2. We bought new chairs for our living room because our old chairs were very uncomfortable. We love our new chairs. They're VERY comfortable.

3. My daughter Lucy didn't finish her milk this morning. She wasn't very thirsty.
4. Fred was very upset this morning. He was late for the bus, and he didn't get to work on time.
5. Hmm. Where are Peter and Mary? They were at work yesterday, but they aren't here today.
6. Our kitchen floor was very dull. Our neighbors recommended Sparkle Floor Wax, and now our kitchen floor isn't dull any more. It's shiny!

Listen and match the products.

ANNOUNCER: And now a word from our sponsors.

WOMAN: I had a problem with my teeth. They were very yellow, and I was upset. I went to my dentist, and she recommended Dazzle. So I went to the store and I bought some. Now I brush my teeth with Dazzle every day. My teeth aren't yellow any more. They're white. They're VERY white! Thank you, Dazzle!

ANNOUNCER: Are YOUR teeth yellow? Try Dazzle today!

TED: Bob! This kitchen floor is beautiful!

BOB: Thanks, Ted.

TED: Is it new?

BOB: Oh, no! This is my old kitchen floor.

TED: But it's so shiny!

BOB: That's right, Ted. It IS shiny, because I bought Shiny-Time!

TED: Shiny-Time?

BOB: Yes. Shiny-Time!

ANNOUNCER: That's right, Ted. YOU can have a shiny kitchen floor, too. Use Shiny-Time . . . every time!

WOMAN: Alan? What's the matter?

MAN: I don't know. I jog all the time, but today I'm really tired. Tell me, Julie, you're NEVER tired. You're always energetic. How do you do it?

WOMAN: Energy Plus!

MAN: Energy Plus?

WOMAN: Yes, Alan, Energy Plus! Before I bought Energy Plus, I was always tired like you. But now I'm energetic all the time!

ANNOUNCER: Tired? Try Energy Plus today! You can find it in supermarkets and drug stores everywhere.

PRESIDENT: Thank you. Thank you very much.

ASSISTANT: That was excellent, Mr. President.

PRESIDENT: Thank you, Ron. You know, I have a terrible sore throat.

ASSISTANT: I can hear that, Mr. President. Here. Try one of these.

PRESIDENT: What are they?

ASSISTANT: Lucky Lemon Drops.

PRESIDENT: Lucky Lemon Drops?

ASSISTANT: Yes, Mr. President. They're really good for a sore throat.

PRESIDENT: Thanks, Ron.

ANNOUNCER: Lucky Lemon Drops. They're good for the president! They're good for you!

WOMAN: My dog's fur was dull. It was VERY dull, and my dog was very sad. Then I bought K-9 Shine! Yes, K-9 Shine. I washed my dog with K-9 Shine, and now his fur is shiny! It's very shiny, and my dog is very happy!

ANNOUNCER: Try K-9 Shine today! YOUR dog's fur can be shiny, too!

Vocabulary List

Numbers indicate the pages on which the words first appear.

Ailments 141

backache
cold
cough
earache
fever
headache
sore throat
stomachache
toothache

Classroom Actions 16a

close *your book*
erase the board
go to the board
open *your book*
put away *your book*
raise your hand
sit down
stand up
take out *your book*
write *your name and address*

Classroom Objects

board 8
book 7
bookshelf 8
bulletin board 8
chair 8
clock 8
computer 7
desk 7
dictionary 8
globe 8
map 8
notebook 8
pen 7
pencil 7
ruler 8
table 8
wall 8

Clothing

bathrobe 77
belt 67
blouse 67

boot 68
bracelet 68
briefcase 68
coat 67
clothing 54a
dress 67
earring 68
glasses 68
glove 68
hat 68
jacket 67
jeans 67
mitten 68
necklace 68
pajamas 67
pants 67
pocketbook 68
purse 68
raincoat 75
ring 77
sandals 77
scarf 77
shirt 67
shoe 67
shorts 77
skirt 67
slippers 77
sneakers 77
sock 67
sports jacket 72
stocking 68
suit 67
sunglasses 73
sweat pants 77
sweater 67
tee shirt 77
tie 67
umbrella 68
wallet 77
watch 68

Clothing Sizes 76b

small
medium
large
extra-large

Colors 70

black

blue
brown
gold
gray
green
orange
pink
purple
red
silver
white
yellow

Community/Civics

community 34a
community meeting 86a
community service day 34a
immigrant 26b
neighbor 34a
neighborhood 34a
stay informed 86a

Continents 16c

Africa
Antarctica
Asia
Australia
Europe
North America
South America

Days of the Week 87

Sunday
Monday
Tuesday
Wednesday
Thursday
Friday
Saturday

Describing Feelings and Emotions

angry 49
annoyed 124
cold 40
depressed 122

embarrassed 107
happy 22
hot 40
hungry 107
nervous 107
sad 77
scared 107
sick 107
thirsty 107
tired 49

Describing People and Things

active 90
athletic 90
average 54a
average height 106a
bad 112
beautiful 22
big 35
blond 102
busy 29
cheap 35
clean 54a
closed 165
comfortable 157
cute 163
dark 165
difficult 35
dirty 72
dry 165
dull 157
easy 35
empty 72
energetic 112
enormous 157
exciting 162
expensive 35
fancy 165
fast 165
fat 35
flexible 140b
foreign-born 26b
frustrated 75
full 157
good 42
handsome 35
happy 22
healthy 54a
heavy 35
high 165
important 54a
inexpensive 75

171

interesting 13
large 26b
late 161
light 165
little 35
long 165
loud 35
low 165
married 35
messy 165
neat 165
new 35
noisy 35
old 35
open 165
outgoing 94
plain 165
poor 35
popular 94
pretty 35
quiet 35
rich 35
rural 78b
sad 77
shiny 157
short 35
shy 94
single 35
slow 165
small 35
strong 54a
tall 35
thin 35
tiny 157
ugly 35
uncomfortable 157
wet 165
young 35

Emergency Numbers 24a

ambulance
fire
poison control center
police

Everyday Activities

act 48
answer the telephone
    114a
baby-sit 87
bake 47

brush *their* teeth 27
buy *groceries* 106a
call 79
clean 27
comb *my* hair 97
cook 17
cry 47
dance 48
deliver 113
do *our exercises* 30
do *the laundry* 106a
do *their* homework 28
do *yoga* 87
drink 17
drive 79
eat 17
enjoy 140b
exercise 148c
feed 27
fix 27
get dressed 97
get up 97
go 89
go *dancing* 87
go to bed 97
go to school 97
go to work 97
greet 140b
have *dinner* 46
help *my children* 106a
jog 87
laugh 50
learn 54a
listen to 17
make *breakfast* 106a
observe 54b
paint 27
pay *the bills* 106a
plant 17
play *baseball* 17
play *cards* 17
play the *piano* 17
read 17
ride 46
see 87
sell 79
shave 135
shop 63
sing 17
skate 118
skateboard 47
ski 118
sleep 17

speak 79
study 17
sweep 106a
swim 17
take a bath 97
take a shower 97
take a taxi 115
take the bus 113
take the subway 115
take the train 115
talk 50
teach 17
type 112
use 53
vacuum 49
visit 79
walk 111
wash 27
watch TV 17
work 79
write 42

Family 54a

divorced
family member
same-sex family
single-parent family
two-parent family

Family Members

aunt 45
brother 45
brother-in-law 54
children 45
cousin 45
daughter 45
daughter-in-law 54
father 45
father-in-law 54
grandchildren 45
granddaughter 45
grandfather 45
grandmother 45
grandparents 45
grandson 45
husband 45
mother 45
mother-in-law 54
nephew 45
niece 45
parents 45
sister 45

sister-in-law 54
son 45
son-in-law 54
uncle 45
wife 45

Food

apple 164a
banana 164a
beans 164b
bread 158
burrito 164b
butter 164a
carrot 164a
cereal 158
cheese 146
cheeseburger 164b
chicken sandwich 164b
coffee 164b
cookie 145
crackers 146
egg 164a
fries 164b
green beans 164b
hamburger 164b
ice cream 158
lemonade 146
lettuce 164a
milk 164a
onion 164a
orange 164a
orange juice 164c
peach 164a
peas 164b
potato 164a
rice 164b
salad 164b
salt 164b
skim milk 158
soda 145
soft drink 164b
soup 164a
sugar 164a
taco 164b
tomato 164a

Food Containers and Quantities 164c

box
can
gallon
pint

Skill Index

BASIC LANGUAGE SKILLS

Alphabet, 1

Language Arts

Capitalization, 140a
Punctuation, 26a
Statements & questions, 78a, 116a, 140a
Subject & verb agreement, 98a
Types of sentences, 26a

Listening, 5, 15, 23, 26, 33, 43, 51, 54, 65, 75, 77, 84, 93, 98, 105, 112, 115, 121, 132, 140, 147, 155, 163, 165

Pronunciation, 6, 16, 24, 34, 44, 52, 66, 76, 86, 96, 106, 114, 126, 137, 148, 156, 164

Speaking
(*Throughout*)

Reading/Document literacy

Abbreviations:
  Compass directions (N.,S.,E.,W.), 6c
  Days of the week, 87, 99, 138c
  Housing ad words, 66c
  Months of the year, 138a
  Streets, 6c
  Want ad words, 126b, 126d
Advertisements, 76c, 164c–d
Articles/Academic reading, 34a, 53, 77, 97, 114a, 115, 139, 148c, 165
Calendar, 87, 99, 138a
Classified ads, 66c, 126b, 126d
Clothing tags, 76b–d
Cloze reading, 86a, 105, 106a, 113, 132, 148a, 155, 156a
Destination signs on public transportation, 96a
Diagram, 52a–b
Email, 25, 54, 78, 98, 116, 140, 166
Envelope, 6d
Food labels, 164c
Forms, 6a, 138c, 156a–b
Help Wanted sign, 126b
Identification (I.D.), forms of, 6c, 16d
Letter, 42–43
Lists, 155
Map, 44a–b, 66a–d
Medical appointment cards, 148b, 148d
Medicine labels, 148b

Menu, 164b
Narratives, short, 4, 13, 15, 16c, 22, 32, 48, 49, 50, 63, 64, 72, 75, 83, 90, 92, 94, 103, 104, 112, 113, 120, 124, 132, 136–137, 146–147, 154, 162
Newspaper, finding information in, 44a
Price tags, 76b–d
Safety signs, 126c
Schedules:
  Business hours schedule, 138c–d
  Work schedule, 96a–b, 138c
Store receipt, 76c
Telephone directory, 24b
Want ads, 126b, 126d

Writing

Addresses, 2, 6, 6a
Autobiography, 163
Charts, writing information in, 5, 16b–c, 34a, 44a, 86a, 126a
Compositions, 23, 33, 34a, 51, 53, 65, 85, 94, 105, 125, 147
Dates, 138b
Email, 25, 54, 78, 98, 116, 140, 166
Envelope, addressing an, 6b
Forms, filling out, 6a–b, 126c, 138b, 156a
Journal writing, 6, 16, 24, 34, 52, 66, 76, 86, 96, 106, 114, 126, 137, 148, 156, 164
Letter, 44
Lists, 9, 121
Months of the year, 138a
Names, 5–6, 6a
Schedule, 96a
Shopping list, 164a
Signs, 126c
Telephone numbers, 6, 24a
Writing process, 54b, 166b

NUMBERS/NUMERACY/MATH

Addition, 76a, 164b
Address numbers, 2–6, 6c–d, 49
Aisle numbers in a store, 77
Cardinal numbers, 1, 16b
Celsius temperatures, 44a–b
Counting items to take inventory, 16b
Dates, 138a–b, 148b, 156a–b
Destination signs on public transportation, 96a
Dosages on medicine labels, 148b
Fahrenheit temperatures, 44a–b

Identification (I.D.) numbers, 6c
Money, amounts of, 76a
Ordinal numbers, 138a–b
Percents, 78
Prices, 76b–d, 164b–d
Quantity, indicating, 60
Route numbers on public transportation, 96a
Salary, 126b, 156a–b
Statistical information, 78, 97, 116
Telephone numbers, 2–6, 24a–b, 26
Temperatures, 44a–b
Time, 127, 134–135, 138c–d, 148b, 154–155
Time zones, 139
Weight, 164c

LEARNING SKILLS

Academic concepts:
  Advertisements, 165
  Continents, 16c
  Families, extended and nuclear, 54
  Statistical information, 78, 97, 116
  Time zones, 139
  Traffic as a global problem, 115
  Urban, suburban, & rural communities, 78
Categorization, 164a
Charts, information, 97, 116, 139, 165
Chronological order, 125
Diagrams, 16, 53
Graphs, statistical, 78
Maps, 16c, 58, 97, 139

LEARNING STRATEGIES

Assessment (Tests and skills checklists), 6d, 16d, 24b, 34b, 44b, 52b, 66d, 76d, 86b, 96b, 106b, 114b, 126d, 138d, 148d, 156b, 164d

Community Connections tasks, 6c, 24a, 34a, 44a, 126c, 138c

Critical Thinking / Problem-solving, 6c, 16b, 86a, 126a, 148a, 153, 164b, 164c

Culture sharing, 26, 54, 78, 98, 116, 140, 166

Picture dictionary vocabulary lessons, 1, 7, 17, 25, 27, 35, 45, 53, 55, 67, 77, 79, 87, 97, 99, 107, 115, 117, 127, 139, 141, 149, 157, 165

Topic Index

Grammar Index

Irregular Verbs: Past Tense					
be	was	get	got	see	saw
begin	began	go	went	sing	sang
buy	bought	grow	grew	sit	sat
do	did	have	had	steal	stole
drink	drank	make	made	take	took
drive	drove	meet	met	write	wrote
eat	ate	read	read		
forget	forgot	ride	rode		

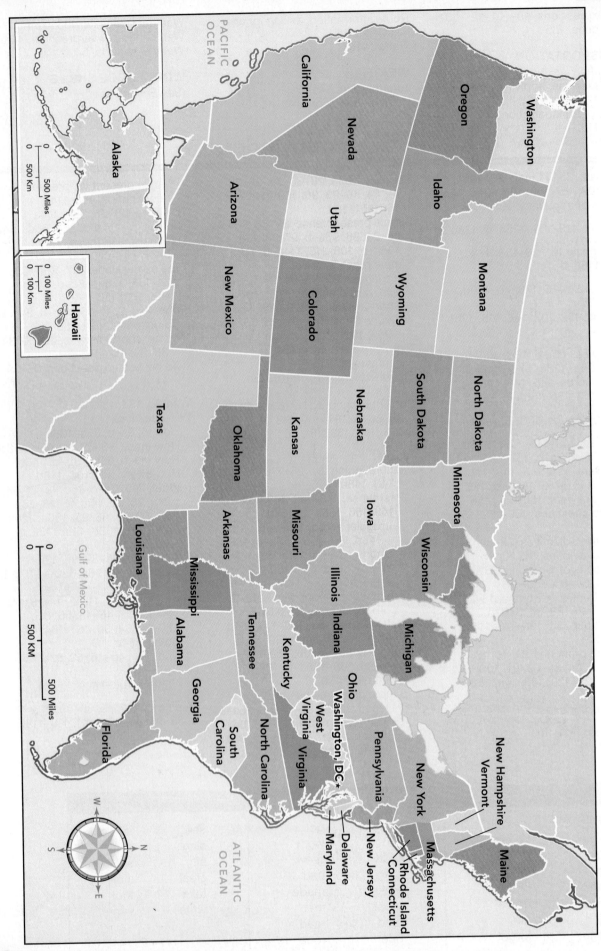

PACIFIC OCEAN

Washington

Oregon

California

Nevada

Idaho

Montana

Arizona

Utah

Wyoming

North Dakota

South Dakota

New Mexico

Colorado

Nebraska

Minnesota

Texas

Oklahoma

Kansas

Iowa

Wisconsin

Arkansas

Missouri

Illinois

Indiana

Michigan

Louisiana

Mississippi

Alabama

Tennessee

Kentucky

Ohio

West Virginia

Virginia

Pennsylvania

New York

Georgia

South Carolina

North Carolina

Washington, DC ★

Delaware

Maryland

New Jersey

Rhode Island

Connecticut

Massachusetts

New Hampshire

Vermont

Maine

Florida

Gulf of Mexico

ATLANTIC OCEAN

Alaska

0
500 Miles
0
500 Km

Hawaii

0   100 Miles
0   100 Km

0
0
500 KM
500 Miles

W
N
S
E